The
Flowers
of Evil

(Les Fleurs du mal)

CHARLES
BAUDELAIRE

Translated by Aaron Poochigian

Introduction by Dana Gioia
Afterword by Daniel Handler

Liveright Publishing Corporation

A Division of W. W. Norton & Company
Celebrating a Century of Independent Publishing

For information about permission to reproduce selections from this book, write to Permissions,
Liveright Publishing Corporation, a division of W. W. Norton & Company, Inc.,
500 Fifth Avenue, New York, NY 10110

For information about special discounts for bulk purchases, please contact
W. W. Norton Special Sales at specialsales@wwnorton.com or 800-233-4830

Manufacturing by Lakeside Book Company
Book design by Chris Welch Design
Production manager: Julia Druskin

Library of Congress Cataloging-in-Publication Data

Names: Baudelaire, Charles, 1821–1867, author. | Poochigian, Aaron, 1973–, translator. |
Gioia, Dana, writer of introduction. | Handler, Daniel, writer of afterword. | Baudelaire, Charles,
1821–1867. Fleurs du mal | Baudelaire, Charles, 1821–1867. Fleurs du mal. English
Title: The flowers of evil = (Les fleurs du mal) / Charles Baudelaire ; translated by
Aaron Poochigian ; introduction by Dana Gioia ; afterword by Daniel Handler.
Other titles: Fleurs du mal
Description: First edition. | New York, NY : Liveright Publishing Corporation, [2022] |
Includes index.
Identifiers: LCCN 2021011573 | ISBN 9781631498596 (hardcover) | ISBN 9781631498602 (epub)
Subjects: LCSH: Baudelaire, Charles, 1821–1867—Translations into English.
Classification: LCC PQ2191.F62 E5 2021 | DDC 841/.8—dc23
LC record available at https://lccn.loc.gov/2021011573

ISBN 978-1-324-09291-9 pbk.

Liveright Publishing Corporation, 500 Fifth Avenue, New York, N.Y. 10110
www.wwnorton.com

W. W. Norton & Company Ltd., 15 Carlisle Street, London W1D 3BS

1 2 3 4 5 6 7 8 9 0

CONTENTS

The Flowers of Evil

SPLEEN AND THE IDEAL

PARISIAN SCENES

WINE

FLOWERS OF EVIL

REVOLT

DEATH

Les Fleurs du mal

SPLEEN ET IDÉAL

TABLEAUX PARISIENS

LE VIN

FLEURS DU MAL

RÉVOLTE

LA MORT

INTRODUCTION

I

Charles Baudelaire was the first modern poet. In both style and content, his provocative, alluring, and shockingly original work shaped and enlarged the imagination of later poets, not only in his native France but across Europe and the Americas. His work guided the Symbolist movement, which became the dominant school of Modernist poetry, and inspired the Decadent and Aesthetic movements. Half a century later, his presence still haunted Surrealism. Nor was Baudelaire's impact restricted to literature. His ideas on the autonomy of art, the alienation of the artist, the irrationality of human behavior, the intellectualization of poetry, the cult of beauty (and the beauty of evil), and the frank depiction of sexuality became central to Modernist aesthetics. He also popularized less exalted cultural trends such as Satanism, sexual degradation, and the use of drugs for artistic inspiration. Not all of these ideas originated with Baudelaire, but his distinctive articulation of these principles became the lingua franca of international Modernism.

Baudelaire's outsize impact is notable because his public career had such limited success during his short life. Little read yet much misunderstood, he survived, just barely, on the margins of the literary world. He never commanded a large audience, though he achieved unwanted notoriety from an obscenity trial. By the time of his death in 1867, however, he had attracted a coterie of admirers who would guide the course of late nineteenth-century French poetry—most notably Paul Verlaine, Arthur Rimbaud, and Stéphane Mallarmé. This devoted cult soon spread Baudelaire's posthumous reputation beyond the poet's own sad fantasies. Rimbaud declared him "the first seer, the king of poets, *a true God.*" Algernon Charles Swinburne elegized him as his strange and somber brother of "Fierce loves, and lovely leaf-buds poisonous." Stefan George translated *Les Fleurs du mal* into German and trained his circle of young intellectual elites in Symbolist principles.

By 1924 poet-critic Paul Valéry would claim that Baudelaire was the most widely translated French poet, the only one whose work could cross borders to win an international audience. "Though there may be French poets greater and more powerfully endowed than Baudelaire," Valéry observed, "there is none more *important.*" In 1939 Walter Benjamin confirmed that verdict, declaring that "*Les Fleurs du mal* was the last lyric work that had a European repercussion; no later work penetrated beyond a more or less limited linguistic area." Benjamin overstated his case—Rainer Maria Rilke's poetry had already begun to exercise its enduring international fascination—but he had made a cogent observation. Baudelaire's posthumous reputation had become the monolith of French poetry, tall enough to be seen from abroad. He had eclipsed his contemporaries; if they were to be seen by posterity, it was mostly in relation to him.

Baudelaire's influence cannot be separated from his position in the artistic vanguard of Paris, the cultural center of nineteenth-century Europe. While the arts thrived from St. Petersburg to Madrid, creators and critics across the continent looked to Paris for innovation and excellence, not only because of the city's wealth, size, and sophistication, but also, paradoxically, because it was in constant cultural and political turmoil. Revolutionary reformers battled social conservatives; secular progressives contended with religious traditionalists. No faction could establish a lasting victory. The vitality of these ineradicable conflicts charged French culture with special energy. The violent dialectic created a milieu more diverse and creative than any other city in Europe or the Americas. Paris was the laboratory for new ideas and cultural institutions—not only in literature but also in painting, sculpture, architecture, opera, theater, and dance. Artists everywhere wanted to come to Paris. Like Hollywood a century later, Paris was where the money and fame were.

Nowhere was the accelerated creativity of Paris more evident than in poetry, which possessed special cultural authority and was expected to articulate the spirit of the times. As French history changed, so did French poetry; each emerging movement offered the vision of a new age. Although Romanticism dominated English and German poetry for most of the nineteenth century, in France the movement was only a single episode in a cycle of artistic innovation. As the century began, French poetry was still dominated by Classicism, which emphasized simplicity of style, clarity of expression, traditional form, and strong emotion held in restraint. Then in rapid succession came Romanticism, Parnassianism, Decadence, and Symbolism. (In fiction, France was also the epicenter of Realism and Naturalism.) The rapid rise of these movements expressed the literary energy of Paris, where successive waves of young writers gathered in cafés, taverns, and salons to argue art and ideas. Meanwhile newspapers and journals—the mass media of the age—had ever more pages to fill. The growth of print media fostered a new urban class of writers. For the first time, a large number of writers could survive without official patronage.

The competing aesthetics of the period merged (and sometimes collided) in Baudelaire's work. He absorbed and assimilated aspects of different literary schools, transforming them into a personal poetics that resists classification. Baudelaire's great achievement was to break the hold of Romanticism, though he was, by nature, a romantic. He created a new poetic style and sensibility that rejected the empty gestures of late Romanticism without losing its heroic energy. He fashioned a new vocabulary of images to describe the modern metropolis in ways that endowed it with sinister beauty and mystery.

Baudelaire did not entirely break with tradition. He crafted an elegant classical style—dense, lyric, and original—to express lurid, repugnant, and even obscene subjects that French literary conventions had either excluded or confined to treatment in the low style. He developed an aesthetic capacious enough to assimilate the novelties, shocks, and conflicts of metropolitan life. He imbued sordid scenes with religious grace. His synthesis of traditional and innovative elements, always animated by the author's desperate sincerity, conveyed the strange and startling beauty of modern Paris.

Baudelaire's posthumous fame has not been limited to the page. Like Vincent van Gogh, his life has come to embody the myth of the doomed and alienated modern artist. The unhappy particulars of his existence—poverty, depression, public censure, alcoholism, drug abuse, sexual license, and disease—personify the *poète maudit*, the "cursed poet." His untimely death from syphilis canonized him as a new sort of tragic hero, the suffering artist who sacrificed all for creative freedom in a heartless bourgeois world. Baudelaire's identity as the ultimate doomed artist brings him into places modern poetry doesn't normally go. There are Baudelaire coffee mugs, T-shirts, and caps. There are posters, pillowcases, corsets, hoodies, socks, and beach towels. There are plaques, statues, rings, and medallions. One can buy a shot glass bearing his image and declaration: *"Il est l'heure de s'enivrer! Pour n' être pas les esclaves martyrisés du Temps, enivrez-vous; enivrez-vous sans cesse!"* (It is the hour to get drunk! Not to be the martyred slave of Time. Get drunk; get drunk without stopping!). What other French poet has enough celebrity to qualify for product endorsement? One can't buy a Paul Valéry corset or a Théophile Gautier hoodie.

Baudelaire died childless and unmarried, but literature even gave him a family, at least in name—the three Baudelaire children—Violet, Klaus, and Sunny—the long-suffering protagonists of Lemony Snicket's witty thirteen-novel cycle, *A Series of Unfortunate Events.* Even young adult readers know that children named Baudelaire are doomed to a miserable existence—*les enfants maudits.* None of this cultural bric-a-brac matters to literary scholars—as Snicket's alter ego, Daniel Handler, acknowledges in his afterword to this volume—but its profusion will strike the average reader as significant. There is something singular and unruly about Baudelaire's legacy that can't be confined to the pages of a book.

Neither Baudelaire's artistic innovation nor his lyric genius, however, adequately explains the mesmerizing impact of his work on posterity. Victor Hugo had equal poetic talent and considerable originality, yet his verse remains unread outside France. There is something fundamentally different about Baudelaire's imagination. *Les Fleurs du mal* portrays the author's experience—and indeed the author himself—with extraordinary candor and unabashed intimacy. Yet the poems have a strange ambiguity that permits contradictory interpretations. The reader can enter Baudelaire's pysche but not make complete sense of it.

Walt Whitman famously declared: "Do I contradict myself? Very well then I contradict myself, (I am large, I contain multitudes.)" In comparison with Baudelaire, Whitman's contradictions seem simple; the reader can discern how the Good Gray Poet feels about any subject. Baudelaire, however, offers contradictions beyond reconciliation. It isn't that his sense of his own existence is confused, though his life was demoralized and disorderly. His ambiguity arises from his refusal to simplify his experience or allow it to be resolved into any one thing. He does not condescend to the reader (or himself) by pretending that human existence is reasonable or consistent.

Baudelaire took pride in the intellectuality of his creative process. (He developed his position from Edgar Allan Poe's "The Philosophy of Composition," which described the composition of "The Raven" as a series of conscious, intellectual decisions.) His versification displays impeccable classical logic. His poems bristle with ideas and opinions. But those external qualities are deceptive. His modes of thought are rarely analytical; they are intuitive, emotional, and even visionary. He presents experience with vivid and unfiltered immediacy. The formal and rhetorical perfection of his verse gives it a surface rationality that belies the agitation and puzzlement underneath.

A conventional myth of modern society is that the individual possesses a unified consciousness; a personality is assumed to be a single entity in which all parts form an indivisible whole. Contemporary neuroscience, however, has demonstrated that human consciousness is an unstable republic of conflicting impulses, instincts, and appetites in perpetual flux. Baudelaire understood, or at least intuited, this unsettling reality before the scientists and psychologists. His poems pull the reader into the vacillation of his consciousness as experienced from the inside.

Music was central to Baudelaire's method. He considered poetry an art of enchantment. A poem should cast a verbal spell that suspends the reader in a trance state of heightened attention and receptivity. That momentary enchantment allows the reader to experience contradictory thoughts and emotions, to feel hidden suggestions and connections that are never fully disclosed or resolved in the poem. The reader interprets the poem—not as a deliberately constructed puzzle, but as a shared experience still in the process of being understood. The verbal music gives the experience a feeling of order beyond the ambiguous scenes and sentiments the poem expresses.

Baudelaire's method places the reader in a more important position than had either the pellucid works of French Classicism or the personal declarations of Romanticism. Of course, readers also had to interpret those poems, but the authors and the tradition gave them careful instructions. When Alphonse de Lamartine announces that he loves a woman, that statement becomes a reliable basis to interpret everything that follows, even if the poem contains some complications. When Baudelaire announces he loves his mistress Jeanne Duval, the assertion is, to quote Flann O'Brien, "nearly an insoluble pancake, a conundrum of inscrutable potentialities, a snorter."

Baudelaire's interpretive difficulty was part of his attraction, especially when it combined with his exquisite music and sensational subject matter. He called for strong readers, and they came. His ambiguity became his legacy; it prefigured the aesthetics of Symbolism, which refined elements of *Les Fleurs du mal* into a style that worked by suggestion rather than statement, music rather than paraphrasable meaning. Symbolism needed even stronger readers. Their advent made Modernist poetry possible.

This ambiguity explains why Baudelaire can be credibly championed by Catholics as a religious poet and by Existentialists as a nihilist. Marxists praise him as a proto-revolutionary who expressed the alienation of the urban masses, and Decadents as an aristocratic hedonist who dismissed bourgeois morality in his search for forbidden pleasures. He is both the Symbolist poet of pure imagination and the patron sinner of Satanism.

Baudelaire is all of these things because he allows the reader to collaborate in the ultimate interpretation of his work. His imagination is not Shakespearean; Baudelaire lacks the "negative capability" of assuming different personalities. He is always and only himself—a real artist in mid-nineteenth-century Paris. Whether transgressive or traditional, sacrilegious or sacramental, Baudelaire eludes explanation. Yet he never eludes the reader. He meets the reader boldly, face-to-face, unembarrassed by his flaws and failures. He knows his songs have made him beautiful.

II

Baudelaire was born in the Latin Quarter of Paris on April 9, 1821. His parents were an oddly matched couple. His father, Joseph-François, was sixty-two years old at the time of the poet's birth. His mother was thirty-four years younger. Joseph-François Baudelaire was a product of the ancien régime. Ordained a priest before the Revolution, he had been a teacher and later a tutor for an aristocratic family. During the Reign of Terror, like thousands of other clergy, he renounced his vows under the threat of imprisonment, exile, or execution. An educated man with influential connections, he obtained a lucrative civil service position in the Senate bureaucracy and then married. He had one son, Claude Alphonse—the poet's half brother. In 1819, after the death of his wife, the prosperous and cultivated widower married again. His new bride was the twenty-six-year-old Caroline Dufaÿs. An impoverished orphan from an educated family, Dufaÿs probably had few prospects for a respectable marriage. The match may not have been passionate, but it was comfortable and affectionate. It also proved brief. The elder Baudelaire died in 1827, when the poet was six.

The young Charles spent his early years in a large house set in a maze of medieval streets on the Left Bank. (Most of the neighborhood was demolished in subsequent renovations of Paris.) The house, which had turrets and high-ceilinged rooms, was full of antique furniture, books, and paintings. The poet remembered his father as a gentle and elegant man who took him on walks to the Luxembourg Gardens. Even after his father's death, Charles's childhood was loving and secure. He was the object of his widowed mother's devoted attention. He also had a large legacy from his father, which he would inherit at twenty-one. The boy lived in what he later called "the green paradise of childhood loves."

His childhood paradise was destroyed by two events. Eighteen months after Joseph-François's death, Caroline remarried. Her new husband was Major Jacques Aupick, an ambitious soldier and diplomat. The couple lived mostly apart for three years while Aupick filled ambassadorial positions abroad. Then, in December 1831, the new family moved to Lyon. The resulting domestic drama has fascinated the poet's biographers. It became a classic Oedipal struggle that could have been scripted by Sigmund Freud. Young Charles, usurped from the monopoly of his mother's attention, resented the stern and practical Aupick. Their relationship remained polite if unaffectionate, but the poet's rancor erupted in his teenage years. Even after they broke off relations, Aupick's conspicuous power and success filled Baudelaire with rage and bitter jealousy.

At school in Lyon, young Baudelaire missed Paris. He disliked his new city, his school, and the locals. Lyon, he later declared, was "a bigoted and fussy city where everything, even religion itself, has to have the calligraphic clarity of a cash register." In 1836, the capable Aupick was promoted to colonel and assigned to Paris, and his stepson was transferred to Lycée Louis-le-Grand in the capital. Although Charles was a prize student, he turned moody, cynical, and stubborn. In his final year he was expelled for refusing to give his teacher a note that had been passed to him in class. The colonel handled the dilemma of his difficult stepson efficiently. Charles boarded with a tutor to finish his *baccalauréat*, the French high school degree.

Baudelaire now had to plan his future. His well-connected stepfather suggested a diplomatic career. Charles declared he must pursue literature. Whatever affection that still existed between the two stubborn men was exhausted in the acrimonious exchange. A compromise was reached; Baudelaire would read law. His half brother had prospered as a lawyer and magistrate. There had also been lawyers in his mother's family. Charles moved to the Latin Quarter, ostensibly to begin legal studies; instead he devoted himself to literature and the pleasures of Paris.

Full of youthful confidence, Baudelaire plunged into bohemian life. He set himself an ambitious reading program. He met writers and painters. He attended plays, concerts, and cabarets. He visited bars and brothels. He drank heavily and smoked hashish. He also contracted venereal disease. He financed his indulgences by borrowing money against his future inheritance. Baudelaire's early adult years in Paris were a period of immense intellectual and artistic growth, but they also established a pattern of dissipation that would burden and eventually shorten his life.

The poet's mother and the newly promoted General Aupick worried about their wayward son. They soon realized his legal studies were a sham, and they understood the temptations young men faced in Paris. When they learned that Charles was borrowing money against his expectations, the family felt an intervention was necessary. His parents decided that a long ocean voyage would both help Charles mature and get him out of his detrimental Parisian haunts. In 1841 the reluctant poet boarded the *Paquebot-des-Mers-du-Sud* bound for India. The voyage proved arduous and uncomfortable. The ship was cramped and filthy, the equatorial heat oppressive. Near the Cape of Good Hope, a violent storm broke the mast and carried away much of the rigging. Slowly the damaged vessel drifted to Mauritius, where the crew spent two weeks making repairs. When the boat stopped next on Réunion, the depressed and homesick Baudelaire refused to continue.

The young poet lingered two months on the lush volcanic island until a boat arrived headed for France. Although the trip had not matured Charles, as his stepfather had hoped, the voyage had nourished his imagination. He had experienced physical danger and privation. He had watched sailors trap, torture, and eventually eat an elegant albatross. He had witnessed the beauty of tropical landscapes and sailed countless leagues of sea and sun and sky. He would never forget the images of his interrupted journey.

In February 1842 Baudelaire reappeared in Paris, to the astonishment of his family. He had returned, he claimed, full of wisdom but with empty pockets. Two months later he came of age and inherited a substantial legacy of approximately one hundred thousand francs, made up of land, investments, and cash. The young poet resolved to live in style. He rented a large apartment, which he filled with furniture and art. He bought stylish clothes and hosted friends at fine restaurants. No city offered so many pleasures, both coarse and cultivated, as Paris, but they came at a cost. Within a year Baudelaire had to sell his land to cover his expenses. His family watched his extravagance with horror and took careful account of his dwindling patrimony.

As a fashionable young man-about-town, Baudelaire indulged in another expensive pleasure—he took a mistress. In 1842 the poet visited the Panthéon, a small vaudeville theater, where he saw Jeanne Duval, a Haitian-born actress and dancer of mixed French and African ancestry. Although she spoke only one line in the play, Duval caught the young writer's attention. He sent her flowers and arranged a meeting for the next day. The two immediately became lovers. In the custom of the time, Baudelaire set her up in an apartment near his rooms at the Hôtel Pimodan. (Paris was a huge and crowded city; lovers preferred to live within walking distance.) Having suddenly come into Baudelaire's life, Duval would never entirely leave.

There followed two years of blissful indulgence. "I cared only for pleasure, for continual excitation," Baudelaire admitted. His romantic infatuation with Duval filled an emotional as well as sexual vacuum. The poet had little experience with women beyond his impersonal dealings with prostitutes. The relationship was initially passionate, but there were cold calculations on both sides. For Baudelaire, Duval provided easy sexual experience without the obligations of marriage. For Duval, a recent immigrant of mixed race, Baudelaire offered much-needed financial security. Their affair was an economic transaction between a rich man and a poor woman, but there was also joy and affection before it became burdened with mutual disappointment and resentment.

Sexual fulfillment did not slow Baudelaire's addictions. His nights with Duval involved consuming huge amounts of wine, brandy, and absinthe. The poet took laudanum, a mix of alcohol and opium. Meanwhile he joined meetings of the Hashish Club at the Hôtel Pimodan. He also indulged in the mundane habit of smoking pipe tobacco. If the poet's pleasures were excessive, so were his expenses. In the two years since coming into his inheritance, he had spent half of his legacy.

As Baudelaire sold his land and investments to pay off debts, the family again intervened. His mother and the general took him to court. The spectacle of a young man squandering his inheritance had a predictable ending in the French legal system. A lawyer took charge of the poet's remaining assets. For the rest of his life, Baudelaire received small regular payments from his remaining capital. The money was sufficient to

cover the expenses of a frugal single man, but Baudelaire's lavish hab-
its and disinclination to find regular employment left him perpetually
in debt and often destitute. Suddenly deprived of affluence and inde-
pendence, Baudelaire raged impotently. He denounced the general,
reproached his mother, and threatened suicide. His brief youthful fling
over, he sank into a state of financial anxiety and emotional instability
that continued until his death.

While Baudelaire's pecuniary humiliations unfolded, he enjoyed
his first literary successes. His poems appeared in *L'Artiste*, first under a
pseudonym, but eventually signed with his own name. Most of his publi-
cations, however, were prose—literary criticism, fiction, and art reviews.
His two major prose works of the period were long essays on the Salons of
1845 and 1846. Sponsored by the Académie des Beaux-Arts, the Salon was
an annual official art exhibition, the largest and most prestigious event
of its kind in Europe. The Grand Salon of the Louvre was hung from
floor to ceiling with new work chosen by a jury of academy members.
In his essays Baudelaire surveyed the state of French art. In particular,
he championed the color and energy of Eugène Delacroix. Published as
individual pamphlets, these outspoken and informed critiques gained
Baudelaire a reputation among the cultural elite.

In 1847 Baudelaire had the most important literary encounter of his
life. He discovered the work of Edgar Allan Poe. His reaction was imme-
diate, overpowering, and permanent. His relationship to Poe was not a
case of literary enthusiasm or influence; it was something akin to posses-
sion. He not only admired Poe's work; he embraced the American writer
as a kindred soul, an alter ego. Baudelaire claimed that in Poe's work he
found subjects he had dreamed about and even actual sentences he had
thought. He could recite Poe's story "The Black Cat" from memory. His
identification was so profound that it is impossible to understand Baude-
laire as a poet, critic, or person without reference to Poe. He considered
Poe a sacred martyr for art and referred to him as "Saint Edgar." In his
morning devotions, Baudelaire prayed first to God and then to Poe.

The remainder of Baudelaire's short life was given mainly to two great
tasks—the composition, expansion, and refinement of *Les Fleurs du mal*
and the translation of Poe's complete prose works. He translated only

a few poems since he felt they were beyond his imaginative powers. In Baudelaire's posthumous *Œuvres complètes*, five of the twelve volumes were translations of Poe. American critics considered Poe a brilliant but decadent, even pathetic, figure. His reputation had been in decline since his untimely death. Baudelaire resolved to establish his genius. "Edgar Poe," he wrote the critic Charles Sainte-Beuve, "who isn't much in America, must become a great man in France."

Baudelaire's championship of his American *frère* was a generous, indeed noble, example of literary advocacy—not a scholar making a career by discovering an author, but a major poet sacrificing much of his creative energy to raise a fellow artist from obscurity. In the course of five years Baudelaire wrote three long essays on Poe. Although some passages were lifted from American sources, these impassioned works stand as brilliant literary criticism; they are also self-revelatory, thinly veiled confessions of Baudelaire's artistic aims and agonies. He saw Poe's tragic life as a prophetic vision of his own future. "There are fatal destinies," his first essay began, "... some men who bear the words 'bad luck' written in mysterious characters in the sinuous folds of their foreheads."

The depiction of Poe as a cursed soul reflects Baudelaire's own self-image. In portraying Poe, Baudelaire enlarged and refined an archetype that came to dominate Symbolist and Decadent literature—*le poète maudit*. The term itself had been coined by the French Romantic poet Alfred de Vigny. Later it would become the title for Paul Verlaine's flamboyant collection of literary portraits, *Les Poètes maudits* (1884). The underlying concept, however, was first fully articulated by Baudelaire. He fashioned the image of the doomed artist too sensitive to survive in a mercenary world. Living outside bourgeois society, impoverished and unrecognized, the *poète maudit* seeks self-destructive solace in drugs, alcohol, and sex, often surviving on the edge of madness. Baudelaire's version of the archetype endures today in contemporary culture's depiction not only of poets, but also jazz musicians, rock stars, painters, and movie actors. Poets often formulate general theories from their personal sorrows. Baudelaire championed the alluring but dubious notion that the surest sign of profound creativity is to be doomed.

In 1848 revolutionary unrest erupted across Europe. In France the people of Paris brought down the constitutional monarchy of Louis Philippe and established the Second Republic. (The new progressive republic soon collapsed into Napoleon III's Second Empire.) As the mobs filled the streets of central Paris, Baudelaire appeared sporting a rifle and shouting, "We must go shoot General Aupick." Given Baudelaire's general distaste for politics, this revolutionary episode has a farcical quality. Aside from this brief and presumably sincere enthusiasm for radical reform, his views were mostly reactionary. "What can be more absurd than Progress?" he asked. "Belief in progress is the doctrine of idlers and Belgians." Baudelaire had genuine compassion for the poor, but he had no confidence that revolution would save them (or any other group) from the sorrows of existence. He often saw the poor and unfortunate as mirror images of his own troubled self. Baudelaire's sudden political engagement may have had more to do with the unhappy poet's emotions than with his ideas—the intoxication of mob violence joined to a ferocious Oedipal resentment toward his stepfather. In his *Intimate Journals*, Baudelaire had no retrospective illusions about the nobility of his motives. They were: "Taste for vengeance. *Natural* pleasure in destruction."

Despite the distractions and difficulties of his Parisian life, Baudelaire deepened as a poet. Although he published mostly prose, he now recognized that verse was his true medium. "Above all," he wrote his mother, "I want to be admired as a poet." For him, poetry represented the supreme human art, an expression of creativity itself. In his journals, he declared, "There are but three beings worthy of respect: the priest, the warrior, and the poet. To know, to kill, and to create."

Baudelaire's revolutionary fervor was short-lived. When Louis-Napoleon Bonaparte seized power in 1851, the poet denounced the coup d'état and then declared himself "depoliticized." To the degree he expressed later political sympathies, they were conservative, Catholic, and aristocratic. Despite his radical poetics and permissive personal mores, Baudelaire was old-fashioned, even reactionary, in everything else. Even his early affectations as a dandy, a well-dressed and idle urban aesthete, reflected the poet's aristocratic aspirations more than any new bohemian liberty. Misanthropy and misogyny also colored his opinions. Fueled by his own unhappiness, he saw human society as foul, selfish, and hypocritical. Poisoned by original sin, humanity was unredeemable. He particularly detested the prophets of the French progressive tradition, Voltaire and Rousseau. It wasn't just progressive ideas he objected to in art. Baudelaire maintained that introducing any political ideas compromised artistic integrity.

Although Baudelaire's life has copious documentation in letters, journals, and literary works, as well as testimonies and memoirs by many friends, the genesis of his masterpiece, *Les Fleurs du mal*, remains murky. The earliest poem in the collection dates from around 1841. A few poems appeared in literary reviews and anthologies over the next few years. In 1851, he published eleven poems under the title "Les Limbes" (Limbo), which he briefly considered as a possible title for his book. Slowly the meticulously patterned collection took shape. In 1855 he gathered eighteen poems in the *Revue des Deux Mondes* under a heading suggested by a friend: LES FLEURS DU MAL. That haunting title stuck. As Baudelaire assembled the poems, he sought to organize them in a way that gave the individual pieces a cumulative power and coherence.

In April 1857, two months before the publication of *Les Fleurs du mal*, General Aupick died. Baudelaire's mother left Paris for a handsome house in Honfleur on the coast of Normandy. She had always been the central woman in his life. Now there was no rival for her love. He again had his "poor dear mother" entirely to himself, though at a considerable distance. As his long, heartfelt letters to her indicate, his mother was his lifelong confidante. He remained fixated in childlike dependence, both emotional and financial, looking to her to solve his perpetual problems. Never doubting her affection, he constantly sought her approval and forgiveness. He often suggested her love could be expressed by a bit of extra cash.

Meanwhile Baudelaire and Jeanne Duval had parted. Their early fervor cooled, and his financial problems undermined the security he had once offered her. The alcohol-fueled relationship deteriorated into violent bickering. She had no regard for his unprofitable artistic pursuits. She mocked him as a failure and even poisoned his cat. He beat her with a candlestick. Nonetheless, Baudelaire could not make a permanent break. He remained "bound like a convict to this chain." He felt a guilty sense of duty to the only woman with whom he had managed an extended romantic relationship. Both of them now suffered from health problems, but Duval's decline was more rapid. In 1859 his "Black Venus" suffered a paralytic stroke, probably from the syphilis that infected them both. He would support her meagerly but faithfully for the rest of his life. Baudelaire never had another intimate or enduring romantic relationship. His poverty, temperament, and reputation made a bourgeois marriage impossible. His other romantic infatuations never went beyond flirtations or brief (and probably platonic) affairs.

In 1857 Baudelaire published the first edition of *Les Fleurs du mal*. The volume appeared in an elegant format printed by Auguste Poulet-Malassis, who became a devoted friend and later provided financial assistance to the perpetually needy poet. Poulet-Malassis sought to revive the art of fine printing in France. His books displayed superb typography on excellent paper, often hand decorated. Determined to have the text published flawlessly, Baudelaire moved to rooms near his publisher. For months he read and corrected successive sets of proofs, infuriating Poulet-Malassis's partner with the expense and delay. He agonized over the punctuation and typeface. "Remember," he wrote Poulet-Malassis, underlining and capitalizing his words for emphasis, that "the purpose of punctuation is not only to indicate the meaning but the WAY IN WHICH IT SHOULD BE READ ALOUD." At the end of June 1857, the book finally appeared in an edition of 1,300 copies. Baudelaire dedicated the volume to Théophile Gautier, "the flawless poet" and "consummate magician of French letters."

Baudelaire had little opportunity to celebrate the publication of his poems. Within weeks of its appearance, the Ministry of the Interior filed a report declaring that the book was "an outrage to public morals" and "an offense to religious morals." Censorship had become a timely issue. Earlier that year Gustave Flaubert had been indicted for immorality after his *Madame Bovary* had been serialized in *Revue de Paris*. After a dramatic trial, the novelist had been acquitted. Baudelaire now emerged as a vulnerable target for the frustrated authorities. *Le Figaro* denounced *Les Fleurs du mal* as a book full of "all the putrescence of the human heart." The Ministry of the Interior, eager to score a victory against what it considered smut and blasphemy, brought the poet and his publisher to trial.

Baudelaire resolved to fight the charges. He maintained that his poems had depicted vice in a way that would be repellent to the reader. He also insisted that earlier authors had published work that was even more scandalous with impunity. He did not dispute the sexual content of the book, which was the explosive issue.

Without General Aupick's political connections, Baudelaire's mother was powerless to help him, and few of the poet's friends were inclined to appear on his behalf. The court ruled against Baudelaire. Six overtly sexual poems were condemned. Both the poet and his publisher received fines. Publicly disgraced, Baudelaire knew the scandal had darkened his reputation. The verdict did not suppress Baudelaire's entire collection. Copies of *Les Fleurs du mal* were removed from sale, the offending verses excised, and the expurgated books returned to stores. The scandal increased sales, but only modestly. *Les Fleurs du mal* had no commercial success in the poet's lifetime.

By early middle age Baudelaire was an incurably unhappy man. His penury, deteriorating health, romantic failures, and lack of recognition weighed on his somber personality. "What I suffer just in living," he wrote his mother in 1861, "is inexpressible." He broiled in disappointments and resentments. "I want to vent my anger in terrifying books. I want to turn the whole human race against me." He claimed to be reconciled to his distorted reputation as the minor author of prurient poems and advocate of hashish and opium, but his superficial equanimity fooled no one. "I am very much at ease in my *stigmatization*," he wrote Victor Hugo, "and I know that from now on, in whatever literature I radiate, I shall remain a monster and a werewolf." The language of his self-presentation is revelatory. His scandalous reputation is the excruciating but sanctifying stigmata of an aesthetic martyr, and it had awakened a dangerous monster inside him.

Baudelaire may have been depressed and tortured, but he was not inactive. Although he claimed to be supported only by his pride and "savage hatred of all mankind," he wrote with the sustained dedication of an absolute artist. Nevertheless, he could not command the public readership necessary to gain either a major reputation or significant income. The second edition of *Les Fleurs du mal* (1860) earned little money, but it attracted a few critical advocates. Swinburne introduced Baudelaire to

English-language readers in a long, carefully argued review that claimed Baudelaire was, with Hugo, Browning, and Tennyson, one of the four greatest living poets. A coterie of young admirers had started to form.

Meanwhile Baudelaire adapted Thomas De Quincey's notorious *Confessions of an English Opium-Eater* (1822) into a pharmaceutical farrago, *Les Paradis artificiels* (1860; *Artificial Paradises*). The book combines a free translation of excerpts from De Quincey with Baudelaire's personal manifesto on drugs as a form of spiritual self-improvement. He describes the effects of opium and hashish and discusses the devious course of addiction—both subjects he knew well. Much of the book is a paean to the power of narcotics to "open up vast perspective, full of new revelations." Although *Artificial Paradises* is a rambling volume, it has had an enduring influence on the literature of drugs and psychedelic experience.

In a more respectable vein, Baudelaire wrote critical articles on his major contemporaries such as Hugo, Gautier, and Leconte de Lisle for Eugène Crépet's anthology, *Les Poètes français*. Not only did this commission produce fine essays, it also created a personal connection with the Crépet family. Years later the editor's son, Jacques Crépet, helped initiate the revival of Baudelaire's reputation.

In 1861 Baudelaire embarked on a futile and foolhardy project. He applied for membership in the Académie Française, the elite official organization charged with preserving the purity of the French language. Composed of forty eminent literati, "the immortals," the French Academy elects new members only when an existing member resigns or dies. Although Baudelaire claimed to scorn official honors, his application reveals how much he craved elite recognition. He hoped his election would remove the public disgrace of his trial. As if his recent conviction of obscenity weren't already an insurmountable obstacle to his election, he chose to apply for the seat left vacant by the death of Henri Lacordaire, a Catholic priest. The application created a scandal. Many believed the shameless poet was seeking publicity. When Baudelaire tried to canvass votes, a few members met him with insincere politeness. The rest either refused to see him or treated him with disdain. On the advice of the kindly Sainte-Beuve, Baudelaire withdrew. His bid for honor had delivered only a new humiliation.

Amid all these personal troubles, Baudelaire maintained the artis-
tic clarity to experiment with a new form, the prose poem. The idea of
the new form was simple but radical—to craft short prose passages that
would communicate the frisson of lyric poetry. Baudelaire announced
his dream of creating "a poetic prose, musical without rhythm and with-
out rhyme, supple and agile enough to adapt to the lyrical movements of
the soul." The notion of a prose poem was not original to Baudelaire. He
borrowed the form from Aloysius Bertrand's *Gaspard de la nuit* (1842). He
would also have known the German poet Novalis's influential *Hymns to
the Night* (1800). Baudelaire, however, brought an intensity and contem-
poraneity to the form, which he used to evoke provocative urban scenes.
His approach popularized the form both in France and abroad. The
prose poem would become part of his artistic legacy, especially through
his impact on Rimbaud, whose *Les Illuminations* (1886) was the first mas-
terpiece in the new genre.

The innovative project made a dramatic break from Baudelaire's ear-
lier poetry. Every poem in *Les Fleurs du mal* was rhymed and metrical.
Nonetheless, Baudelaire saw the "little poems in prose" as a "pendant"
or companion piece to *Les Fleurs du mal*. He intended to write one hun-
dred pieces, the same perfect number that had governed the design of
the first edition of *Les Fleurs du mal*. Like most projects from his final years,
however, it was never finished. He wrote only fifty pieces, which were not
collected until after his death. They are lesser works than the poems in
verse, but, as he had hoped, they add imaginative context to *Les Fleurs du
mal*. When they were published in 1869, they were given the generic title
Petit poèmes en prose (*Little Poems in Prose*). That timid description did not
last long. His feverish views of the modern city were reissued in 1917 as
Le Spleen de Paris.

Meanwhile Baudelaire worked intermittently on a private project,
a confessional book to be called "Mon cœur mis à nu"—"My Heart Laid
Bare." The title and the idea came from Poe, who had claimed that if any-
one could write a book that told the naked truth about the human heart,
it would revolutionize literature. For years Baudelaire filled notebooks
with candid observations about himself and the world. He intended to
publish his testament, but the work never went beyond a gathering of

pensées, notes, and short fragments. Nonetheless, the notebooks burst with irreverent ideas and aggressive energy. Baudelaire ponders theology, love, power, and society, but he has little to say about poetry. He does, however, make many provocative remarks about his ideas of beauty. "I can scarcely conceive," he wrote, "a type of Beauty which has nothing to do with Sorrow." Combined with other fragments, the work was published posthumously, under the more neutral title *Journaux intimes* (1887; *Intimate Journals*). The volume remains the most revelatory source for the poet's spiritual, emotional, and imaginative inner life.

Baudelaire had suffered a small stroke in 1860. A year later, symptoms of his syphilis returned. He lived in constant pain and also experienced brief bouts of disorientation. He expressed dark satisfaction in his decline. "I have cultivated my hysteria," he wrote, "...I have felt the wind of the wing of madness pass over me." Disease, drugs, and alcohol had ruined his health—at forty he was already an old man. One acquaintance described him as "aged, faded, weighed down although still slim, an eccentric with white hair." His other troubles increased. In 1862 Poulet-Malassis went bankrupt, which forced the publisher to flee to Belgium to avoid prison. Meanwhile *La Presse*, which had published twenty of Baudelaire's prose poems, dropped him as a regular contributor. The financial emergency forced the poet to sell all rights to his Poe translations, past and future, for two thousand francs. He then sold the rest of his work, including *Les Fleurs du mal* (which was actually owned by Poulet-Malassis), to another publisher for an equally small sum. Most of the money went to pay his debts.

In 1864, in a final attempt to secure financial independence and escape his Parisian creditors, Baudelaire moved to Brussels. He planned to give a lucrative series of lectures. He also hoped to secure a commercial publisher who would promote his works. Bourgeois and bureaucratic Brussels was not a city known for literary culture. The lectures proved badly paid and poorly attended. By the third event, the audience was so small that the depressed poet stopped in mid-lecture. Further talks were canceled. The sponsors paid him only a fraction of the promised fee. His other project also failed; the publisher declined to meet with him.

Baudelaire hated Belgium, but he did not leave. He had nowhere else to go, and he couldn't pay his hotel bills. He toyed with the idea of writing a devastating satire of Belgium, to be titled "Pauvre Belgique!" (Poor Belgium!), but he was too ill and exhausted to pursue the notion. Poulet-Malassis provided some temporary help by publishing the censored poems from *Les Fleurs du mal*, supplemented by some recent verses. The French prohibition against *"les poèmes condamnées"* did not hold in Belgium. There was always demand for stylish erotica. *Les Épaves* (*The Wreckage*) was published in February 1866 in an edition of 260 copies. The slim volume was the last book Baudelaire was to see released before his death.

In March, while visiting the Church of Saint-Loup in Namur on a holiday with friends, the poet suffered a stroke that paralyzed his right side. He was placed in a convent hospital, but his fits of swearing so scandalized the sisters that he had to be moved to a hotel. His mother, seventy-three years old and infirm, came to Brussels with her maid to care for him. It soon became obvious he would never fully recover. By April he had lost the ability to speak coherently, though his mind remained lucid. His friends sadly noted that the master of language was now bereft of words. In June the poet was brought back to Paris and placed in a hydro-therapeutic sanatorium in Chaillot. He lived another year, but his condition slowly deteriorated. On his deathbed he requested the Catholic last rites. He died in his mother's arms on August 31, 1867. He was forty-six.

III

To an unusual degree, Baudelaire's reputation rests on a single work, *Les Fleurs du mal*. Most poets of similar stature have a larger body of verse illustrating the stages of their careers. Baudelaire channeled his creative energy into the three successive editions of *Les Fleurs du mal*. The volume contains all of his mature verse, with the exception of his prose poems and a few minor works. From its first edition of 1857 to the posthumous volume of 1868, *Les Fleurs du mal* chronicles the development of the poet's imagination. It is difficult to follow that evolution, however, because the poems are arranged thematically, not chronologically. As the author revised the book, he inserted new poems among the existing ones. He considered the book's structure more important than documenting the stages of his own imaginative development.

Although Baudelaire meticulously planned the structure of *Les Fleurs du mal*, the size and scope of the final edition were the result of several historical accidents. Baudelaire had not originally written a large or inclusive book. He arranged the first edition of *Les Fleurs du mal* to contain exactly one hundred poems (not including his verse preface, "Au lecteur"). He considered 100 (or 10 × 10) a golden number symbolizing perfection. It is unlikely Baudelaire would have revised his elegant structure had not the government censor removed six poems. The author's numerological design was thereby destroyed, and his masterpiece sullied. At first, he considered writing six new poems, but he soon envisioned the more ambitious scheme of integrating all of his new work into future editions. Baudelaire spent the rest of his life expanding and rearranging *Les Fleurs du mal*. He died before the third edition was published; his literary executors made the final editorial decisions.

The history of the *Les Fleurs du mal*, therefore, was complicated, but it followed a simple course—each edition contained more poems. The first edition arranged its 100 poems in five thematic sections: "Spleen et Idéal" (Spleen and the Ideal), "Le Vin" (Wine), "Fleurs du mal" (Flowers of Evil), "Révolte" (Revolt), and "Mort" (Death). For the second edition in 1861, Baudelaire added a new section of eighteen descriptive urban poems, "Tableaux parisiens" (Parisian Scenes), and otherwise expanded the volume to 126 poems in total. The posthumous collection, subtitled *Édition définitive*, contained 151 poems. The six-part structure remained, but the editors added a "supplement" at the end that included a dozen new poems from *Les Épaves*.

The problem remained, however, of Baudelaire's six condemned poems—"Les Bijoux" (The Jewels), "Le Léthé," "À celle qui est trop gaie" (To One Who Is Too Cheerful), "Lesbos," "Femmes damnées: Delphine et Hippolyte" (The Damned Women: Delphine and Hippolyta), and "Les Métamorphoses du vampire" (The Metamorphoses of the Vampire). They could still not be included for legal reasons, so the "definitive" volume lacked those striking works. With a bitter irony Baudelaire might have appreciated, the complete and definitive edition of his masterpiece was neither complete nor defined according to his careful framework. Only in 1949 did French censorship law change so that a truly complete version of *Les Fleurs du mal* could be published—ninety-two years after the obscenity trial. The final version contains 158 poems.

The title of Baudelaire's collection is itself a microcosm of the poet's aesthetic. The phrase *"les fleurs du mal"* is evocative, contradictory, and allusive. "Flowers of evil" creates an image that is simultaneously beautiful and dangerous, pleasurable and corrupting. (In French the title phrase also carries the meaning "the flowers of sickness.") The title subverts the classical view that identifies the beautiful with the good; instead, it asserts there is a different kind of beauty associated with evil and sickness. The title is also sexually suggestive; the flower is the traditional poetic image for budding sexuality. (The fourth section of Baudelaire's collection, which is also called "Fleurs du mal," deals with the destructive lure and dangerous consequences of sexual desire.) Using the term *fleurs* to refer to his verse, Baudelaire alludes to the Greek root of *anthology*, "a gathering of flowers." The poet, therefore, positions his new collection as part of the classical tradition while simultaneously subverting it with *"du mal."* Unlike traditional collections of lyric verse, *Les Fleurs du mal* is not a gathering of beautiful poetic flowers, but a bouquet of evil blossoms.

All editions of *Les Fleurs du mal* begin with the prefatory poem, "Au lecteur" (To the Reader). Here Baudelaire follows a custom of introducing a book of poems with a verse dedication. In this case he does not address it to a particular individual, but to all future readers of the poem and book. Nothing in the tradition, however, prepares a reader for the author's offensive, aggressive, and rudely intimate assault. In the opening stanza Baudelaire accuses the reader (and himself) of folly, error, avarice, and vice. He mocks their weak remorse for these sins. He compares their vice-ridden selves to lice-infested beggars. More accusations of depravity and pusillanimity continue in each stanza. The poem ends by personifying their ennui as an idle but malevolent demon:

C'est l'Ennui! — l'œil chargé d'un pleur involontaire,
Il rêve d'échafauds en fumant son houka.

Tu le connais, lecteur, ce monstre délicat,
— Hypocrite lecteur, — mon semblable, — mon frère!

Boredom! Moist-eyed, he dreams, while pulling on
a hookah pipe, of guillotine-cleft necks.
You, reader, know this tender freak of freaks—
hypocrite reader—mirror-man—my twin!

Significantly, the poem is written in the first-person plural; there is no distance between the author and the audience. Everyone is implicated in the collective depravity and damnation.

"Au lecteur" has become one of the most influential poems in the modern canon. In these deliberately repulsive yet strangely seductive verses, Baudelaire not only announces the troubling themes of his book; he also offers a transgressive vision of human nature—weak, vicious, self-deceiving, irrational, and doomed. Baudelaire's dark worldview reflects his unorthodox and inverted Catholicism. He sees humanity as mired in original sin, but the suffering finds no redemptive savior. There is only boredom, self-destructive vice, and longing for oblivion. Baudelaire's accomplishment is to make this horrifying vision beautiful through the enchantment of language. In "Au lecteur" he violates traditional rules of poetic taste and decorum; he presents graphic images of death, decrepitude, and putrefaction in sonorous and brilliantly rhymed alexandrine lines. Moral transgression accompanies the aesthetic violation: Satan, "Trismegistus," rules the fallen world, and he leads humanity like puppets through sin toward death. The poem's famous final line, *"Hypocrite lecteur, — mon semblable, — mon frère,"* makes the reader complicit in both moral and aesthetic revolution. The *poète maudit* has called forth the *lecteur maudit*. The first flower of evil has bloomed and scattered its seeds.

There are few poems in which one can actually see the course of literary history change: "Au lecteur" is one of them. In many ways the poem should not work. Baudelaire employs an elegant style to present a repugnant view of humanity. He expresses shocking contemporary content in a controlled classical style. He perverts Catholic imagery to acknowledge

satanic power. He packs the poem with unpleasant imagery—an open
sewer of human misery and depravity. What unifies the caustic com-
bination is the commanding presence of Baudelaire's speaker, a man
characterized by alienation, anger, depression, and disgust for life. The
persona, however, is not merely autobiographical; the speaker is also a
literary creation. Baudelaire has distilled a tougher version of himself
to narrate *Les Fleurs du mal*—more audacious, intense, and determined
than the harassed and vulnerable man one finds in his letters. Baude-
laire's tortured, amoral, and often sardonic persona became one of the
models of the modern antihero. His descendants appear in thousands of
subsequent stories, poems, play, and novels. It would be hard to imagine
the novels of Louis-Ferdinand Céline, Jean-Paul Sartre, Jean Genet, or
Michel Houellebecq without Baudelaire's example.

"Spleen et Idéal," which opens *Les Fleurs du mal*, is the longest and most
diverse of the volume's five sections. The eighty-five poems in this section
make up more than half of the entire book. Although "Spleen et Idéal"
begins *Les Fleurs du mal*, it is in many ways the heart of the collection, pre-
senting nearly all of Baudelaire's themes in memorable form. The sec-
tion contains many poems that have achieved canonic status, not just in
France but internationally, including "L'Albatros" (The Albatross), "Cor-
respondances" (Correspondences), "Une Charogne" (A Carcass), "Chant
d'automne" (Autumn Song), "L'Invitation au voyage" (The Invitation to the
Voyage), "À une madone" (To a Madonna), "La Géante" (The Giantess), "Har-
monie du soir" (The Harmony of Evening), and the four parts of "Spleen."

The term "spleen" requires some explanation since the word in
English no longer carries the meaning it did for Baudelaire. No term is
more important in understanding *Les Fleurs du mal*, which may accurately
be described as a poetic exploration of spleen. In French, *spleen* is an
anglicism, but the original root is Greek. Greco-Roman doctors believed
that the black bile secreted by the spleen produced melancholy, one of
the four humors or temperaments of classical medicine. In French, *spleen*
came to mean a depression or melancholy characterized by guilt, ennui,
isolation, and despair. In English, the term also suggested outbursts of
splenetic anger. Spleen is the dominant mood of the Baudelairean persona
in *Les Fleurs du mal*, not merely in the opening section, "Spleen et Idéal,"

but throughout the book. "I sought to express," Baudelaire wrote his mother, "some of my sources of anger and melancholy." This dark temperament has become so closely associated with *Les Fleurs du mal* that in French the term is often called *spleen baudelairien*.

"Correspondances" deserves particular attention because it became one of the foundational texts of Symbolism. The poem proposes that the sounds and images of nature create mysterious correspondence between the visible and invisible worlds. The concept is not original to Baudelaire; it has its source in Plato and was a central tenet in Emanuel Swedenborg's mystical writings. (The eighteenth-century Swedish visionary claimed that God and the planets had revealed to him the secrets of the spiritual world.) Baudelaire also found this occult notion in Poe. "Imagination is an almost divine faculty," Baudelaire wrote, "that perceives immediately and without philosophical methods the inner and secret relations of things, the correspondences, and the analogies."

"Correspondances" creates the image of the world as a living temple, made up of a forest of symbols in which humanity wanders experiencing sights, sounds, and scents that suggest hidden connections. The poem presents a modern version of the neo-Platonic concept that physical reality is a projection behind which an ideal world waits, toward which we naturally aspire. No poem by Baudelaire had greater impact on literary history.

Although Baudelaire's ideas and poetry inspired the Symbolist movement, he is not, strictly considered, himself a Symbolist. Instead he (with Poe) is the movement's precursor and source. The term "Symbolist" was not even coined in relation to poetry until 1886, when Jean Moréas published the Symbolist manifesto for the movement in *Le Figaro*. (Before Moréas's influential article, Baudelaire and Verlaine were known as "Decadent" poets.) Symbolism came to be associated with a range of poetic styles that did not express ideas, emotions, or situations overtly, but instead communicated them indirectly by evoking them in the reader's mind. "Don't paint the thing," advised Mallarmé, "but the effect that it produces." Since conventional exposition was avoided, poets relied on image, symbol, and the hypnotic spell of verbal music. Symbolists also avoided didacticism, especially moral or political exhortation. The object was to enchant the readers to unlock their imagination, memory, and emotions. Verlaine's declaration, "Music above all things," became the movement's motto.

All of those Symbolist characteristics appear in Baudelaire's poetry, but they are neither his exclusive nor dominant procedures. His sensibility is larger and more omnivorous. In terms of literary history, Baudelaire is the transitional figure from Romanticism to early Modernism in a period dominated by the Realist novel. Romanticism and Realism meet and struggle in his work. The young Baudelaire had been formed by Romanticism with its emphasis on personality, emotionalism, and sincerity expressed in bold and colorful style. Romanticism, Baudelaire observed, was primarily "a manner of feeling." It was not, however, the way the adult Baudelaire felt about the world, himself, or poetry. He wanted to escape the hyperbolic emotionalism and Napoleonic obsessions of French Romantic poetry. His poetic ideal was more controlled and intellectual. Yet he never escaped the visionary impulse of the Romantic imagination. What tempered Baudelaire's Romantic longings was his attraction to the Realist mode of Honoré de Balzac. In Balzac, he found a modern imagination that encompassed both the stylish and sordid aspects of modern Paris, including its vast underworld of the poor and criminal classes. Baudelaire took the prose content of Realism and cast it into verse.

Although Baudelaire is not a Symbolist, certain poems in *Les Fleurs du mal* exemplify the ideals of the movement. "Harmonie du soir," one of the most exquisite lyrics in the French language, mesmerizes the reader through the radical purity of its lyric design; it is all verbal music and suggestive images. Baudelaire's poems often have strong intellectual content; they bristle with opinions, observations, and arguments. "Harmonie du soir," however, unfolds only through sensual imagery and emotion—sights, sounds, and scents all imbued with gentle sadness. The scene acquires additional resonance through religious images (censer, altar, blood) that suggest a mysterious sacrament of romantic sorrow. The poem is a pantoum, a Malayan form in which each line is repeated in a complex pattern to create an interlocking chain of sound and statement. The form was still new in French when Baudelaire employed it. The haunting melancholy of "Harmonie du soir" helped popularize the pantoum across Western literature.

A distinguishing feature of Baudelaire's poetry is the rich texture of his lines. French style, in both prose and verse, has historically been characterized as *clair, simple et logique* (clear, simple and logical). These qualities were especially evident in French poetry of the eighteenth and early nineteenth centuries. Poets crafted lines of remarkable elegance, balance, and lucidity. By contrast, Baudelaire's lines are more densely packed. They often contain words more typical of prose than the purified literary vocabulary of traditional French verse. Baudelaire shows less concern with the clarity and ease of his lines than with how much meaning he can concentrate into musical shape. In the process he created a new poetic style—richer, slower, less transparent than the work of his predecessors. The poems are not obscure, but neither are they entirely *clair* or *simple*. The dense texture contains more associative meanings. A reader catches the general sense of the poem immediately, but it requires repeated readings to comprehend the full range of the associations. Consider the opening lines of the second "Spleen" poem:

J'ai plus de souvenirs que si j'avais mille ans.

Un gros meuble à tiroirs encombré de bilans,
De vers, de billets doux, de procès, de romances,
Avec de lourds cheveux roulés dans des quittances,
Cache moins de secrets que mon triste cerveau.

More memories than if I'd lived a thousand years!

A massive chest of drawers crammed with lines of verse,
court summonses, love letters, novels, balance sheets
and locks of ample hair rolled up in old receipts
hides fewer secrets than my melancholy brain.

The rich texture and mixed diction give the lines a deliberate, authoritative, yet lyrical effect. This aspect of Baudelaire's style had a great impact on English-language poets. One sees his influence on poets as diverse as T. S. Eliot, Robert Lowell, Edna St. Vincent Millay, Richard Wilbur, and Weldon Kees.

The "ideal" of "Spleen et Idéal" may be less obvious than the "spleen." The Baudelairean ideal was not political or religious. He had no faith in political transformation or the redemptive power of Christianity. Likewise, love promised an ideal it failed to deliver. "Love is the desire to prostitute oneself," he wrote. Baudelaire's "ideal" was the "eternal clarity" of beauty. By beauty he did not mean something merely pretty or decorous. For him, beauty was both a visionary and sensual experience. Beauty was the intoxicating pleasure of perceiving the hidden order of the universe—either through nature or art. Once again Baudelaire borrows and refines this transcendent idea from Poe, who saw art as "the reproduction of what the senses perceive in nature through the veil of the soul." For Baudelaire, beauty represents the highest ideal of consciousness and the only true goal for art.

The later sections of *Les Fleurs du mal* are shorter and more unified than "Spleen et Idéal." Each part augments and explores themes presented in the opening section. "Tableaux parisiens" consists of eighteen poems that were mostly written during Baron Haussmann's renovation of Paris. The colossal urban renewal project built the modern Paris of wide boulevards and spacious parks, but the architectural achievement came at the expense of destroying most of the medieval city and displacing much of the urban population. Baudelaire's poems present the experience of the alienated and disenfranchised poor and elderly—the workers, beggars, prostitutes, infirm, and disabled. In the spirit of Balzac, Baudelaire presents a realistic street-level view of the modern city.

Baudelaire believed that modernity in art could be achieved by using the city as subject matter. There could be no ambitious innovation in style or form without new content: new subject matter facilitates artistic originality. In depicting Paris, the writer must go beyond "the spectacle of fashionable life" and include "the thousands of stray souls—criminals and kept women—who drift about in the underground of a great city." The sheer originality of the urban poems may be hard for contemporary readers to appreciate since Baudelaire's innovations have become conventional aspects of today's poetry. In "Tableaux parisiens," however, Baudelaire invented the language and perspectives of the modern city.

After the five "Le Vin" poems comes the book's title section, "Fleurs du mal." In the original edition, these twelve erotic poems appeared immediately after "Spleen et Idéal." For the second edition, Baudelaire placed them later in the book. This section had been at the center of the obscenity trial; three parts of it—"Lesbos," "Les Métamorphoses du vampire," and the first "Femmes damnées"—had been banned from publication. Baudelaire had protested that the poems did not encourage vice but condemned it. In the second edition, he positioned his erotic poems more carefully. The shift in placement demonstrates the importance Baudelaire gave to the volume's structure: where a poem appears influences how a reader interprets it. The "Fleurs du mal" sequence now appears only after the poet has explored the destructive ecstasy of intoxication in "Le Vin." To Baudelaire, *ennui* and *spleen* were the representative spiritual diseases of the modern age. Humanity seeks to cure them with dark fantasy and sensual pleasures—wine, drugs, sadism, and sex. The vices, however, provide only momentary respite from emotional pain or paralysis. The only true escape is death.

The dozen poems in the "Fleurs du mal" section form a cycle that explores sexual desire and its consequences. The cycle begins and ends with short, dark poems—the sonnet "La Destruction" and "L'Amour et le Crâne" (Love and the Skull), which describes a macabre engraving of Cupid sitting on a skull blowing bubbles. These bookends communicate that desire, decay, and death are the unifying themes of the cycle. The poems in "Fleurs du mal" show Baudelaire at his highest level of artistry dealing with his most sensational subjects. "Une Martyre" (A Martyr) describes a vicious sex murder in voyeuristic terms. "Lesbos" offers a melancholic sexual fantasy about Sappho's island, a paean to erotic awakening. The two "Les Femmes damnées" (The Damned Women) poems present compassionate portraits of lesbianism in a society where such romances end tragically. "Les Métamorphoses du vampire" presents a lubricious seductress who, once the sexual act is consummated, is revealed to be a rotted skeleton. "Un Voyage à Cythère" recounts a trip to Venus's island of love, which proves to be an island of death; Cythera is now inhabited by carrion birds devouring dead men hanging from a gibbet. The poems in "Fleurs du mal" are both deliberately disgusting and lasciviously beautiful. This is Baudelaire's hothouse of gorgeously exotic but evil flowers.

Baudelaire's views on love and sex are dark, disturbing, and contradictory. Sex is a brief rapture after which one wakes in a chamber of horrors. Some of his statements on love are intriguing; most are repellent. "The sole and supreme pleasure of Love," he claimed, "lies in the absolute knowledge of doing evil." His declaration that "Love is the desire to prostitute oneself" is not surprising from someone who knew sexual love only through prostitutes and demimondaines. His fear and loathing of erotic attachment reflected his own unhappy experiences. Baudelaire viewed sexual relations as a power struggle in which one party dominates the other. The best one can hope for in the sadomasochistic situation is that power might shift in one's favor. In his notes for "My Heart Laid Bare," he conflates sex and violence: "It would perhaps be pleasant to be alternately victim and executioner." Sex is not the foundation of love or marriage, and it is never associated with the renewal of life in children. It is rapture, regret, and laceration. In "La Destruction," the demon of lust brings the speaker to ruin and damnation. Sexual desire has left the narrator wounded in filthy rags. Who writes such a poem? A young man who knows that he will die from syphilis.

Yet Baudelaire is always the poet of contradiction. Wherever there is *spleen*, there is also the *idéal*. However doomed and disgusting the actual outcome of erotic love, the dream of it is ecstatic and ennobling. Jorge Luis Borges's exquisite line, "love, and the imminence of love, and intolerable remembering," could have been composed to describe Baudelaire's attitude. The imminence of love excited his gentlest emotions and highest ideals. In "L'Invitation au voyage," for example, the speaker invites his beloved to an imaginary world shaped to the heart's desire. Each stanza ends in the blissful refrain:

Là, tout n'est qu'ordre et beauté,
Luxe, calme et volupté.

There will be nothing but beauty and leisure,
harmony, calm and pleasure.

If the idea of romantic love excited his imagination, the bitter reality he found disgusted him. As the poet Pierre Emmanuel observed, "Erotic tenderness in *Les Fleurs du mal* is a ritual of idealization or of recollection; the sexual embrace precipitates degradation and oblivion."

The first four sections of *Les Fleurs du mal* present Baudelaire's doomed vision of modern life—a perspective that would color French literature for the next century. Trapped in a fallen world, we are paralyzed by boredom and melancholy. We long for unreachable transcendent meaning. God exists but is indifferent to our suffering; the Devil rules our daily world. To feel alive we seek intoxication, voyeuristic violence, and sexual debauchery. These indulgences provide momentary oblivion, but they ultimately corrupt us. There is no escape from our decline into death. What can we do in such a world? Baudelaire's answer is to revolt.

"Révolte" is the shortest section of *Les Fleurs du mal*, consisting of only three poems; it is also the most outrageous and transgressive section. Baudelaire's revolt is not against any temporal authority; it is an existential rebellion against God. "Révolte" proclaims the poetry of blasphemy. When *Les Fleurs du mal* was prosecuted, the poems in "Révolte" were cited as offensive to religious morals, but they were not ultimately censored. Post-revolutionary France was inured to sacrilege and anti-religious satire, though Baudelaire's poems pushed that tolerance to its limits. In "Le Reniement de saint Pierre" (Saint Peter's Denial), he presents the Crucifixion with respectful compassion, but then congratulates Peter for denying Christ. (The poem implicitly celebrates Baudelaire's elimination of Christ and the Redemption from his personal cosmology.) In "Abel et Caïn" (Abel and Cain), Baudelaire praises Cain for killing his own brother to protest God's plan.

"Révolte" ends with the most notorious poem in the collection, "Les Litanies de Satan" (The Litanies of Satan). This sonorous chant unfolds for fifteen stanzas, each of which ends with the refrain "*Ô Satan, prends pitié de ma longue misère!*" (Satan, have mercy on my endless grief!). Demonic parody is the method of satanic worship. Baudelaire models the refrain of his infernal prayers on the *miserere nobis* ("have mercy on us") of Catholic liturgy. Baudelaire's litany cast a spell on later literary Satanists such as Joris-Karl Huysmans and Aleister Crowley.

The strange power of "Les Litanies de Satan" comes from its tortured sincerity. Genuine blasphemy, as T. S. Eliot observed in regard to Baudelaire, needs to be "genuine in spirit and not purely verbal... the product of partial belief." In his rebellious and unorthodox way, Baudelaire believed in God and Satan. Seeing himself as irrecoverably flawed, he chose to embrace his own damnation. "There is in every man always," Baudelaire maintained, "two simultaneous allegiances, one to God, the other to Satan." Without abandoning his belief in God, he changed his allegiance. His Satanism was not a literary pose; it represented a genuine religious and existential rebellion against an indifferent God. Satanism offered a solution—however tragic and futile—to the intolerable human condition. As Eliot commented, "Damnation itself is an immediate form of salvation—of salvation from the ennui of modern life." Baudelaire revolted to make his damnation mean something beyond the sum of his own sins. Satanism was his existential leap to create a free and independent self in an absurd world. One of the central motifs of *Les Fleurs du mal* is Baudelaire's perverse and sardonic delectation of his own damnation.

"Révolte" unavoidably brings up Baudelaire's strange and inverted Catholicism. It is impossible to understand him as a secular poet. He remained inside the Catholic worldview even as he violently tried to escape it. "Nothing upon the earth," he wrote, "is interesting except religion." There were "two fundamental literary qualities," he asserted, "supernaturalism and irony." Both of those qualities insist that the surface of a thing is only part of its meaning. Baudelaire saw the world through a double lens where every material element had a supernatural correspondence. He reinvented his childhood religion in the same way— inverting it to reflect his own traumatic psychohistory with his stepfather, General Aupick. God the Father is rejected, and Satan the rebellious sinner is elevated.

"I am the spirit who denies," says Goethe's Mephistopheles. The symbols of Satanism are Christian images inverted; their power is not to redeem but to negate. Those reversals and rejections typify Baudelaire's worldview, which is simultaneously Catholic, satanic, secular, and supernatural. Denying the Redemption, he proposes a Catholicism without Christ—a faith, therefore, that lacks the power to redeem humanity from original sin. As Erich Auerbach observed, Baudelaire is seeking "not grace of eternal beatitude but either nothingness, *le Néant*, or a kind of sensory fulfillment, the vision of a sterile but sensory artificiality." Marcel Proust astutely described *Les Fleurs du mal* as "that sublime but sardonic book in which piety sneers, in which debauchery makes the sign of the cross; in which Satan is entrusted with the task of teaching the most profound theology."

One of the most potent and enduring images of European art has been the *danse macabre*, or dance of death. In this allegorical image, representative members of the social classes—emperor, knight, priest, lover, peasant—join hands with Death and dance to the grave. Mortality is the universal human fate. The final section of *Les Fleurs du mal*, "La Mort," is Baudelaire's *danse macabre*. In the original edition, it consisted of only three poems, but in the 1861 reprinting, he expanded it to six—five sonnets followed by Baudelaire's longest poem, "Le Voyage" (Voyaging). Four of the sonnets present classic *danse macabre* tableaux, the deaths of representative types—lovers, artists, poets, and the poor. In a tragic and absurd world, the oblivion of death becomes a sort of secular salvation: "It is the open doorway to unknown Heavens."

"Le Voyage" represents a more novel, ambitious, and inclusive enterprise than the sonnets since it carries the heavy responsibility of finishing the book. The poem begins in the child's infatuation with maps, prints, and travel. The poem then introduces another representative assembly—a group of travelers who embark on a voyage, each driven by a different motivation. They experience the beauties, boredom, dangers, and discoveries of their journey, but on returning, they feel mostly disappointment. Questioned about the journey, they report wonderful sights, but what impressed them most was universal folly and "*Le spectacle ennuyeux de l'immortal péché*" (immortal sin—a rather boring sight). All that awaits them now is a joyful final journey across the sea of shadows toward the nothingness they desire. This summary does little justice to Baudelaire's magnificent music, imagery, and invention. He sought to end his great book with a masterpiece, and he succeeded. Among its many splendors, "Le Voyage" astonishes the reader of Baudelaire's dark collection by concluding the section titled "Death" with joyful radiance, a final vision of death as the ideal realized only in oblivion.

In "The Poetic Principle," Poe maintained that a long poem could not exist because it was impossible for the reader or the poet to maintain the necessary "pleasurable elevation or excitement *of the soul*." Beyond half an hour, Poe claimed, attention flags and "revulsion sets in." Poe's essay was a cornerstone of Baudelaire's own aesthetic. "Le Voyage" represents Baudelaire's power to sustain the lyric elevation and excitement to its maximum length. For thirty-five stanzas he maintains his radiant enchantment. He casts a spell at once sublime and intimate. Baudelaire never wrote a more exquisite poem. Its tragic music brings *Les Fleurs du mal* to its logical and inevitable conclusion.

IV

Baudelaire was one of the most important critics of the nineteenth century. His views—some original, some adapted from earlier authors—radically changed the course of European literature. He wrote extensively on literature and the visual arts. Although posterity views him as a poet, his contemporaries knew him mostly for his prose and translations, except for the scandal of the *Fleurs du mal* obscenity trial.

Baudelaire is not a systematic theorist. Even his best work is often digressive, disorganized, and repetitious. Yet his writing carries authority. His forceful prose style conveys the originality and perspicacity of his insights. "Always be a poet," he wrote, "even in prose." Although Baudelaire prized pure intellect in the creative process, he did not see criticism as a cool, analytical enterprise; he admired "the religious intoxication of the great critics." Such spiritual inebriation informs his best essays, which pulse with emotional energy. Baudelaire explored poetics from the perspective of a practicing poet. He searched for clarity on the issues that obsessed him as an artist. As he explored his own creative dilemma, he articulated ideas that proved decisive to posterity.

The central idea of Baudelaire's poetics is the autonomy of art. He insisted that literature and indeed all art has no specific moral purpose. He understood that his theory contradicted the popular opinion that literature should have an ethical, religious, or political aim. "Most people assume," he observed, "that the object of poetry is some kind of teaching, that it must now fortify conscience, now perfect manners, now, in sum, demonstrate something useful." The didactic impulse, Baudelaire declared, was an aesthetic heresy. "Poetry," he insisted, "... has no object but itself." His conviction influenced the kinds of verse he wrote; for him, poetry was a lyric medium. As Valéry observed, *Les Fleurs du mal* was an unusual book for its era; it contained no historical poems, narratives, philosophical poems, or political opinions—a radical break from the norms of French Romanticism. Instead, it presented "charm, music, powerful abstract sensuality."

Baudelaire's theory of the autonomy of art is more nuanced than posterity's simple "art for art's sake" slogan. Although he believed true art had no moral aims, he recognized that individual works of art might nonetheless have moral consequences. In his notes for an abandoned preface to the second edition of *Les Fleurs du mal*, he struggled to respond to his criminal indictment for obscenity and blasphemy. Although the public scandal had wounded him, he professed indifference: "Some have told me these poems might do harm; I have not rejoiced at that. Others, good souls, that they might do good; and that has given me no regret." Baudelaire doesn't dispute the moral impact of his work; he declares it doesn't matter to him. The positive or negative moral consequences of a poem are immaterial to its artistic value. As Oscar Wilde wrote thirty years later in his preface to *The Picture of Dorian Gray*, "There is no such thing as a moral or immoral book. Books are well written, or badly written." That view remains as controversial today as it was during legal prosecutions of both authors. Neither Baudelaire nor Wilde won society's support or forgiveness for their aesthetic.

Artists find some ideas more useful than others. Baudelaire's belief in the autonomy of art and his rejection of didacticism spoke powerfully to the best poets of the next generation, who wanted to escape the traditional burden of addressing moral and political ideology, including the nationalism that had obsessed the Romantic era. Artistic autonomy became an animating principle of the Symbolists as well as the Decadent, Aesthetic, and early Modernist movements. Although Baudelaire's earliest followers were French—first Verlaine, Rimbaud, and Mallarmé, then Valéry, Jules Laforgue, and Paul Claudel—his impact was international. Symbolism influenced a diverse cohort of poets, including W. B. Yeats, T. S. Eliot, Wallace Stevens, Hart Crane, Stefan George, Rainer Maria Rilke, Gabriele D'Annunzio, Eugenio Montale, Alexander Blok, Osip Mandelstam, Émile Verhaeren, Federico García Lorca, and Antonio Machado.

If the purpose of poetry is neither moral nor didactic, does the art have any goal beyond the excitation of the senses, emotions, and imagination? However memorable as a phrase, "art for art's sake" is a circular assertion. Is there anything at stake other than a self-contained microcosm of sensation? At the center of Baudelaire's poetics is an emphatic response to this question. He recognized that narrow aestheticism encourages art that is merely decorative—mood painting in verse; it devolves into evanescent notions such as *poésie pure* (pure poetry) made of lovely sound and evocative images unattached to any exterior reality. Such aestheticism fosters a deliberately minor poetry. One might fault Baudelaire for many things, but never for minor aspirations.

For Baudelaire, the goal of poetry is beauty, but beauty is not an end in itself. Through beauty, poetry brings the reader into a new relationship with reality. The experience of beauty changes consciousness; it allows one to perceive qualities and correspondences of things not apprehensible in quotidian existence. There is an almost mystical sense of transcendent consciousness in Baudelaire's notion of beauty. Art is so ecstatic that it momentarily annihilates the self, freeing human awareness from its ennui and egotism. "In certain almost supernatural states of the soul," he wrote, "the profundity of life reveals itself, completely in any spectacle, however ordinary it may be, upon which one gazes. It becomes its symbol." The ecstasy of beauty, in Baudelaire's poetics, creates a consciousness that apprehends the hidden correspondences between the physical and spiritual realms of existence.

Scholars debate whether Baudelaire's theory of beauty was meant to be understood in literal or figurative terms. Perhaps here, as so often in his work, Baudelaire endorsed two contradictory ideas at once. He could never replace God in his worldview. (Why else did he need to "revolt" against divine order rather than merely ignore it?) He believed in a numinous supernatural level of reality toward which art aspired. This conviction gave the revelations of beauty an objective quality; one actually participates in something real, even if the experience is difficult to articulate in conceptual terms. To borrow Jacques Maritain's haunting phrase, beauty represents "the splendor of the secrets of being radiating into intelligence." From this perspective, beauty has redemptive power; it allows fallen humanity to participate briefly in a mysterious grace.

If Baudelaire's theory is understood on a figurative level, however, then beauty offers only the forms of meaning, which the individual fills with subjective significance. This interpretation, which has found favor with Freudians and Postmodernists, uses ideas that the poet himself explored. Baudelaire understood the allure of altered states of consciousness from stimulants and narcotics. He analyzed the ways in which those substances change private perceptions of reality. Art offers a similar, though more edifying, escape from the burdens of existence. Art illuminates the imagination, memory, and sensory perception. In this figurative interpretation, however, it does not transcend human consciousness by connecting it to a higher or ideal realm of existence.

Now comes the revolutionary twist in Baudelaire's poetics that gave his work its transfigurative impact on his early readers. If beauty is a heightened form of perception that reveals the occult correspondences of reality, then such intense consciousness can also transform the perception of objects considered ugly or evil. Discovering the beauty in such objects—disease, vice, intoxication, decay—reveals the secret purposes of their troubling existence. If art is to redeem human existence from purposelessness and ennui, then it must develop the capacity to accommodate the sordid and evil aspects of modern life. Art must develop, therefore, a poetics of evil.

Surely the darker aspects of Baudelaire's poetics originated in his own character. His melancholic temperament had always colored his sense of the beautiful—witness his passionate, early attachment to Poe. Baudelaire, however, developed his personal perspective into a general theory. *"Le beau est toujours bizarre,"* he declared. "The beautiful is always bizarre." His poetic project became to find the beauty in evil and repellent things. That ambition required the creation of a sensibility so capacious it could encompass both the grotesque and the sublime. A poetics of evil also demanded a style that could present his bleak material and yet give pleasure. *"Aux objets répugnants nous trouvons des appas,"* he wrote. "In repugnant objects we find charm." In his notes for an unfinished preface to *Les Fleurs du mal,* he boasts of his achievement, "I have found it amusing, and the more pleasant because the task was more difficult, to extract *beauty* from *Evil.*"

Baudelaire's celebration of the beauty of evil marked a revolutionary moment in European aesthetics. He overturned conventional notions of beauty and offered for admiration "objects repugnant" in both sensory and moral terms. The repercussions of this idea continue to echo through art and literature. The contemporary notion of transgressive art traces its lineage back to *Les Fleurs du mal.* Before Baudelaire, poets had presented the grotesque, ugly, and evil in their work, but these subjects had not been deliberately connected to the beautiful or sublime; nor had poets declared these subjects beyond moral judgment. The aestheticization of evil became central to Baudelaire's literary legacy, with enduring impact on fiction and drama as well as poetry.

Baudelaire's poetics of evil, however, possesses its own ambiguity. As an isolated idea, it appears quite simple, but how should it be interpreted in the larger context of his poetics? That integration poses a series of fundamental questions. Is the aestheticization of evil an end in itself, or must it be connected to a broader frame of values? Is the discovery of beauty of evil transgressive or redemptive? Does Baudelaire's aesthetic revolution destroy the traditional notions of beauty, including its inherent relationship with the true and the good? Or does Baudelaire instead only broaden the aperture of beauty to reconcile all that exists to an ideal order?

The purpose of beauty in Baudelaire's worldview is to provide a glimpse of ideal order. He affirmed Poe's rapturous description of humanity's "wild effort" to reach beauty, "an ecstatic prescience of the glories beyond the grave ... to attain a portion of that Loveliness whose very elements, perhaps, appertain to eternity alone." Baudelaire, however, specifies that evil and sickness are also beautiful. The contradiction seems irreconcilable until one remembers the poet's obsession with original sin and the fallen nature of humanity.

Baudelaire saw an essential duplicity in human nature, with its "simultaneous allegiances" to both God and Satan. His poetics sought to reconcile their contradictory claims. In this synthesis, his vision represents a secularization of the Christian notion that everything that exists, including evil, serves a divine purpose. Baudelaire relocates the theological concept from God to humanity. Since his poetics is human, it must reflect the duality of fallen humanity, half spirit and half animal. The individual exists in a perpetual tension between the two antithetical forces. "Invocation of God, or Spirituality, is a desire to climb higher," he wrote in his journals, "that of Satan or animality is delight in descent." Baudelaire did not conceive of one force without the other; neither was sufficient by itself to encompass reality.

For Baudelaire, beauty exists in an endless dialectic between the spiritual and animalistic elements of human nature. The energy of that dialectic animates Baudelaire's work. It also explains why his poetry is so difficult to interpret; it does not present static insights, but a dynamic relationship between contradictory forces. He believes that art needs to embody and express both the divine and demonic sides of human nature without entirely separating them.

The profound ambition and originality of Baudelaire's poetic vision suggests why *Les Fleurs du mal* has exercised such powerful fascination over posterity. In its design and execution, the book embodies the author's transformative aesthetic. Individually his poems are remarkable lyric works, animated by the author's musical genius and emotional candor; dozens of the poems live as independent works in anthologies and textbooks. Read together in Baudelaire's carefully arranged collection, however, they present the complexity and contradictions of the human condition. They tremble with the pleasures, sorrows, and angers of his foreshortened life. Baudelaire did not seek to go beyond good and evil; he strove to see both clearly as part of the dialectic of reality. He understood the power of ambiguity to express the double nature of the human soul.

In the final lines of "Le Voyage," Baudelaire brings *Les Fleurs du mal* to its visionary conclusion. Even on the final journey toward death, the poet rejoices in the "ecstatic prescience" of being fully alive, open to the mysterious beauty of mortal existence:

> *Nous voulons, tant ce feu nous brûle le cerveau,*
> *Plonger au fond du gouffre, Enfer ou Ciel, qu'importe?*
> *Au fond de l'Inconnu pour trouver du nouveau!*

> Our minds are burning, and we want to go
> into the magnitude of Heaven or Hell,
> to fathom the unknown, to find *what's new.*

Dana Gioia
Sonoma County &
Los Angeles, California
November 2020

A NOTE ON THE TRANSLATION

All of the poems in *Les Fleurs du mal* are formal. One might expect the great rebel poet to have been the inventor of *verse libre* (free verse), but the poems in this volume emphatically establish that Baudelaire was not only a formalist but a virtuoso formalist. (He collected his unmetrical and non-rhyming poetry in a separate volume of prose poems, *Le Spleen de Paris*.) There are many English translations of *Les Fleurs du mal*. I will not comment on them other than to say that, since the incantatory effect of meter and rhyme are essential to Baudelaire's aesthetic, and since form and content are inseparable, I felt it was imperative to preserve the full formality of the originals by translating them into metrical and rhyming poems.

The most prevalent meter in *Les Fleurs du mal* is the French alexandrine, a line of twelve syllables in which syllabic patterns are artfully arranged around a caesura or caesurae. In every instance I have rendered Baudelaire's French syllabics as English accentual-syllabics. That is, rather than just considering syllable count, I have taken word stress into consideration and introduced iambs (units of two syllables, unstressed and then stressed), the most common meter in English. In translating alexandrines, I at times shorten the line to a pentameter (ten or eleven syllables), and at times use our English hexameter (twelve or thirteen syllables). Not all of Baudelaire's poems are in alexandrines. He is a master of shorter, lyric meters as well. For those poems, I shortened my lines in an attempt to replicate their various syllabic lengths with accentual-syllabic dimeters, trimeters, and tetrameters. Since it is easier to rhyme in French than in English, I decided not to go for true rhymes in my translations, but a mixture of true and off rhymes that would replicate the original schemes. The license of off-rhyming allowed me to avoid contorting syntax in order to achieve true rhymes. Furthermore, English has a far larger vocabulary than French. Rather than translate each French word with the same English word each time it recurs, I have, partly out of formal considerations and partly in the interest of nuance, allowed myself to use the full breadth of the English lexicon. I also strove to give readers a Baudelaire who, though clearly still a writer of the nineteenth century, speaks without poetic inversions and diction in our contemporary idiom. Above all, my intention with these translations is to replicate in English the almost magical effect of the originals and to render beautiful in English Baudelaire's nontraditional beauties—disease, vice, intoxication, and decay.

The publication history of *Les Fleurs du mal* is complicated. I will summarize it here and explain how I have presented the poems in it. The first edition (1857) consisted of one hundred poems, in addition to the prefatory poem, "To the Reader." In that same year, after an obscenity trial, six of the poems were banned: "The Jewels" (21x), "Lethe" (31x), "To One Who Is Too Cheerful" (43x), "Lesbos" (110x), "The Damned Women: Delphine and Hippolyta" (110xx), and "The Metamorphoses of the Vampire" (115x). Baudelaire subsequently made minor revisions to the poems in the original edition and composed thirty-five new ones. He published this book as *Les Fleurs du mal* (without the banned poems) in 1861. This edition has come to be regarded as standard by scholars, and it is the one I use as the basis for my translations. However, I have inserted the banned poems (only removed from the ban by a legal decision in 1949) in the positions they occupied in the original 1857 edition.

I regard the translator as a medium, a vessel to be possessed by the original author's spirit. The months I spent summoning and submitting to Baudelaire (the months of March, April, May, and June of 2020, as the COVID-19 pandemic raged) were intense and exhausting. As the levels of infection surged around me, I worked on this bouquet of "sickly flowers." So strong is Baudelaire's personality, that he will never be fully exorcised from me. I am grateful for that.

Aaron Poochigian
New York City
November 2020

The
Flowers
of Evil

TO A FLAWLESS POET,

CONSUMMATE MAGICIAN OF FRENCH LETTERS

AND MY MUCH LOVED AND HIGHLY ESTEEMED

TEACHER AND FRIEND

THÉOPHILE GAUTIER,°

WITH FEELINGS

OF DEEPEST HUMILITY,

I DEDICATE

THESE SICKLY FLOWERS.

C.B.

To the Reader

For all of us, greed, folly, error, vice
exhaust the body and obsess the soul,
and we keep feeding our congenial
remorse the same way vagrants nurse their lice.

Our sins are stubborn; our repentance, weak.
When we confess, we ask high premiums.
Assuming cheap tears will expunge our crimes,
we gladly walk the same old muddy track.

Thrice-potent Satan, cushioned on perdition,
lulls our enchanted minds incessantly.
A perfect alchemist, he boils away
the valuable ore of our volition.

The Devil guides us like a puppet master.
Disgusting objects please us very well.
Each day we take another step toward Hell,
unflinching, through a putrid lack of luster.

In just the way that some broke debauchee
kisses and nips an old whore's martyred tit,
we steal, in passing, off-limits delight
and squeeze it, like a seasoned orange, dry.

The ranks of demons reveling in our brains,
like multitudes of maggots, swarm and seethe,
and Death, invisible river, when we breathe,
descends into our lungs and softly keens.

Why haven't arson, poison, rape, the knife
embroidered their enticing images

into our sad lives' tedious tapestries?
Sadly, our spirits don't have nerve enough.

There among all the jackals, panthers, mutts,
monkeys and vultures, scorpions and snakes,
those howling, yelping, grunting flocks and packs,
that infamous menagerie of our rots,

there's one most ugly, false and dirty birth!
Though hardly moving, uttering no grand sound,
he'd gladly make a shambles of this land
and, yawning, swallow the entire earth:

Boredom! Moist-eyed, he dreams, while pulling on
a hookah pipe, of guillotine-cleft necks.
You, reader, know this tender freak of freaks—
hypocrite reader—mirror-man—my twin!

SPLEEN
AND THE
IDEAL

1 Benediction

Whenever, by some holy proclamation,
the Poet is born into this tedious sphere,
his cussing mother, full of indignation,
holds up her fists to God (who pities her):

"Dammit! I wish that I had nursed a mess
of vipers rather than have spawned that runt!
Cursed be the night of evanescent joys
when he was thrust in me as punishment.

Since, from all womankind, you lit on me
to cause my shamefaced husband so much woe,
and I can't chuck this warped monstrosity
into the fireplace like a billet-doux,

I'll make the hatred that you heap on me
redound upon the agent of your doom.
Yes, I'll so twist this miserable tree
that its repulsive buds won't ever bloom!"

She swallows thus the foaming spit of spite
and, ignorant of Heaven's larger scheme,
constructs a pyre in the infernal pit
and consecrates it to maternal crime.

But, with an unseen angel as protector,
the outcast child drinks in the wine-like light
and finds ambrosia and vermilion nectar
in all that he is given to drink and eat.

He sings ecstatically from Calvary,
plays with the winds, discourses with the clouds.
His journey's guardian spirit loves to see
him happy as a songbird in the woods.

The people he would hold dear fear to love him
or, confident in his naïveté,
look for a way to wring a scream out of him.
They try out every sort of savagery.

They mix ash in or grossly hack and spit
on bread and wine intended for his mouth.
All he has touched those hypocrites throw out.
They chide their feet for walking in his path.

His wife keeps blabbing in the squares and quads:
"Well, since he thinks I'm worthy of a cult,
I'll act like one of the barbaric gods
and tell him that I want my image gilt.

Yes, I'll get drunk on genuflections, wine,
and sacrifices, incense, myrrh and nard,
all so that, laughing at him, I can own
the worship that he ought to give the Lord.

When I get bored with this impious show,
I'll lay my bold frail hands on him and start
ripping, with nails like those the Harpies grow,
a path the whole way inward to his heart.

I'll tear that heart, as if it were a red
and trembling baby bird, out of his chest,
then cruelly drop it in the dirt to feed
whichever vicious beast I like the most."

The pious Poet raises his serene
hands heavenward toward a refulgent throne,
and glamorous flashes from his spirit screen
from him how nasty everyone has been:

"Blessings on you, my Lord, who send us pain
to cure, divinely, our impurities—
a balm that helps the stalwart best sustain
the potency of holy ecstasies!

I know that you prepare a special spot
for poets up there in the holy zones,
and you will call me to an infinite
party with Dominations, Virtues, Thrones.°

I know our one nobility is pain,
and neither earth nor Hell can make it worse.
What's more, to plait my transcendental crown,
I need to tax time and the universe.

But all Palmyra's lost antiquities°—
the precious ores, the pearls out of the sea—
though you yourself arrange them, can't surpass
this crown of ever-dazzling clarity,

since it is made of perfect purity,
a holy metal from the primal blaze.
The eyes of man, majestic though they be,
are its obscure, sad mirror images."

2   The Albatross

Often, for fun, the sailors on a ship
catch albatrosses, big seabirds, who trail
languorously, for the entire trip,
some vessel sailing on the ocean swell.

Soon as the crew has caught him on the deck,
this despot of the sky, bereft of pride,

lets his expansive white wings dangle, like
a pair of oars, clumsily at his side.

The feathered traveler is a lame and weak
joke now who had been beautiful before.
One sailor holds a pipe up to his beak;
another limps to mock the crippled flier.

The Poet is like this royal of the clouds
who rides on storms and scorns all archery:
once he is exiled to the earth, shrill crowds
abuse him, and his giant wings are in the way.

3   Elevation

Over the ponds and over the ravines,
over the mountains, forests, clouds and seas,
beyond the sun, beyond ethereal space,
beyond the starry hemispheres' confines,

you fly, my spirit, with agility
and, like a good swimmer who loves the tide,
plow through immeasurable amplitude
with an ineffable and virile joy.

Fly far away from this depressing stink
and purify yourself in upper air.
Imbibe the holy fire that fills the clear
regions, as if it were a heavenly drink.

Happy is he who vigorously soars
beyond the boredom and the vast distress
so burdensome to our befuddled race
and dashes into those serene, bright spheres.

Happy is he whose lark-like intellect wings
into the vault of morning, who ascends
above this life and freely understands
the language of the flowers and silent things.

4 Correspondences

Nature, a temple in which porticoes
are growing, gives at times confounding talks.
The figurative groves through which man walks
look back at him with understanding eyes.

Hues, sounds and perfumes discombobulate
the senses just as far-off echoes fuse
into a deep and hazy synthesis
vast as the light of day and dark of night.

There are perfumes fresh as a baby's skin,
sweet as an oboe's skirl and green as grass,
while others are corrupt, imperious

and capable of infinite expanses,
like ambergris, musk, incense, benjamin,
which sing the rapture of the soul and senses.

5 I love recalling those antique, nude times . . .

I love recalling those antique, nude times
when Phoebus' gilded statues with his beams.
Then men and women played at games of speed
and no one was a cheater or a prude.
Yes, with the loving sunlight on their loins,
they exercised their excellent machines.

Back then prolific Cybele° did not
find all her sons so burdensome a weight,
but, like a she-wolf brimming with compassion,°
fed, from her dark brown nipples, all creation.
Like fruit without impurities or blots
whose smooth but firm rinds begged for little bites,
man, a refined, robust and mighty thing,
proudly exhibited what made him king.

Today, though, when the Poet would assess
such primal grandeurs in the nakedness
of man- and womankind, he feels a chill
despondency well up and grip his soul.
He meets with mournful and obscene tableaux.
O monstrous figures crying out for clothes!
O torsos suitable for travesties!
O bodies warped or morbidly obese
which the serene, grim god of Usefulness
swaddles like infant flesh in clothes of brass!
What of the tallow-pallid females whom
indulgence eats and feeds? And what of them,
the virgins, heirs to all their mothers' sins?
Pregnancy makes a hideous difference!

We moderns do have, in our time, it's true,
some charms the ancient peoples never knew,
like faces gnawed away by syphilis
and beauties, one might say, of listlessness,
but these inventions of a latter muse
can't ever make such invalids refuse
tribute to sacred Youth whose pleasing face
is simple and untroubled and whose eyes
are bright and bracing as a flowing stream.
Youth pours on all things music and perfume
and warm vitality insouciantly,
like birds and clear skies, flowers and the sea.

6   The Beacons

Rubens,° sloth-garden, river of oblivion,
pillow where young flesh never ends up making love
but where the primacy of life flows on and on
like waves in seas and breezes in the big Above.

Leonardo,° deep and solemn looking-glass
where, in the shadows of the glaciers and the pines
framing the countryside, there are mysterious
and winsome angels wearing irresistible grins.

Rembrandt,° sad hospital with murmuring corridors
and one immense crucifix fastened to the wall,
a place where prayers ascend in filth and breathe through tears
and winter sunlight passes brusquely down the hall.

Michelangelo,° vague place where Hercules
mingles with Jesus Christ, and dead men's mighty shades
rise from the earth, stand stiffly in the twilight haze
and, pointing with their fingers, tear their funeral shrouds.

A raging boxer with the brashness of a faun,
you showed us there is beauty in vulgarians;
O great heart filled with pride, O sickly, sallow man,
Puget,° you were the outlaws' melancholy prince.

Watteau,° a carnival where many famous hearts
go flitting here and there like butterflies ablaze,
while in an airy room a chandelier imparts
insanity to dancers spinning on their toes.

Goya,° nightmare full of things unknown and wicked,
of fetuses sautéed for midnight witches' revels,
of hags in front of mirrors and children wholly naked
who dress themselves most carefully to lead on devils.

Delacroix,° lake of blood where evil seraphim
live in the shade of ever-flourishing fir trees,
where curious fanfares fade away into the gloom
and disappear, like one of Weber's stifled sighs.°

Lamentations, maledictions, cries of hate
and ecstasy, entreaties, sobs and hymns of praise
are sounds with which a thousand mazes resonate.
They are a holy opiate for the human race!

They are the watchword of a thousand sentinels,
an order that a thousand speaking horns have brayed;
they are the beacon on a thousand citadels,
the shout of hunters lost inside an endless wood.

Without a doubt, Lord God, this is the most sublime
assurance we can give you we are of some good—
that this impassioned sob rolls on and on through time
and dies out on the shore of your infinitude.

7   The Sick Muse

Poor muse, the sun is up. What's wrong with you?
Your eyes are full of what you dreamt last night.
I see, reflected in your present hue,
cold, taciturn insanity and fright.

Have the green succubus and crimson fiend
emptied on you their urns of love and dread?
Has Nightmare's impish and despotic hand
plunged you into Minturnae's famous mud?°

I pray your breast, fragrant with healthiness,
constantly be the home of fine thoughts; may
your Christian blood flow just as strictly as

the measured music of an ancient ode
over which Phoebus, lord of melody,°
presides, and also Pan, the harvest god.°

8   The Muse for Sale

O muse of mine, you love rich palaces,
but, when all January whips its wind
through drifts and twilight boredom, will you find
some half-burnt sticks to warm your purple toes?

When moonbeams struggle through your windowpanes,
will your blue shoulders find their former tint?
Knowing your throat is dry, your money spent,
will you change coffered ceilings into coins?

To earn your daily bread you have to swing
the censer like an altar boy and sing
those holy hymns in which you don't believe,

or vend your charms to eyes that don't perceive
your tear-stained laughter—an emaciate fraud
who somehow pleasures the splenetic crowd.

9   The Bad Monk

Long ago cloisters had the sacred Truth
of Holy Scripture painted on their walls.
These pictures warmed the hearts of men of faith
and eased the chill inside their stringent cells.

Back when the Word of Christ was prosperous,
more than one famous monk, unknown today,

setting his easel in a charnel house,
glorified death in a straightforward way—

my soul's the tomb in which I live and walk
forever on and on, bad eremite.
No pictures cheer this miserable retreat.

O lazy monk! When will I learn to make
what my hands write and what my eyes adore
out of the living vista of despair?

10   The Fiend

My youth was nothing but a dark storm, shot
through, now and then, by brilliant bursts of sun.
Thunder and flooding worked such total ruin
that ripe fruit's tough to come by in my plot.

Here in my fall, my mental harvesttime,
I have to rake and shovel to regain
bits of the sodden soil in which the rain
dug holes, each one as spacious as a tomb.

Who can say if the flowers of which I dream
will find in dirt washed like an ocean shore
the mystic nurture that would make them bloom?—

The pain! The pain! Time eats our lives. What's more:
a secret Fiend, our hearts' devourer, grows
stronger by feeding on the blood we lose.

11   Bad Luck

You'll need a lot of initiative
to lift that great weight, Sisyphus.°
However much one works for success,
Art takes time and Life is brief.°

My heart beats like a muffled drum
that leads a funerary march
far from the famed tombs near the church
to the graveyard where no mourners come—

but, deep in mantle, gems are dozing
in uncollected obscurity
out of the reach of pick and spade,

and the sweetest flowers are releasing
their secret perfume reluctantly
in the remotest solitude.

12   The Past Life

I lived for years beneath a vast arcade
which ocean suns lit with a thousand hues.
At dusk the columns—tall, straight, sumptuous—
transformed the scene into a grotto made

of basalt. Rolling mirrors of the skies,
the waves mixed, in a solemn, mystic way,
their opulent, all-powerful harmony
with sunset hues reflected in my eyes.

I lived there in voluptuary ease,
amid the heaven and sea, in gorgeousness,
and naked slaves, breathing exotic scent,

waved palm leaves up and down to cool my brow.
They had one purpose only: to augment
the mournful secret that had laid me low.

13   Traveling Gypsies°

The fire-eyed tribe of prophets left last night.
Some had their kids strapped to their backs, while others
fed powerful infant famishment a mother's
opulence from a loose and dangling tit.

The men now walk with gleaming weaponry
alongside wagons loaded with their kin.
Their eyes, eyes rendered heavy by a wan
regret for lost illusions, scan the sky.

The cricket in his sandy solitude,
seeing them passing, plays a louder tune.
Cybele,° doting, makes the trees more green,

makes rock jet water and the desert bloom
before these travelers for whom, like home,
the coming darkness's dominion opens wide.

14   Man and the Sea

Free man, you will forever love high seas.
They are your mirror; you can see yourself
tossed in the endless tossing of a gulf.
Your soul is no less bitter an abyss.

You like to dive to the reflection's core.
Your eyes and arms embrace it, and the cry

of its unmanageable misery
distracts your heart, sometimes, from its own roar.

You both are shadowed and mysterious:
man, none have plumbed your void the whole way through;
O sea, who sees the wealth inside of you?
You two prefer to keep your secrets close.

Yet pitilessly for unnumbered eons
you have attacked each other, so do both
of you delight in homicide and death,
O timeless warriors, O ruthless twins!

15   Don Juan in Hell°

When Don Juan tumbled to the nether flood
and gave Charon the ferryman° his fare,
a man fierce as Antisthenes,° a sad
beggar, laid vengeful hands on either oar,

and women with their robes undone, breasts showing,
convulsed beneath the black sky overhead
and skulked behind him with a long, loud lowing
like cows soon to be slaughtered to some god.

Sganarelle,° laughing, sought what he was owed
while, with a trembling finger, Don Luis°
revealed to all the shore-wandering dead
the son who'd mocked his gray senility.

Beside the traitor who was once her man,
Elvira° shook with grief and, virtuous,
asked for a last smile, one that had the shine
and sweetness of his erstwhile promises.

While, stiff and armed with steel, a man of stone
stood at the helm and cleaved the dusky tide,
Juan, leaning on his sword and looking on
the wake behind them, never deigned to look aside.

16   Punishment for Pride

Some years back when Theology was in full bloom
and flourishing with utmost energy and vim,
a famous doctor of religion,° it is said,
since he had salvaged souls that had been mostly dead
and roused them from the depths of lightless lethargy,
went on to thrust himself toward sacred ecstasy,
seeking by mystic pathways, to himself unknown,
a state pure souls alone were able to attain.
Like someone who had climbed too high and was afraid,
he cried out in the raptures of satanic pride:
"O little Jesus, how I have exalted you!
But if I chose to lay your helpless body low,
I'd mix disdain in with your all-too-sacred state
and leave you merely an outrageous neonate."

Suddenly his intelligence was cracked in two.
His solar brilliance was concealed in weeds of woe.
Utter disorder rolled into the gifted mind
that once had been a precious temple where, enshrined
beneath illustrious ceilings, he had reigned supreme.
Now speechlessness and night set up their camp in him,
as if he were a vault to which the key was lost.
Henceforth he walked the city like an idle beast
and, when he passed through gardens without fathoming
the things he saw, as blind to winter as to spring,
he was as negligible as a broken tool,
and children jeered at him as if he were a fool.

17 Beauty

Men, like a stone-dream, I am beautiful.
My breasts, which bruise hand after hand, are made
to give the poets an inhibited
love that, like matter, is perennial.

Like an unfathomed sphinx,° I rule the sky
and make my heart of snow as white as swans.
I hate excitement that displaces lines.
I know no laughter and I never cry.

Before the grandiose poses that my body
strikes with a fierce and monumental air,
poets will waste their days in serious study,

because I have, to keep my lovers close,
pure mirrors in which all is lovelier:
my eyes, eyes with eternal limpidness.

18 The Ideal

The various charms of trivial portrayals
in worn vignettes,° works of passé design—
the feet in brogues, the fingers clacking zills—
never will fascinate a heart like mine.

Let Paul Gavarni, artist of chlorosis,°
keep all his prattling invalids, his pale
paragons, since among such bloodless roses
I never find my rubicund ideal.

What does my heart, my Hell-deep heart, demand?
It's you, Lady Macbeth,° a killing mind,
a storm-born dream of Aeschylus,° or you,

great Night, offspring of Michelangelo,°
who calmly twist, in an eccentric pose,
flanks fashioned to be fed to Titans' maws!°

19   The Giantess

Back when prolific Nature birthed large-size
progeny daily, it would have been fun
to live beside some girlish giantess
like a luxurious cat beside a queen

and watch her body blossom with her soul
as she enjoyed her frightful exercise
and fathom if she felt a loving zeal
from the vague moisture swimming in her eyes,

to wander her colossal form at ease
and mount the slopes of her enormous knees,
and, in the summer, when the harsh sun laid

her out, lethargic, over her estate,
to sleep casually in a vast breast's shade
like a quaint village at a mountain's foot.

20   The Mask

An Allegorical Statue in the Style of the Renaissance
For Ernest Christophe, Sculptor°

Let us admire this Tuscan masterpiece:
Two sisters, Elegance and Strength, present
a cascade of the body, rippling thews.
This woman, this astounding monument,

winningly slim, yet with a buxom shape,
was made to couch on a refulgent throne
and charm the spare time of a prince or pope.

O look at the refined, voluptuous grin
where Self-conceit parades its ecstasies;
that sly, mocking and apathetic stare.
Those dainty features, wholly veiled in gauze,
proclaim to us with a triumphant air:
"Love crowns my head, and Pleasure asks for me!"
Look closely at this noble work: what charm
is flowing out of her gentility.
Come walk the whole way round her lovely form.

O blasphemy of art! O fatal trick!
This woman, this celestial lure toward joy,
is at the top a double-headed freak!

—But no, it's just a mask, a visual ploy,
that face lit up by an exquisite grin,
and, look, the features on the actual face,
crushed miserably underneath a screen,
seem to seek shelter in deceptiveness.
Poor gorgeous thing! The river of your tears
voluminously wets my worried soul.
Your slyness thrills me, and I slake my fierce
thirst in your eyes' tormented waterfall.

—Why is she weeping, she, pure pulchritude,
who forces mankind to obey her laws?
What secret evil chews her sinewy side?

She weeps, you fool, because she's lived, because
she still is living. But what makes her grieve
the most, what really brings her to her knees,

is that tomorrow she must be alive
still, and the next day, and the next—like us.

21   Hymn to Beauty

O Beauty, do you come from Paradise
or Hell? Your gaze, infernal and divine,
brims over with benevolence and vice,
and that's why people liken you to wine.

Your eyes are full of sunrise and sunset;
you strew fragrances like a stormy night.
Your mouth is like a flask; your kiss, a draught,
makes heroes weak and children resolute.

Are you here from the stars? From the abyss?
The dog of Fate attends your daily stroll.
You sow at random jubilance and woes.
You rule all things but aren't responsible.

You mock the corpses that you trample on.
You wear Abomination as jewelry,
and Homicide, your favorite precious stone,
jigs on your belly in an amorous way.

Candle, the dazed moth seeking out your glow
ignites and utters: "Blessed be my doom!"
Panting above his love, the handsome beau
looks like a sick man hugging his own tomb.

Beauty, you simple, vile monstrosity,
I cannot care about your origin,
provided that your gaze, smile, feet show me
a sweet infinity I have never known.

Angel or Siren?° Satan? God? Who cares,
so long as you, O queen with eyes of satin,
O scent, light, rhythm, make the universe
less loathsome and the lapse of time less leaden?

21x   The Jewels

My love was nude but, since she knew my heart,
had kept her jewels on—that was all she wore.
This rich array displayed the conquering art
slave girls might use in kingdoms of the Moor.

This gleaming world of precious stones and gold,
when it performs its pert and mocking dance,
drives me out of my mind. Yes, I go wild
over the back-and-forth of lights and tones.

She lay alluringly, prepared for love,
and from a couch looked down on my desire
which, like a sweet and oceanic wave,
rose for her, as the tide climbs up the shore.

She watched me with a vanquished tiger's eyes
and posed and posed in an indifferent way.
Candidness, mixed in her with artifice,
endeared her metamorphoses to me.

First it was arms and shoulders, back and thighs,
laved as with oil and rippling like a swan,
that moved before my calm and probing eyes.
Then belly and breasts, grape clusters on my vine,°

advanced and urged me more than demons could
to smash the peacefulness my soul had reached,

to smash to bits the crystal colonnade
in which it had been all-too-calmly couched.

Her waist so thickened into either hip
that I observed what seemed a new design—
A buxom girl below, a boy on top.
The blush was perfect on her fawn and brown.

Because the sun was fixed on going out,
we two were seeing by the hearth alone,
and, every time it sighed a sigh of light,
it flickered crimson on that amber skin.

22   Exotic Perfume

When, on a warm fall evening, I breathe in,
eyes shut, the perfume of your balmy breast,
I see a very happy stretch of coast
lit by the fires of an unsubtle sun:

a lazy island on which Nature grows
peculiar trees and fruits that taste like bliss,
sinewy males whose limbs are vigorous,
and females flashing candor from their eyes.

Led by your fragrance to this charming place,
I see a wharf with ships and rigging still
worn out from riding on the ocean swell;

meanwhile the scent of verdant tamarind,
swelling my nostrils, riding on the breeze,
mixes with sailors' chanteys in my mind.

23 Her Hair

O tumble to the collarbone, O fleece,
O locks, O fragrance full of "I don't care,"
what ecstasy! To stuff a gloomy place
with all I know is rife within this mass,
I'll shake it like a kerchief in the air.

Africa: torrid; Asia: languorous—
whole worlds half-dead and very far away
live in your depths, redolent wilderness.
While other spirits sail on melodies,
mine, O my darling, swims in your bouquet.

I'll go to where both resinous man and tree
lose consciousness beneath a tropic blast.
Strong, swelling tresses, carry me away!
O onyx sea, O dazzling reverie,
made up of sail and pennant, oar and mast:

a sounding harbor where my soul can swill
colossal waves of sounds and scents and hues,
where vessels on the silk and golden swell
open their arms wide to the sky to cull
the heat there making an eternal daze.

I'll dunk my lust-besotted head in this
dark sea where what I want is kept in prison.
My subtle soul that rolls in its caress
will rediscover you, ripe languidness,
O endless rest, ambrosial intermission.

Indigo tresses, you, O shadow tent,
lend me an ever-azure, open sky.
I'll gladly sink into the mingled scent

the little wisps along your neck ferment—
cocoa oil, musk and tar in harmony.

A long time! Always! In your mess of hair
my hand will scatter every precious stone
so that you not be deaf to my desire.
Paradise of my dreams—that's what you are,
my gourd for drinking memory's best wine.

24   I love you as I love nocturnal skies . . .

I love you as I love nocturnal skies,
O grandiose reserve, O tear-filled vase.°
Attractive one, midnight accessory,
I love you more the more you run from me,
the more mockingly you expand the breach
between the big blue and my farthest reach.

I rush you, climb you, outrage you as if
I were a choir of worms, and you, a stiff.
Implacable, cruel creature, I adore
your chill—it makes you even lovelier.

25   Adulterated woman, you would screw the whole . . .

Adulterated woman, you would screw the whole
world in an alley. Boredom makes you mean of soul.
Merely to work your teeth, as if you're at some sport,
you spend the whole day gnawing on a lover's heart.
Lit up like a boutique's front windows or like trees
adorned with lanterns for outdoor festivities,
your eyes use borrowed power in a haughty way,
utterly mindless of your beauty's monarchy.

O blind and deaf machine, fecund in cruelties,
drinker of all creation's blood, wholesome device,
why are you not embarrassed? Why have you not seen,
in every mirror that you pass, your charm's decline?
Has the immensity of every wicked plot
you brilliantly conceive not filled your heart with fright,
when Nature, mighty in her secretive designs,
uses you for her own ends, O you queen of sins,
foul beast, to knead out men of ingenuity?

O muddy grandeur! O sublime ignominy!

26 *Sed non satiata*°

Bizarre and shadowy divinity,
musky mélange of perfume and Havana,
work of an obeah, Faust° of the savannah,
child of the night, witch cut from ebony,

love dancing on your lips is more to me
than opium and Malbec, Cabernet.
Whenever my desires parade your way,
your eyes, like cisterns, slake my great ennui.

Yes, large and dark, they pour your spirit out.
—O ruthless demon, serve a drink less hot.
I am no river Styx° to wrap you round

nine times, nor can I, so that I could wound
your will and lay you low, dire debauchee,
on your infernal mattress play Persephone.°

27   When she, a billow of bejeweled clothing . . .

When she, a billow of bejeweled clothing,
enters, it seems that she is dancing like
an endless snake some charmer has got writhing
rhythmically up and down a shaken stick.

She understands our misery as well
as a dark morning does, or desert air.
Like long networks of breakers in the swell,
she moves about without the slightest care.

Fine stones have gone into her polished eyes,
and in that strange symbolic nature where
classical sphinxes° mix with seraphim,

where everything is keen steel, gold and gem,
there shimmers always, like a useless star,
a sterile woman's frigid stateliness.

28   A Serpent Dancing

I love to take you in,
indolent one,
to watch your gorgeous skin
glint like chiffon.

In the depths of your curls that smell
of oil and scent,
in that vagabond dark sea-swell
with an indigo tint,

my dreaming soul is cruising
toward distant skies

like a ship in the morning rousing
before a breeze.

Your eyes are gems where gold
and iron meet,
where nothing is revealed
of bitter or sweet.

Whenever you move, entrancing
paragon,
you seem a serpent dancing
along a baton.

Your head, resembling a smooth
young elephant's,
sways like a child's beneath
your indolence,

and your body leans and stretches
like a trim ship
that rolls and rolls and drenches
its yards in the deep.'

When the waters of your mouth
mount to your lips
like the sea rising beneath
thawed ice caps,

I know I am drinking a red
wine, strong and tart—
a night sky over my head
spangling my heart.

29   A Carcass

Do you recall, my love, the thing we saw
that fine morning in luscious June?
Right where the pathway turned, a carcass lay
on a bed made of cobblestone.

Her legs akimbo like a harlot's, she,
a boiling, toxic, sweating mass,
exposed, in an aloof, ironic way,
a belly puffed with noxious gas.

The sun was shining on that heap of rot
as if to cook it thoroughly
and pay back Nature many times for what
she had arranged in pregnancy.

The sky kept gaping as the noble stiff
opened, flower-like, to the dawn.
The stench was so intense it seemed as if
you just might pass out on the lawn.

The blowflies in her bowels made a hum;
there also was a horde of seething
maggots flowing like a busy stream
across her ripped and living clothing.

The whole ensemble burgeoned with a rasp
or swelled and tumbled like the sea.
It seemed her flesh, filled with a sort of gasp,
thrived on its own fecundity.

This cosmos loosed a curious music-making,
like running water, or a gale,
or grain a farmhand with a rhythmic shaking
keeps moving in a winnowing pail.

Such evocations, like a dream, diffused—
a challenging, half-done design
some artist had forgot and later must
complete from memory alone.

A restless mongrel, crouched behind a rock,
studied us with a greedy stare,
biding her time until she could get back
the chunk she had abandoned there.

—And you, my being's center, you, my love,
the star and angel of my eyes,
someday will match that offal. You will prove,
at last, unsightly putridness.

Yes, charming princess, you will look like that
when the last sacraments are over
and you go down among the dead and rot
beneath the grass and flowering clover.

Then tell the maggots, O my gorgeous one,
as they consume you kiss by kiss,
that I preserve the beauty and divine
essences of my mistresses.

30 *De profundis clamavi*°

Please show me pity, you, my only passion.
Here in the dark pit where my sad heart lies
I see a glum realm rimmed by leaden skies
and rife with all-night terrors and damnation.

For six long months a cold sun casts its beams.
For six long months night hides away an earth

even more naked than the polar north
—no animals, no greenery, no streams.

No horror in the world is crueler than
the frigid torture of that glacial sun
and that night vast as ancient Anarchy.

I envy most the lower beasts because,
sunk deep in ignorance, they doze and doze.
My skein of time unwinds so sluggishly!

31   The Vampire

Yes, you are one who like a blade
has gotten into my sorrowful heart.
Yes, you, as forward as a crowd
of demons, are at hand, dressed smart,

to make your bedroom and estate
in my humiliated soul.
—You monstrous thing, you bind me as tight
as manacles bind a criminal,

as card games bind a gambling man,
as bottles of red wine bind a sot,
as carcasses bind blowfly and rat.
—Cursed woman, I am wholly your own.

To win my freedom back from you,
I have begged mercy of a blade.
I have decanted poison, too,
to fix my lack of fortitude.

Scorning the cowardice I showed,
both knife and poison said to me:
"You are not worthy to be freed
from your detestable slavery.

If either one of us should strain
to liberate you from her empire
—fool!, the carcass of your vampire,
beneath your kisses, would live again!"

31x   Lethe°

Come to my heart, you cruel and sullen thing,
loved tiger, creature with a lazy air.
How long I've longed to plunge my trembling
fingers into the thickness of your hair!

I want to stash my much tormented head
beneath your fine apparel, in your scent,
and breathe, as if out of a flower that's dead,
the redolence of what our love once meant.

I want to sleep, to sleep instead of live,
and, in a state as sweet as lifelessness,
to dream of kissing you without reproof,
kissing that body with the copper gloss.

If I should choke down my oppressive sighs,
it would be in your couch's deep abyss.
Your breath is fragrant with forgetfulness.
Lethe itself is in your every kiss.

My destiny from now on, and my bliss,
will be to suffer like an innocent

and doomed convict, a docile martyr, whose
desire intensifies his punishment.

To cure my bitterness, I'll suck in drugs
of oblivion, of all-consuming rest,
from your ungentle breast's bewitching dugs.
There never was a heart inside your chest.

32   Once, sleeping with a horrid Jewish crone ...

Once, sleeping with a horrid Jewish crone
(we lay like corpses), I began to dream,
beside that flesh bought for a given time,
of someone beautiful who once was mine.

I saw afresh her native majesty,
her gaze armed with vitality and grace,
her hair a scented casque around her face.
These memories reanimated me.

I would have wildly kissed your noble skin,
and rolled out treasuries of deep caresses
from your young feet to your dusky tresses,

if you had been able to devise,
one night, some easy tears, O wicked queen,
to dim the splendor of your frigid eyes!

33   Postmortem Remorse

After you go to sleep, my shady sweet,
in the dark stone of your memorial
and come to own as bedroom and estate
only a leaky vault and funeral hole,

when, by squeezing tight your panting breast
and lithe, sloth-graceful haunches, slabs annul
your heartbeats and volition and arrest
the feet that went out looking for a thrill,

the tomb, intimate with my infinite
reveries during long nights without sleep
(tombs understand the poet's mind, of course),

will say, "Flawed courtesan, what good was it—
your ignorance of why the dead ones weep?"
And worms will gnaw your carcass like remorse.

34   The Cat

Come to my lovesick lap, my cat, my dear.
Retract the talons of your paws
and please, please drown me in that gorgeous stare
made out of steel and glass.

Whenever my fingers pet, with perfect ease,
your head and supple derriere,
whenever they excitedly caress
your electrifying fur,

I seem to see my woman. Her scrutiny,
cold and unending, like your own,
affable creature, flays me like a blade,

and, from her feet up to her head,
a subtle air, a dangerous bouquet,
radiates from her dark brown skin.

35   *Duellum*°

Two warriors in a duel: steel has struck,
and blood is flowing. Sparks are in the air.
The clang of metal and the give-and-take
are youth in service to some loud amour.

Their blades are broken, like our youth, my love,
but teeth and fingernails avenge the lost
sword and the shattered dagger soon enough.
—O hearts mature in ulcerated lust!

Our brawling champions have tumbled down
into a gorge where lynx and panther dwell.
The dry thorns bloom with skin—that pit is Hell;

our friends are in it. Savage Amazon,°
let's roll around down there without regret
till we immortalize our ardent spite.

36   **The Balcony**°

Lover of lovers, mother of recollection,
you who are all my pleasure, all my duty,
remember now the depth of my affection,
sweet hours beside the fire, and twilight beauty,
lover of lovers, mother of recollection.

Evenings lit only by a glowing coal,
rose-scented evenings on the balcony—
how sweet your breast was, how sublime your soul.
We uttered phrases that will never die
on evenings lit only by a glowing coal.

Sunlight is gorgeous in the balmy dusk!
Our hearts are big; the views are limitless!
I swear I smelled your blood (it smelled like musk)
when I came close, princess of princesses.
Sunlight is gorgeous in the balmy dusk!

A wall arose that was the thickening night.
Your eyes were there—my own eyes felt them out.
I drank your breath, O poisonous delight!
My loving hands were on your sleeping feet.
A wall arose that was the thickening night.

Calling up happy moments is an art.
Head resting on your knees, I live again.
Your languid beauty lives inside your heart
and body—what else would I find it in?
Calling up happy moments is an art.

O vows, O scents, O everlasting kisses—
will they arise from the unfathomed pit
as sunlight lost inside the sea's abyss is
born again each morning, opposite?
O vows, O scents, O everlasting kisses!

37 The Possessed

The sun has dressed himself in funeral clothes.
Moon of my life, muffle yourself like him.
Sleep, if you wish, or smoke. Be mute, be dim.
Plunge your whole self into Ennui's abyss.

That's how I love you best. But, if you swagger,
like an eclipsed star stepping from the murk,
into insane debauchery on a lark,
how perfect! Leave your sheath, you charming dagger.

Kindle your eyes from all the lights that shine.
Enkindle lust in random dunces' glances.
Morbid or wild, to me you are a joy.

Go on. Be what you will: black night, red dawn.
Everything in my trembling flesh pronounces,
"My dear Beelzebub, you are for me!"

38   A Phantom

I. The Darkness
Inside the cave of sad oblivion
where Fate has sentenced me to make my home,
where no rose-colored sunbeams ever come,
where, with my sullen hostess Night, alone,

I am a great artist whom God, the smart-
aleck, has forced to paint, alas!, the dusk,
where, like a cook who favors the grotesque,
I have to boil and then devour my heart,

sometimes a specter made of grace and light
flickers a spell, then lengthens, grows and grows.
When it has reached its fullest width and height,

I recognize the gorgeous visitor
by its distinctive, Eastern, weird allure:
it's Her! Pitch-black, but somehow luminous.

II. Perfume
Reader, have you inhaled, from time to time,
like an indulgent glutton, like a souse,
the incense wholly filling up a house
of God or a sachet's age-old perfume?

A deep, deep magic where the days of yore,
restored, intoxicate the mind afresh.
Thus does the lover from his lover's flesh
gather up memory's exquisite flower.

An alien and fearsome scent would rise
out of my lover's thick, resilient hair,
a censer in a niche, living sachet,

and, whether plush or muslin, all her clothes,
redolent with her pure naïveté,
would set at large, for me, the scent of fur.

III. The Frame
In just the same way as a frame can give
even a very celebrated painting
something remarkable, something enchanting
by setting it apart from things that live,

gems, metals, gilding, furniture became,
perfectly, her exquisite elegance.
Nothing obscured her spotless radiance.
Everything worked to serve her as a frame.

And one could say that she at times had faith
all things adored her, in that she would bathe,
with great extravagance, her nudity

in kisses given by chiffon or lace
and, with each movement, whether leisurely
or quick, display a monkey's childlike grace.

IV. The Portrait
Disease and Death make ashes of the fire
that once was burning for us. Of those grand

but tender eyes that flickered with desire,
of that mouth in which my heart was drowned,

of kisses active as a healing cream,
of rapture more intense than radiance,
what's left behind? O soul of mine, how grim!
A pallid picture done in just three tones,

a picture which, like me, is perishing
alone, and which that ancient vandal, Time,
erases daily with insulting wing . . .

O murderer of life and art, dark one,
I'll never let you blot out of my brain
the woman who was my delight and fame!

39   I dedicate this poem to you so that . . .

I dedicate this poem to you so that
if my renown, a ship blown by a gust
out of the north, should chance to reach the coast
of future days and make men dream some night,

though chat of you, vague and outdated tales,
will bore the reader like a dulcimer,
my lofty verses will suspend you here
in interlacing, mystic manacles.

Damned being, I am all that heeds you now,
I only from the pit to paradise.
You, though you leave no traces when you pass,

mincingly trample, with a tranquil face,
fools who have criticized your nastiness.
O dark-eyed angel with a polished brow!

40   *Semper eadem*°

You asked me, "Why is there a haunting gloom
in you, like breakers washing dark, bare stone?"
—Because, once we have brought our harvest home,
life is an evil. A secret widely known.

A very simple and straightforward pain
that, like your joy, is sparkling for us all.
Stop asking me of it, my curious one,
and, pleasant though your voice is, please be still.

Hush up, you silly, winning soul whose mouth
yields childish laughter. Very often Death,
still more than Life, holds us in subtle ways.

Let the great lie besot my dizzy head;
let me descend into your dreamlike eyes
and drowse a long time in your lashes' shade.

41   All Together

The Devil himself stopped by my flat
this morning as if to say hello
and, trying to catch me in a fault,
probed me with: "Here's what I want to know:

Of all those lovely qualities
of hers that charm you and set you reeling,
of all the rose and dusky hues
that make her body so appealing,

which is the sweetest?" O my soul,
you answered the Abhorrent One:

"Since all is luscious in the whole,
no separate piece can be fixed upon.

Since the totality sweeps me away,
I cannot name one part most sweet.
She dazzles me like the break of day
and gives me solace like the night.

The harmony is so exquisite
that holds sway over all she is
that nobody could analyze it
or single out the melodies.

That dazzling unity drives all
my senses wild with astonishment
so that her breath is musical
and words she says are full of scent."

42   What will you say tonight . . .

What will you say tonight, poor lonesome soul?
What will you say, old withered heart of mine,
to her, most good, most dear, most beautiful,
beneath whose sacred eyes you bloom again?

—Now we will proudly magnify her fame:
nothing excels the sweetness of her sway;
her holy body smells like cherubim;
her gaze wraps us in clothes as bright as day.

Whether it be at night in solitude
or on a thoroughfare among a crowd,
her ghost precedes me like a torch's flame:

"I, who am beautiful, urge you to adore
all that is beautiful through me. I am
your Virgin, Muse and Angel Overseer."

43   The Lit Torch

They march before me—brilliant eyes some keen
angel has gifted with magnetic powers.
Divine fraternal twins, brothers of mine,
they pull my eyes up toward their gem-like fires.

They save me from the snares of vice and crime
and guide me down the path of Beauty. They
attend on me; I am enslaved to them.
They are a lit torch which I must obey.

The mystic light you shine, Alluring Eyes,
is candles in the daytime, and a red
sun never puts out your fantastic blaze.

But you are bracing; candles serve the dead.
Stars of a flame the sun cannot excel,
the song you pipe while marching stirs my soul.

43x   To One Who Is Too Cheerful

Your head, your attitude, your ways
are lovely as the countryside.
Like breezy days without a cloud
the smiles that animate your eyes.

The passerby your presence warms
is smitten with you in your prime

that radiates with so much vim
out of your shoulders and your arms.

The bright hues and the radiance
in which you dress yourself make all
the poets out there, heart and soul,
see, in their minds, a flower dance.

Those crazy clothes are emblems of
the extravagance of you, the thrill.
Madwoman, I am mad as well,
and I abominate you, love.

Sometimes in green and pleasant places
to which I have lugged my great ennui,
I have suffered as, like irony,
rays of the sun chewed me to pieces.

And then the springtime greenery
has so demoralized my heart
that I have ripped a flower apart
to punish Nature's pomposity.

So in the hour of sensuousness,
late, late at night, I wish I could
glide thief-like over to your bed
and climb your body's treasure-house

and spoil your all-too-healthy rind
by mutilating your tempting breast
and cutting, in a haunch, a vast
and terribly unshallow wound,

and then, O dizzying temptation,
by parting those lips of yours, my dear,

those lovely, vivid lips you wear,
passionately inject my poison.

44 Reversibility

Glad angel, do you know disquietude,
sighs, degradation, penitence, vexations
and frightening nights' obscure abominations
which crumple up the heart into a wad?
Glad angel, do you know disquietude?

Angel of kindness, do you know distemper,
fists clenching in the dark and tears of gall,
when Vengeance beats out rhythms born in Hell
and makes, of all our faculties, his empire?
Angel of kindness, do you know distemper?

Healthy angel, do you know disease
which, like an outcast, limps through hospital rooms?
Hoping to see sunlight, a few stray beams,
he does his best to speak but just makes noise.
Healthy angel, do you know disease?

Angel of beauty, do you know the fear
of wrinkling, aging, and the hideous
torment of seeing, in a person's eyes,
a former passion turning to a chore?
Angel of beauty, do you know the fear?

Angel of light and mirth and happiness,
the dying David would have claimed the bloom
that radiates from your tantalizing prime,
but all I want to ask of you is grace,
angel of light and mirth and happiness.

45   Confession

Sweet and endearing friend, one time, just once,
you placed your fine arm on my own
(and deep down in my spirit's dark confines
the memory of that touch lives on):

midnight and, like a medal made of silver,
the harvest moon was shining down.
It seemed the hour's sincerity, like a river,
was flowing through the sleeping town.

There were some cats that crept about like thieves
among the houses and the stalls.
Their ears were pricked; like specters out of graves,
they followed slowly at our heels.

All of a sudden, in the confidence
born of the night surrounding us,
from you, most resonant of instruments,
a fiddle filled with joyousness,

from you, as vigorously as at dawn
a bugle sounds the reveille,
a funny tone, a melancholy tone,
escaped your lips and limped away

as if it were a sickly, foul, obscene
child, an entire family's shame,
one whom they, to conceal it from the sun,
keep locked up in a basement room.

It sang, poor thing, the selfsame note you sighed:
"Nothing is trustworthy down here.
Self-interest always rears its ugly head,
whatever paint it tries to wear.

Being a beauty is a full-time job,
a boring job, the tedious toil
of the crazed dancer who can only sob
behind a mechanistic smile.

Trusting in others is preposterous
since love and loneliness break down,
and Darkness bags the rubble, piece by piece,
and lugs it to oblivion."

I still recall her quiet apathy,
the moonlight like a witch's spell,
and the dread secret that she hissed to me
as if in a confessional.

46   The Spiritual Dawn

When, partnered with the rodentine Ideal,
white-rosy dawn reaches the drunkards' dive,
an angel, to fulfill some punitive
decree, wakes in a sleepy animal.

The distant azure of the Sacred Sky
opens and yawns with infinite allure,
for downcast men who ache and still aspire.
That's how, pure Being, darling Deity,

over the ruins of a drunken rout,
the rosier, more enticing memory
of you glints always in my widened eyes.

The rising sun has put the candles out.
You, soul who always shines triumphantly,
are equal to the sun that never dies.

47   The Harmony of Evening°

Right now the stems are quivering; right now
flowers, like censers, loose, each, a bouquet.
Sounds and perfumes are mingling in the sky,
a mournful waltz, a languid vertigo.

Flowers, like censers, loose, each, a bouquet;
the trembling violin is full of woe,
a mournful waltz, a languid vertigo.
The sky, an altar cloth, is shadowy.

The trembling violin is full of woe,
a tender heart that hates vacuity.
The sky, an altar cloth, is shadowy.
The sun is sliding down like dark blood flow.

A tender heart that hates vacuity
gathers up embers of a bygone glow.
The sun is sliding down like dark blood flow.
You, like a monstrance,° light my memory.

48   The Perfume Bottle

There are intense perfumes to which all matter is
pervious. You could say their savors pass through glass.
For instance, opening a chest brought from the East,
a chest whose old lock squeaks and squeals because of rust,

or in an empty house while searching an armoire
rife with the dark and dusty fragrance of the days of yore,
you sometimes find an age-old bottle filled with lost
memories. Pick it up, and you revive a ghost.

A thousand thoughts were sleeping in obscurity,
a thousand gently trembling cocoons, and they,
tinted with azure, glazed with rose, gold-glittering,
fledge themselves of a sudden and are on the wing.

Intoxicating memory leaps into the nose
on currents of disturbance; you must close your eyes.
Vertigo wrestles the already vanquished soul
through the abysmal recesses of human smell

and drops it to the bottom of an ancient pit
where, just as Lazarus once tore his winding-sheet,
a ghostly corpse comes back to life—the specter of
a long-dead and seductive, rancid sort of love.

So it will be for me that, when I am no more
in people's memories, when, in the woeful drawer
in which I have been left behind, I lie, an old
bottle—decrepit, cracked and dusty, ringed with mold,

I will become, O luscious pestilence, your grave
and testify to the intensity you have.
O poison mixed by seraphim, like alcohol
you gnaw my senses! You begin and end my soul!

49 Poison

Wine can invest a foul depression with
most marvelous luxuries
and make fantastic rows of columns rise
from its alchemic breath,
breath crimson as the sun in dirty skies.

Opium spreads beyond all boundaries,
expands on boundlessness,
makes hours never-ending, augments bliss,
and with dark, dismal joys
surfeits the spirit with expansiveness.

But those are nothing to the venom flowing
out of your eyes, those round,
green and reflective lakes that warp my mind…
My dreams are always going
into those bitter fathoms to be drowned.

And yet the miracle of your saliva
by far exceeds them all.
It sinks its teeth in, shakes and hurls my soul
ruthlessly down a river,
and I go tumbling all the way to Hell!

50   Cloudy Sky

One could describe your gaze as "lost in rain."
Your baffling eyes (are they blue, gray or green?)
by turns compassionate, dreamy or merciless,
reflect the tedium of pallid skies.

Dear, you evoke white-veiled and lukewarm hours
that make the hearts of the entranced shed tears
and make their nerves, stirred by some undefined
and racking pain, jeer at the sleeping mind.

You seem at times a beautiful horizon
lit up at sunset in a misty season…
O cloudy patch, touched by a few stray beams,
despite the rainfall, you go up in flames!

Dangerous women, ravishing milieu,
will I adore, in time, hoarfrost and snow?
Will I extract, from stubborn winter, joys
even more keen than those of iron and ice?

51   The Cat

I.
A strong, sweet, handsome and glamorous
cat is strolling inside of me
as if I were his property.
You scarcely hear when he meows;

his voice is so soft and amiable.
But, when he utters a purr or growl,
it becomes very powerful.
Such is his secret and his spell.

Those sounds, turned into liquid, sink
into the darkest depths of me.
They fill me up like poetry
and refresh me like a magic drink.

Able to slake the keenest anguish,
his voice holds many ecstasies
inside itself. It can express
epics without the use of language.

My heart is like a violin,
and there is no bow anywhere
that plays a concert in me more
sublimely and resonantly than

the sound of you, mysterious,
bizarre and seraphic animal.
As in the nature of angels, all
of you is fine and harmonious.

II.
His patchwork coat emits so sweet
a fragrance that one night I was
embalmed in much perfume because
I gave him just one little pet.

My household's guardian spirit, he
presides and judges, rules in glory
over his whole territory.
Is he an elf? A deity?

My eyes, as if by magnetic attraction,
gape at the loved beast. But, when they
are able to look tamely away,
and I succumb to self-reflection,

I see, surprising, inside of me
his pale irises up in flames,
illustrious beacons, living gems,
that contemplate me fixedly.

52   The Beautiful Ship

Soft sorceress, I will describe to you
that youth of yours where many graces glow.
I want to paint an elegance
where ripeness is allied with innocence.

When you, with your full skirts, go sweeping by,
you seem a fine ship putting out to sea
with full sails, rocking on the tide
lazily, slowly, sweetly, side to side.

Atop plump shoulders and a stout, round neck
your head bobs with a quaint grace when you walk.
O regal child, how placidly,
how gloriously, you go your way.

Soft sorceress, I will describe to you
that youth of yours where many graces glow.
I want to paint an elegance
where ripeness is allied with innocence.

Your breasts push out whatever dress you wear,
triumphal breasts much like a fine armoire
endowed with bright round bosses that,
like shields for soldiers, give back sparks of light:

exciting shields, inset with tips of rose!
And, in the drawers, sweet secret luxuries,
perfume and fine liqueur and wine,
that stupefy the hearts and minds of men.

When you, with your full skirts, go sweeping by,
you seem a fine ship putting out to sea
with full sails, rocking on the tide
lazily, slowly, sweetly, side to side.

Your noble legs, beneath the silks they chase,
arouse and torment vague proclivities
like twin enchanters mixing up
a dark elixir in a drinking cup.

Your arms, like those of infant Hercules,
like glistening boa-snakes, are made to squeeze
the life out of your prey, as if
you wanted printed on your breast—your love.

Atop plump shoulders and a stout, round neck
your head bobs with a quaint grace when you walk.
O regal child, how placidly,
how gloriously, you go your way.

53   The Invitation to the Voyage

Dream of the joy
of living with me,
my child, my dear. We two
will love all day,
love and then die,
in a land that looks like you.
To me at least,
the overcast
and sweet sun there appears
as mysterious
as your lying eyes
shining through your tears.

There will be nothing but beauty and leisure,
harmony, calm and pleasure.

Shined by the years,
bright tables and chairs
would furnish our shared bedchamber.
Exquisite blooms,
mixing perfumes,
would smell vaguely of amber.

Each sumptuous ceiling
and mirror revealing
Oriental style
would mutely intone
its very own
sweet language to the soul.

There will be nothing but beauty and leisure,
harmony, calm and pleasure.

The ships that dream
on river and stream,
each, in an errant way,
is waiting to bear
your least desire
wherever it wants to be.
—The glorious sun,
as it goes down
on rivers, fields and streets,
will empurple and gild
all we behold
in its hot-blooded glitz.

There will be nothing but beauty and leisure,
harmony, calm and pleasure.

54   The Irreparable

How can we choke Remorse, the die-hard one,
who lives and moves tortuously?
Much like a worm, he gets beneath our skin,
much like a mite, invades the tree.
How can we choke Remorse, the die-hard one?

What nostrum or what vintage or what draught
can drown an age-old nemesis
as nasty as a greedy prostitute
and ant-like in its stubbornness?
What nostrum or what vintage or what draught?

Darling enchantress, speak out if you can
to this my soul that seeks relief.
It's moribund, both crushed by wounded men
and trampled by a horse's hoof.
Darling enchantress, speak out if you can

to me, a wretched man that wolves sniff at
and circling crows look down upon.
Speak to this ravaged soldier. Must he not
own even a funerary stone?
It's me, a wretched man that wolves sniff at.

Can one light up a sky this dense and black?
Rip through a murkiness in which
there is no sun to vanish and come back,
no shooting star to cleave the pitch.
Can one light up a sky this dense and black?

The Hope that lights up windows at the Inn
is snuffed out now and gone for good.
No sun is shining on its grounds; no moon
shows sufferers the proper road.
Satan has darkened windows at the Inn.

Sweet sorceress, do you adore the cursed
and grasp the sin we can't forbear?
I mean Remorse, whose toxic shafts have pierced
our target hearts and rankle there.
Sweet sorceress, do you adore the cursed?

The Irreparable grinds his nasty jaws
upon our souls, inept creations,
and, like a termite, frequently destroys
structures by striking their foundations.
The Irreparable grinds his nasty jaws.

—I've witnessed in a common theater,
as instruments played on and on,
a fairy, lost in an infernal blur,
suddenly enkindle dawn.
I've witnessed in a common theater

a being made of light and gold and mesh
swoop down and drive great Satan out,
but in the tawdry playhouse of my flesh
(a place untouched by rapture), I await
always that being fledged with wings of mesh.

55   A Conversation

You are a clear and rosy autumn sky,
but sorrow breaking on me like a tide
leaves on my sad lips, when it flows away,
the burning memory of brackish mud.

—No use your reaching for my panting chest.
What you are after has been rooted out
by savage female teeth and claws. Desist.
My heart is gone; the beasts have eaten it.

That heart is now a place where, in a rout,
rowdies get drunk and pull hair, even kill!
—What scent hovers around your gorgeous throat? ...

Beauty, this flagellation is your will.
Come, use your eyes, bright as a festival,
to roast the bits the beasts refused to eat.

56   Autumn Song

I.

Now we will plunge into a dark, dark chill.
Goodbye, short summer. Goodbye, vivid glare.
I can already hear the funeral knell
of logs tumbling to the courtyard floor.

All winter will possess my being: gall,
hate, forced and stubborn toil, much shivering,
and, like the sun in his Antarctic Hell,
my heart will be a frozen, blood-red thing.

I tremble listening to the thud of fuel.
Builders of gallows make no worse a sound.
My spirit, like a tower, reels to a cruel
ram's obdurate percussion: *Pound. Pound. Pound.*

To me, lulled by those tiresome thuds, it seems
a coffin's quickly being nailed. But whose?
Summer was yesterday; now autumn comes.
There is departure in that eerie noise.

II.

I do adore your large eyes' emerald glow,
my sweet, but all is bitterness to me,
and nothing, not your love, hearth, bedroom, now
is worth the sunlight shining on the sea.

But, tender darling, love me anyway.
Be mother to a sour, unthankful man.
Lover or sister, be what just won't stay,
the joy of autumn or the setting sun.

Short work! The tomb waits, keen for her repast.
When I have laid my head down on your knees
to mourn bright, torrid summer, let me taste
late autumn's luscious and unhealthy rays.

57   To a Madonna

A Votive in the Spanish Style°

O mistress, O Madonna, I would build for you
a secret altar in the chasm of my woe,
then cut a niche out in my dark soul's corner, far
from all contemptuous looks and everyday desire,
gild it and decorate the shrine with azure hues.
There you, amazing statue, will assume your pose.
Next, from my highly polished, steely poetic lines
meticulously set with rhymes like precious stones,
I would assemble an impressive diadem.
Then, Virgin, in my Envy, I would cut and hem
a fancy robe for you in the barbaric style,
stiff and grotesque, lined with Suspicion. Like a jail,
it will imprison all the charms on which I dote.
Instead of pearls, my weeping will bedazzle it.
My trembling Desire will serve you for a gown,
waves of Desire that buoy up and tumble down,
mount to the top of summits, fall into abysses.
It will invest your fair and rosy flesh with kisses.
From Deference I would make some handsome slippers, shod

in silk, in which your little sacred feet will tread.
This footwear, by surrounding them in an embrace,
will come to take the imprint of their loveliness.
If I cannot, with all the artistry that's mine,
carve out a silver moon for you to stand upon,
I will insert the snake that rips my insides out
right underneath you, and you will crush beneath your feet,
O queen of matchless power, rich in restitution,
that round monstrosity charged up with hate and poison.
All of my thoughts, set out like votive lights, will shine
before your florid, virginal and noble shrine,
spangle the blue-enameled ceiling with their rays
and always watch you, watch you, with their fiery gaze.
Because I love and cherish you so much, my dear,
all will be benjamin and jasmine, incense, myrrh.
My stormy spirit will ascend in fragrant smoke
around your slopes and settle on your snowy peak.

At last, so that you can perfect the role of Mary
and mix some ardor in with dark voluptuary
barbarity, I will take the Seven Sins and make
knives from them, seven freshly whetted points, and, like
a callous knife-thrower in an amusement park,
taking your sweet love's inmost places as my mark,
fix each of them inside your panting heart, inside
your sobbing heart, inside your heat that streams with blood.

58 Song of the Afternoon

Although your mischievous brows
give you a curious air
that seraphs do not share,
O witch of the tempting gaze,

odd one, you conquer me
with extravagant desire.
I love you as if you were
a heathen deity.

Your every fragrant tress
evokes wild lands and woods.
You take on attitudes
of riddles and mysteries.

Scent varnishes your skin
as incense fills a nave.
Warm nymph, the charms you have
are like the setting sun.

No potion hits my head
as hard as your languidness.
You could, with a caress,
reanimate the dead.

Your haunches ardently
desire your back and bust.
You even stuff with lust
the cushions on which you lie.

Sometimes, while appeasing
a strange ferocity,
stern girl, you ambush me
with nibbling and kissing.

Sometimes, dark one, you flay
my heart with bitter laughter,
then cast, a moment after,
your moonlight gaze my way.

I place my entire fate,
my genius, my happiness,
beneath your satin shoes,
beneath your silky feet.

You set my spirit right
with your various lights and shades.
The heat of you explodes
my long Siberian night.°

59 Sisina°

Picture Diana° in majestic clothes
off-trail and beating hedges with a stick
or, hair loose, breasts exposed, and drunk on noise,
driving the fiercest cavalrymen back!

What of Théroigne° of the rapacious heart,
stirring the shoeless multitude to war?
With fiery eyes and cheeks, she plays her part
by mounting, sword in hand, the royal stair.

Such is Sisina. But, forgiving fighter,
she is as charitable as murderous.
Her violence, roused by martial drums and niter,

knows how to yield to people's desperate pleas.
Though burnt by passion time and time again,
her heart keeps tears in store for worthy men.

60 *Franciscae meae laudes°*

Now I will make a novel sort
of music for you, O you hind
gamboling through my empty heart.

You should be adorned with flowers,
you invigorating woman
who washes away these sins of ours.

I will drink kiss after kiss
from you, magnetic one, as from
the river of forgetfulness.

When a storm of vice and crime
was sweeping through our every path,
goddess of goddesses, you came

and, like the lodestar, shared your shine
with our benighted frigate. I
will place my heart upon your shrine.

O fountain of eternal youth,
O reservoir of excellence,
return my lost voice to my mouth.

You have burnt what was obscene,
smoothed out what was harsh and warped
and made the weak man strong again.

When I am starved, you are the inn;
when I am lost, you are the lamp.
O lead me from paths of sin.

O sweet bath scented pleasantly
with every sort of sweet perfume,
come reinforce the strength in me.

Chaste corselet of continence
dipped in the angels' sacred water,
gleam your protection of my loins.

O salted bread to dine upon,
O goblet glittering with gems,
O my Francisca, holy wine.

61   To a Creole Lady°

Off in a sun-touched, scented land, I've known,
inside an altar made of crimson boughs
and palms from which indifference rains down,
a Creole lady of unsung loveliness.

This warm enchantress sheathed in pale dark skin
moves her neck nobly, as a princess would.
Much like a huntress, she is tall and thin.
Her smiles are calm; her glances, unafraid.

Madame, if you should travel to the Seine
or green Loire in the land of true renown,
O beauty worthy of antique châteaus,

you'd draw, inside the shadows of the groves,
a thousand odes from poets whom your eyes,
your giant eyes, had left more servile than your slaves.

62   *Moesta et errabunda*°

Agatha,° tell me, do you want to fly
far from the brackish ocean of this town
toward other waves where a resplendent sky
shines deep and blue and makes us chaste again?
Agatha, tell me, do you want to fly?

The vast sea is a comfort to our grief.
What devil makes the sea, a hoarse chanteuse
accompanied by an organ's groan, relieve
our miseries with sacred lullabies?
The vast sea is a comfort to our grief.

Train, frigate, bring me to a different home,
since here and now the mud is mixed with tears.
Your heart, Agatha, does sometimes proclaim:
"Vice prospers here, and torment and remorse.
Train, frigate, bring me to a different home."

Sweet paradise, why are you so far off?
O place where love plays under cloudless skies,
where what one loves is worthy of that love,
where hearts succumb to an immaculate bliss.
Sweet paradise, why are you so far off?

But the green paradise of childhood loves,
of songs, games, kisses, flowers that smell like musk,
of brimming cups of vintage in the groves
and fiddles echoing from the hills at dusk—
but the green paradise of childhood loves,

the blameless paradise of stolen delights,
is it already farther than Cathay?
Can we invoke with melancholy notes

or animate with a silver melody
the blameless paradise of stolen delights?

63   The Revenant

I'll slip into your bedroom like
an angel with a savage look
and with the midnight shadows glide
silently over to your bed,

where I'll give you, my dusky one,
kisses as chilling as the moon
and caresses that a snake might give
the dirt heaped up around a grave.

In the discolored light of dawn
you'll find my place beside you void
and cold until night comes again.

I want to hold authority
over your life and youth by dread
as others do by delicacy.

64   Autumn Sonnet

Your crystal-bright eyes utter, "What in me,
eccentric lover, do you most admire?"
—Hush up. Be sweet. My heart, which all things tire
except for bestial simplicity,

wants to conceal from you its trust with Hell,
its midnight promise handwritten in flame,
since you would cradle me a long, long time.
Lust rankles. Knowledge makes me feel unwell.

Let us love sweetly. Ambushed in his lair,
dark Cupid pulls his lethal longbow tight.°
I know the weapons that he keeps in there:

Crime, Horror and Insanity! —O pale
daisy, are we not like the sun in fall,
my oh-so-white, so frigid Marguerite?°

65   The Sorrows of the Moon

Tonight the moon is dreaming, dreaming much
more idly than a lovely woman on a heap
of cushions who, with light and listless touch,
brushes her breasts before she falls asleep.

Thus, fading on a cloud bank's satin back,
the moon succumbs to lengthy reveries.
Before her eyes white ghosts appear that, like
a bed of flowers, bloom into the skies.

When she at times, in utter sloth, lets drop
a single tear (a surreptitious one),
some pious poet, enemy of sleep,

takes it, a pale thing gaudy as a shard
of opal, and conceals it in his heart
far from the prying vision of the sun.

66   The Cats

True lovers and exacting scholars both,
in their maturer years, love grandiose
sweet cats, who are their houses' pride, because
they, too, dislike the cold and tend toward sloth.

True friends of learning and immoderation,
cats hunt the frightening silence darkness breeds.
Darkness° would use them as his funeral steeds
if their hauteur could stomach subjugation.

While meditating, they augustly strike
the pose of sphinxes in a no-man's-land
and look like they are lost in reveries.

Their fecund flanks, like magic, spark and shock,
and particles of gold, like grains of sand,
flicker obscurely in their mystic eyes.

67 The Owls

Under the black-boughed yew trees' shade
the owls have settled down in rows
and, like exotic deities,
dart crimson from their eyes. They brood.

And there they will remain, stock-still,
until the wistful hour comes on
when mighty darkness drives the sun
slantwise and rules the land awhile.

The poise they show instructs the wise
that in this world one must avoid
both agitation and restlessness.

Drunk on the frivolous, our race
suffers, as punishment, a need
to move always from place to place.

68   The Pipe

I am the pipe of a writer. Like
the skin of an Abyssinian—
that's how I look. My hue makes plain
my owner is fond of having a smoke.

Whenever he is possessed by gloom,
I puff and puff like a kitchen where
a meal is being cooked up for
a workman soon to come back home.

Coiling, I cradle my owner's soul
in the expanding azure film
that issues from my burning flue.

What I unfold is a potent balm
that charms his heart and remedies all
the things that fill him up with woe.

69   Music

Music moves me like the ocean swell.
Whether in open air
or under heaps of cloud, I spread my sail
and coast toward a pallid star.

My proud chest puffed out like a figurehead
and the cloth of my lungs pulled tight,
I ride on the back of an ascending flood
that is hidden under night.

I feel, alive inside me, all the passions
of a ship in distress.
A strong wind and a storm with its convulsions

cradle me on the sea
sometimes. At others, pure tranquillity
mirrors my hopelessness.

70   The Burial

If on a dense, dark night some godly
Christian soul is charitable
enough to bury your vaunted body
behind some ancient shanty's rubble

just as the immaculate
stars close their tired eyes to rest,
the spider will be weaving her net,
and the viper birthing in her nest.

You will hear throughout all time to come,
above your accursed skeleton,
dire wolves lugubriously howling,

emaciated witches wailing,
old lechers having too much fun,
and dim thieves plotting to do crime.

71   A Fantastical Engraving°

This ghastly thing has nothing on at all
except some cheap crown from a carnival
preposterously balanced on his skull.
The specter rides astride a spook as well—
a doomsday hack he guides without a bit.
(The beast drools like a madman in a fit.)
The pair are charging at a breakneck pace

through what appears a vast, vast, endless space.
Waving a flaming sword, the cavalier
mocks bodies he has trampled down before.
A prince surveying his domain, he flies
over a cold and sizable necropolis
where lie, beneath a pale and mournful sun,
all who have died since history began.

72   The Happy Corpse

In rich soil, snail-infested soil, I hope
to dig myself a deep informal grave
where I can stretch my old bones out and sleep
forever like a great white in the wave.

To me, all wills and tombs are odious.
Sooner than beg the world to weep and grieve,
I would, while still alive, invite the crows
to drain the blood out of my filthy stiff.

Maggots, companions without ears and eyes,
my flesh is coming to you. I am glad.
Rot-offspring, dissolute philosophers,

run through my ruin then, without remorse.
Tell me if any ache remains for this
old soulless corpse, the dead among the dead.

73   The Cask of Hate

Hatred is the Danaïdes' wine cask.°
Insane Revenge, with muscles red and fierce,
lifts up and dumps into her gaping dusk
pail after pail of dead men's blood and tears.

The Fiend bores secret holes in it, and they
would drain a thousand years of sweat and strain,
even if Hatred could revive her prey
and plump their husks to squeeze them dry again.

Hatred is an inebriate in a dive
who feels thirst multiply with every drink,
like the Lernaean Hydra's heads in fable.°

Happy the drunk who knows when he is sunk,
but Hatred, sadly, has been doomed to live
without the hope of passing out beneath the table.

74   The Cracked Bell

At night in winter it is bittersweet
to hear old recollections gently rise
around the whitening fire's wisps of light
when church bells launch their voices through the haze.

Happy the bell that has a lively throat.
Alert and dignified, despite its age,
it utters its ecclesiastic note
faithfully, like an old guard keeping watch.

My soul is cracked. When, in her boredom, she
fills up the cold night air with melodies,
it often happens that her fragile voice

rasps like a wounded man unseen beside
a lake of blood, among a heap of dead.
He cannot move. He dies in agony.

75   Spleen (I)

Pluvius, mad at Paris, pours down waves
of chilling rain out of his waterpot
onto the pale inhabitants of graves.
He pours, too, doom on the suburban street.

Scrabbling at the tiles, my restless cat
prepares some comfort for his mangy hide.
A poet's ghost inside a gutter spout
complains wretchedly like a frozen shade.

A bell is keening, and a smoking log
pipes to accompany a grinding clock,
and, all the while, in a malodorous deck

of cards (the dire bequest of some sick hag)
the jack of hearts and queen of spades converse
portentously of long-dead love affairs.

76   Spleen (II)

More memories than if I'd lived a thousand years!

A massive chest of drawers crammed with lines of verse,
court summonses, love letters, novels, balance sheets
and locks of ample hair rolled up in old receipts
hides fewer secrets than my melancholy brain,
which is a pyramid, a mound that must contain
more dead than pits where thousands have their final home.
A graveyard hated by the moon—that's what I am,
a potter's field where always, like remorse, a host
of worms is gnawing on the flesh I love the most.
I am an old boudoir perfumed with withered roses,
a room extravagant in antiquated dresses,

where only sad pastels and pale Bouchers° inhale
the fragrance emanating from an opened vial.

Nothing can move more slowly than the limping hours
when, under the oppressive drifts of snowy years,
ennui, the fruit of melancholy lethargy,
takes on the magnitude of immortality.
From now on, living matter, you are nothing more
than granite that, fenced in by enigmatic fear,
is sleeping in a dim Saharan desertscape,
or a primeval sphinx° that, stricken from the map,
lost to the careless world, with an indignant frown
sings only in the long light of the setting sun.

77   Spleen (III)

It's like I am the monarch of a rainy land.
Young and yet somehow old, of great means but unmanned,
he scorns his sycophantic tutors' bows and whiles
his days away with dogs and other animals.
Nothing delights him, not the hunt, not falconry,
not subjects dying right before his balcony.
The dirty ballads of a favorite buffoon
never evoke a chuckle from this mean, ill man.
His bed, adorned with fleur-de-lis, is like a grave,
and ladies' maids, to whom all kings are handsome, have
no dresses in their wardrobes impudent enough
to drag a smile out of this youthful-looking stiff.
The alchemist who makes his gold cannot invent
anything that will purge his toxic element,
and baths of blood in which the Romans used to lie,°
and which, in their infirm days, royals often try,
have never warmed this corpse's lethargy because
his veins, instead of blood, pump green Lethean ooze.°

78   Spleen (IV)

When, like a coffin lid, the dense low sky
weighs on a mind that long ennui has caught,
and the horizon's whole periphery
pours out a day gloomier than the night,

when all the land becomes a humid cell
where Hope herself, like an imprisoned bat,
beats, with her meek wings, rhythms on a wall
and knocks against a ceiling lost to rot,

when rainfall stretching out its endless train
looks like the bars of a gigantic jail,
and taciturn and loathsome spiders spin
webs in the depths of everybody's soul,

bells of a sudden swing up in disgust
and fling a frightful clamor at the sky,
while, here and there, an exiled, vagrant ghost
emits, insistently, a whimpering cry.

—Long hearses without music, without drums,
file slowly through me. Hope can only howl
(since she has lost) and queenly Anguish comes
to plant her black flag in my lowered skull.

79   Obsession

Vast woods, you scare me like cathedrals. Winds
blow through you like an organ. Our cursed hearts (endless
chambers of mourning where the last gasp sounds)
resonate with your solemn *De profundis.*°

Ocean, I hate the way you toss. My soul
tosses in just that way. What I hear in
the massive laughter of the salt-sea swell
is laughter wheezing from a vanquished man.

I love you, night, but wish your stars weren't there.
Their light speaks in a tongue I recognize.
Nakedness, darkness—that's what I prefer,

but even blankness is a canvas where
thousands of beings spring out of my eyes.
Though vanished, they are quite familiar.

80   The Taste for Nothingness

Sad soul, you once were quick to join the fight,
but Hope, whose spur at one time urged you on,
no longer mounts. There's no shame. Come lie down,
old stallion who trips on every rut.

Give in, my heart, and sleep, sleep like a brute.

Tired old marauder, you have done it all
but now are fit for neither love nor war.
Goodbye to flute song and the bugle's blare.
Pleasure, release my dour and brooding soul.

Succulent Spring has lost its pleasant smell.

Moment by moment Time envelops me
just as the falling snow conceals a stiff.
I, when I search the round world from above,
can find no shelter or security.

Avalanche, will you carry me away?

81   The Alchemy of Grief

Nature, while one man makes you a bright
fire, another paints you as gloom.
What signifies, to some, the tomb
for others stands for life and light.

You, secret Hermes,° who assist
and at the same time frighten me,
have made me, like his majesty
King Midas,° a sorrowful alchemist.

I change gold back to slag because
of you and make a Paradise
a Hell. I find my darling dead

in clouds like a shroud above my head,
then, on the sea coast of the sky,
construct impressive sarcophagi.

82   Reflected Horror

What thoughts, descending from a pale
strange sky as tortured as your fate,
pass into your forsaken soul?
Answer me now, you profligate.

—Although intemperately avid
for puzzles and uncertainties,
I refuse to whine like Ovid
chased from the Roman paradise.°

Skies torn up like a torn-up shore,
you are the mirror of my hauteur.
Your clouds, clad in funeral attire,

fly like the hearses of my dreams,
and, when you glint, I witness gleams
of the hellish regions I adore.

83   *Heautontimoroumenos*°

To J.G.F°

I'll strike you without rage or spite
the way a butcher hacks his block,
the way that Moses hit the rock.°
For irrigation's sake, I'll let

the tears of your solicitude
wet my Saharan desertscape.
My lust for you, a thing of hope,
will swim into that saline flood

just as a ship puts out to sea.
The echoes of your sob will roll
through my inebriated soul
like drumbeats rousing the infantry.

But am I not a dissonant note
in the celestial symphony,
since Irony voraciously
gnaws on me, eats me, bite by bite?

Yes, Irony is in my voice.
My veins pulse with her poison now.
I am a looking-glass of woe
that shows her her own nastiness.

I am the dagger and the scar.
I am the slap, I am the cheek,
I am the limbs, I am the rack,
the convict, the executioner.

I am the vampire of my own soul
—one of those grand forsaken men
doomed to keep laughing on and on,
though they can never crack a smile.

84   The Irremediable

I.
A Form, an Idea, an Essence, shot
from the azure heavens, falls into
the river Styx°—a muddy slough
no eye of Heaven can penetrate;

an angel, a reckless voyager
drawn by a passion for the maimed,
and deep in a gulf that he has dreamed,
strains, like a swimmer, toward the shore

while, full of anxiety, he fights
against a whirlpool that, circling,
emits a sort of madman's song
while doing dusky pirouettes;

a man, bewitched and wretchedly
groping and groping at random, seeks
to escape a room brimming with snakes
without a lantern or a key;

damned and benighted, another man
descends a stairway without a railing
on the edge of a blankness smelling
distinctly of a humid lagoon

from which slime-covered monsters stare
with large bright eyes that render night
darker by contrast with the light
(they only make themselves appear);

a vessel trapped up near the pole
in a hibernal crystal net
forever quests for the only strait
that will release it from its jail

—pure symbols, an accurate tableau
of an irremediable evil,
they make us confident the Devil
does well whatever he aims to do.

II.
A somber and limpid tête-à-tête,
a heart as its own looking-glass!
A clear, dark well of truthfulness
in which a pale star drops its light.

An ironic beacon, a torch of Hell
whose glow is diabolic grace,
the only glory and means of peace,
—the consciousness of doing ill.

85   The Clock

The Clock, a sinister, aloof and stark
deity, points at us and says, "Recall!"
Soon enough shafts of grief will strike your soul,
your frightened soul, as if that were their mark.

A misty pleasure glides toward the horizon
much like a sylphid° saying her goodbye.
Each instant eats a morsel of the joy
a man is granted for his earthly season.

Three thousand and six hundred times an hour
the thin hand clucks "Recall!," then moves on fast
and, like a droning insect, says, "It's past!
My trunk has sucked up more of what you were!

Remember! *Souviens-toi! Esto memor!*°
(All tongues are spoken through my metal throat.)
Let every minute count, you profligate—
You must extract the ingot from the ore."

Recall Time is a gambler. His every throw
wins without cheating. That's just how it goes.
Recall, as day diminishes, night grows.
The pit thirsts always; the water clock runs low.

Soon will sound the hour when sublime
Virtue, sacred Chance, and your chaste spouse,
when even Penitence (the hospice house),
all say, "Go on, you coward. Die. It's time."

PARISIAN
SCENES

86 Landscape

So as to write my eclogues° in the most chaste way,
I want, like an astrologer, to be up high,
far up among the clock towers. Lying lost in dreams,
I would take in the church bells' solemn windborne hymns.
Chin propped on either hand, I would observe the shops
where people sing and chatter, and the chimney tops,
the belfries, all the city's masts, and that vast sky
that turns eternity into a reverie.

Yes, it is sweet to see, far off across the gloom,
a star birthed in the blue, a lantern in a room,
rivers of smoke and soot ascending through the air
and the anemic spell the moon casts everywhere.
Spring, summer, autumn—I will watch them come and go,
and then, when winter drags in its unvarying snow,
unsash the drapery, lock up the shutters tight
and build my fairy palaces indoors all night.
There I will dream of pleasure-gardens, blue horizons,
fountains weeping into alabaster basins,
kisses, songbirds at twilight and the break of day,
and Idylls° when they most suggest naïveté.
Riot raging vainly against my window glass
will fail to make me look up from my desk, because
I will be deep inside the art of conjuring,
all of my own volition, a fantastic spring,
extracting sunshine from my heart and making warm
days out of my tempestuous intellectual storm.

87 The Sun

All through this worn-out neighborhood, where cottages
wear shutters to conceal clandestine lecheries,

just as the fierce sun pummels with redoubled heat
both cityscape and countryside, rooftops and wheat,
I daily take a solitary walk to hone
my fencing wit. I search for words beneath a stone,
sniff into corners for the gamble of a rhyme,
and find, with luck, a line I've dreamed a long, long time.

Our wholesome father, the destroyer of chlorosis,°
falls on the fields and rouses worms as well as roses.
He breaks angst down and blows it toward the big Above.
He stuffs a brain with honey, as he does a hive.
He is the one who breathes new life into old men
condemned to crutches till they smile and laugh again
like little girls. He authorizes plants to sprout
in those immortal souls that live to germinate.

When, like a poet, he descends on cities, he
invests even the vilest things with dignity
and, king-like, enters, without retinue or noise,
all of the hospitals, all of the palaces.

88   To a Red-Haired Beggar Girl°

White-skinned girl with auburn hair,
your dress is tattered here and there,
and every hole shows me you are
both fair and poor.

Sickly poet that I am,
I see myself in your sickly frame.
Your ginger and befreckled complexion
holds much attraction.

You wear your thick clogs better than
the legendary sort of queen
would wear a pair of boots made of
much fancier stuff.

Instead of the patched rags you have on,
may a flounced and majestic gown
endow you with a train that trails
over your heels.

Instead of those decrepit socks,
sport, for the lusty eyes of rakes,
a bright and garter-belted knife
along your calf.

Let that ineptly tied brassiere
reveal, to pleasure our desire,
your twin breasts, as illustrious
as shining eyes.

Let your arms that make men pray
all your clothes be stripped away
defiantly fight off the demands
of roguish hands.

Lovers bound by your fetters offer
you presents: pearls that divers recover
from beautiful waters and ballads scored
by Belleau the Bard.˙

And there are lowborn rhymers, too,
who dash off poetry for you
after discovering, under a stair,
a shoe you wear.

More than one love-smitten lord,
more than one page boy and Ronsard°
will turn into peepers staking out
your airy hut.

In your bedroom you would enjoy
far more kisses than fleurs-de-lis.
You have the power to entrance
past kings of France

—Meanwhile you have to beg to eat
rotten refuse handed out
from some saloon's back-alley door,
run-down Véfour.°

While walking about, you always eye
the cheapest sort of jewelry.
Sorry I can't afford to bestow
those gifts on you!

Go, then, without any ornament,
no pearls, no diamonds, no rich scent,
only, my beauty, your naked body
abroad in the city!

89   The Swan

For Victor Hugo°

I.
My thoughts all turn to you, Andromache°—
that little stream, the mournful looking-glass
that caught your whole widowhood's majesty,
the tears you shed to feed that "Simoïs"°

had quickened in my fecund recollection,
as I walked through the modern Carrousel.°
The old Paris is gone. A town's complexion,
like human hearts, never stays put at all.

I picture in my mind the camp of shacks,
the rough-hewn column drums and capitals,
the weeds, the puddles mossing up huge blocks
and mirroring the bric-a-brac and frills.

The place once hosted a menagerie,
and here's what I saw there at just the hour
when Work wakes up and greets the cool black sky
and sweepers push dust storms into the air:

a swan, who had somehow found freedom, passed
clumsily, wings laid flat, along the walk.
His wealth of feathers draggled in the dust.
Right by a ditch, he opened up his beak.

Flapping excitedly, wings on the ground,
heart roused by lakes he once was giddy with,
he said, "Come on and rain, sky! Thunder, sound!"
I see him as a strange and fatal myth.

Toward the ironic sky, as in some book
of Ovid,° toward the cruel blue, his head
kept bobbing up atop a shaky neck
as if he were abominating God!

II.
Though Paris changes, nothing in my sorry
state has budged. Blocks, palaces tacked on,
old districts, all to me are allegory.
My dear remembrances weigh more than stone.

A sight outside the Louvre hits home: I think
of that big swan who struggled in his woe,
an exile, a sublime and antic thing
consumed by longing, and I think of you,

Andromache, torn from a husband's love,
base property of Pyrrhus's rough pride,
head bowed to rave beside an empty grave,
widow of Hector, Helenus's bride.

I think of a black girl, tubercular,
searching with tired eyes, as she slogs through mud,
for palms she knew in Africa somewhere
behind a massive barrier of cloud;

of all deprived of something they may not
find ever, ever again—whose tears are streams,
who suck a grief-milk from the she-wolf's tit;°
of skinny orphans, of decaying blooms.

Thus in the woods that house my exiled soul,
hoary Remembrance blares a cri de coeur!
I think of sailors stranded on an isle,
of captives, the defeated ... many more!

90   The Seven Old Men

For Victor Hugo°

Dream-stuffed and ever-swarming cityscape
where ghosts by daylight tug at wanderers,
everywhere mysteries run much like the sap
that fills this great metropolis's sewers.

One morning, while I strolled a bleak back road,
houses, because of mist, looked very tall,
looked much like harbors on the riverside.
The mise-en-scène was like an actor's soul.

A filthy pale miasma filled the place.
While I was walking, with a virtuous heart's
courage to fight against my laziness,
through district streets disturbed by rumbling carts,

all in a flash a codger who had on
rags that were look-alikes of stormy skies
and might have made much alms come raining down
if evil didn't glitter in his eyes

appeared to me. I'd say his eyes were rife
with bile; his gaze, like frost, was sharp and hoar.
His polished beard was pointed like a knife,
and it was like the one that Judas wore.

He seemed to be less bent than cut in half.
His spine was pointed opposite his feet
so that the cane on which he propped himself
gave him the attitude and awkward gait

of some ill beast, or a three-legged Jew.
He made his clumsy way through snow and smut
as if his shoes trod on the dead below,
not through indifference of it all, but hate.

A second followed—beard, back, eyes, rags, cane,
no different traits—out of the selfsame Hell.
This look-alike grim centenarian
tramped in the same way toward their secret goal.

What person out there had been making fun
of me? What wicked con job was in play?
I had to see all seven, one by one—
one wretched codger multiplied that way.

All who would laugh at my excited state
and who are not struck cold by them like me
ought to consider that, despite their gait,
they looked like creatures of eternity.

How could I see an eighth one and go on
living—another look-alike, a foul
phoenix,° his own father, his own son?
—I turned away from that cortege from Hell.

All worked up, like a double-visioned souse,
I shuffled home and shut the door, awestruck,
trembling and ill, my spirit feverous,
moved by the mystery of that freakish shock.

My reason vainly tried to grasp the helm.
The keen storm mocked me with its every blast
and, as when monstrous storm winds overwhelm
a dancing frigate, I had lost my mast!

91   The Little Old Ladies

For Victor Hugo°

I.
Deep in the windings of a capital
where even horror has some elegance,
I often serve a fatal whim and tail
quaint and decaying human specimens.

These wrecks were women at an earlier time,
Laïs° or Eponine.° Though cracked misfits,
they still have souls. We ought to cherish them.
Under their tattered wraps and petticoats,

they creep along, lashed by a wicked gale,
or cower as an omnibus goes past.
They clutch a floral bag or reticule
as if it were a remnant left by Christ.

Like marionettes, they shamble to and fro
or drag themselves along like wounded things
or do a dance without intending to,
sad bells that a remorseless demon rings.

Though tired, their eyes can penetrate like drills
or shine like brimming potholes in the street.
They are the bright eyes of a girl who trills
with sudden awe at anything that's bright.

Think why a coffin for a crone should be
as small as one in which a child is placed.
Thus witty Death sets up a simile
that is in crazed and captivating taste.

So when I see some feeble phantom straying
through swarming Paris, lost in the urban hub,
I always think this shatterable being
is gently heading back into her crib,

unless, distracted by geometry,
I see, in each discordant warp and twist,
how woodworkers will have to modify
the boxes where such stiffs will come to rest.

—Their eyes are pits filled with a million tears,
crucibles where a once-hot ore abates . . .
The mystery of them powerfully allures
the man who sucks at Tribulation's teats.

II.
Vestal virgin° of the gambling house;
priestess of comedy whose name the dead
announcer knows; celebrity who was
everyone's pleasure in Tivoli's shade°—

they daze me. But among these fallen things
some squeeze a share of honey from their grief:
they ask Devotion, who has lent them wings,
to lift them up; they call him Hippogriff.°

One woman whom the state trained in defeat;
another whom her husband pushed too far;
one, a Madonna martyred by her brat;
the tears of each could fill a reservoir.

III.
Such ancient ladies I have walked behind!
I saw one, as the sun was going down
and gushing crimson as if from a wound,
pensively settle on a bench alone

to hear a concert, rich in brass, the sort
that soldiers sometimes put on in a park
at dusk, the sort that charge the civic heart
with roused feelings and a heroic spark.

Upright and animated by the cause,
she avidly inhaled the warlike tune.
Her eyes gleamed like an ancient eagle's eyes.
Her marble brow begged for a laurel crown.

IV.

You shuffle on, without complaint, outdoors
through the disorder of the teeming town—
mothers with bleeding hearts, great saints and whores
whose names, in bygone days, the world had known.

You who were full of beauty and renown
no one remembers now. A drunk reviles
your passing with a mock-seductive line;
a child does antic dances at your heels.

Backs hunched, shrunk shades, and keeping to the walls,
you are ashamed of living on and on.
Nobody says hello to you, doomed souls,
human debris, ripe for oblivion.

But here I am, with ever-restless eyes
and tender feelings, watching over you
as though I were your father. How marvelous!
I taste a secret joy you do not know:

I see your youthful passions just beginning;
I see your sad or sunny days gone by.
Heart multiplied, I share in all your sinning.
I feel your many virtues shine on me.

O wreckage, O my kin, my fellow brains,
each evening I say good night to you.
What fate is yours, octogenarians,
O Eves, crushed by the Lord God's dreadful claw?

92   The Blind

Just look at them: how horrible they are!
Absurd as mannequins, repulsive, they
sleepwalk through life in a peculiar way,
darting their orbs of night one knows not where.

Their eyes, in which no spark of life is found,
seem to be aimed far off into the sky.
One doesn't ever see them dreamily
direct their heavy noggins toward the ground.

They scuff through days of darkness without bound,
the kin of endless silence. City, as
you shout and laugh and trumpet everywhere,

you profligate, look how I shuffle—yes,
I who am even more dazed than the blind.
I say, "What are they looking for up there?"

93   To a Woman Passing

The street around me thundered on and on.
A tall, slim, regal woman in profound
mourning went by me, while her jeweled hand
held up the hem and flounces of her gown.

Her fine, lithe legs displayed a marble poise.
Thrilled as a drunk, I sucked out of her eyes—
fair heavens in which hurricanes arise—
seductive sweetnesses and killing joys.

A lightning flash . . . then darkness!—Fleeting belle
whose gaze rejuvenated me, shall I
see you no more before oblivion?

Far elsewhere! Too late! Never! I cannot say
where you have fled, nor you where I have gone.
You whom I might have loved—you knew it well!

94   Skeleton Laborers

I.
Anatomical plates are sold
in stalls along the dusty docks
where lots and lots of cadaverous books
sleep their sleep like the mummies of old.

The old engraver's distinctive skill
and a pervasive mood of gloom
render them, though they are quite grim,
incontrovertibly beautiful.

One sees in these mysterious scenes
(and it makes their horrors still more wild),
like laborers working in a field,
flayed frames and digging skeletons.

II.
Out of the soil you are breaking there,
resigned and melancholy drones,
with all the effort of your spines,
with all of your open musculature,

tell us what your harvest might be.
Convicts recovered from the slab,
what farmer hired you for the job
of filling up his granary?

Do you reveal (a vivid sign
of the destiny we soon will reach)
we'll lack, when buried in a ditch,
the sleep we were told would be our own?

Nothingness is treacherous.
Even Death is a deceiver.
Alas, forever and ever and ever,
work may be awaiting us

in some anonymous estate:
to scratch up acres, clod by clod
and drive the insubordinate spade
under our bare and bloody feet?

95   Twilight

Sweet evening, friendly to the cutpurse, like a wolf
or an accomplice, enters. Shutting on itself,
the sky becomes a massive cell with no great haste,
and restless man transforms into a feral beast.

Evening, kind evening, keenly counted on by all
those whose undissembling arms can say: "We've toiled our toil
today!" Yes, it is dusk that offers solace to
those spirits who must chew a savage sort of woe:
the tired but stubborn scholar with his heavy head;
the wrecked construction worker sinking into bed.
Meanwhile, foul fiends are slow to wake but wake again
heavily in the atmosphere like businessmen.
Flying, they bump the eaves and shutters of the houses.
Against the streetlamps' gleamings, taunted by the breezes,
Prostitution, madame of the back streets, blazes.
She opens up her ever-busy enterprises.

Much like a hostile army on a sneak attack,
she drains the bad parts of the city, block by block.
She operates inside these quarters made of mud
just as a parasite robs people of their food.
One has to hear a kitchen hissing here and there,
a blaring orchestra, a screeching theater.
The tables of the inns where gamblers play roulette
are full of sluts and charlatans and all that set.
Remorseless thugs who never pardon anyone
are getting ready to go back to work again—
they gently jimmy doors, crack open safes, so as
to live a few days more and dress their mistresses.

Soul, pull yourself together in this serious time
and close your ears, block out the shrillness of the slime.
This is the hour when sick men gasp most poignantly—
but black night grasps their throats and no one hears them cry.
Each of them has been marked to fill an unmarked plot.
Their hospital is full of coughing. They do not
need to consider soup with spices anymore
or evenings with a loving friend beside the fire.

Yes, most of them have not enjoyed even a dull
hearth light; yes, most of them have never lived at all.

96   Gambling

In faded armchairs, pale, old courtesans
with painted brows and eyes demure but fierce
simpered so as to make the garish stones
and metals tinkle in their withered ears.

Around the green felt there were lipless faces,
lips without any color, toothless jaws,

and fingers palsied by accursed diseases
fumbling through a pocket or heaving dress.

Chandeliers (how begrimed the ceiling was!)
and giant lanterns cast a gaudy glare
over the dusky and distinguished brows
of poets, who waste their sweat and earnings there.

There, in a dream, I saw this very scene
unfold before my visionary eyes.
I, in a corner of that quiet den,
leaned in and felt cold, mute and envious

both of the gentlemen's tenacious passion
and of the old harlots' sepulchral mirth.
That they should vend in such a jolly fashion
beauty or honor—all that they were worth!

I shuddered at my envy of that lot
dashing so rashly into the abyss.
Drunk on their own blood, they choose to set
pain over death, Hell over nothingness.

97   *Danse Macabre°*

To Ernest Christophe°

Much like the living, she enjoys her height.
She has a kerchief, gloves and many flowers.
She has the grace and balance that befit
a gaunt coquette who puts on lavish airs.

At dances does one see a build so taut?
Her long gown, in a grand majestic style,

flows with abandon toward an arid foot
pinched in a pom-pommed, rose-like kitten heel.

The frill that runs along her clavicle,
like some lewd river passing over rocks,
demurely shields from public ridicule
the funerary turn-ons of her sex.

Her eyes are sockets of oblivion.
Her skull, artfully dressed in irises,
gingerly sways atop her jutting spine.
The charm of wildly stylized nothingness!

Some passersby will call you a "cartoon,"
but how can they, the wholly flesh-obsessed,
fathom the grandeur of a skeleton?
Superb bones, you are much more to my taste!

You with your grimace, do you hope to ruin
life's festival? Does some extinct love still
invigorate your living carrion
and drive you toward the human carnival?

Will you expel that dark, insulting dream
with singing violins and candle glow?
And will you use your fresh libidinous stream
to quench the Hell that burns inside of you?

O endless pit of foolishness and crime,
O old and constant sorrow's crucible,
I see the ever-hungry serpent climb
from ribs resembling a latticed wall.

I fear your coquetry will never win
any trophy truly worthy of it.

Who of these mortals gets it's all for fun?
Only the strong can bear the charms of fright.

Vertigo spirals from your absent eyes,
pits full of horrid thoughts. What beau could join
the dance with you and not puke when he sees
those rows of teeth fixed in a constant grin?

But who has not embraced a sack of bones?
Who has not eaten from a sepulcher?
What good are clothes, makeup and luscious scents?
Disgust just shows how fine prudes think they are.

Noseless geisha, irresistible slut,
tell all those whiny dancing fools the truth:
"Proud pretty ones, though you put on a coat
of rouge and talc, you wholly reek of death.

Redolent skeletons, plucked dandies, blown
Antinoüses, snowy-haired manwhores—
the *danse macabre* whirls round and round and soon
will sweep you off to never-heard-of shores.

From torrid Ganges to the frigid Seine
the leaping, gasping mortals do not see
the angel's trumpet like an all-black gun
aimed at them from above, maliciously.

Death sees you writhing, foolish Humankind,
under whatever sun you chance to be.
Quite often, just like you, she makes a blend
of uncut craziness and irony."

98 The Love of Lying

When I see you walk by, my lazy one, my dear,
accompanied by music bouncing off the ceiling,
poising harmonious attractions in the air
and showing, in your eyes, an apathetic feeling,

when I consider, by the gaslight's flames, your wan
forehead embellished only with your wan allure
as evening torches offer up a sort of dawn,
and find your eyes as striking as in portraiture,

I think, "How lovely she is! How bizarrely fresh!
A thick and royal tower, massive recollection,
crowns her, and her heart, bruised as mellow peach,
is ripe, just like her flesh, for masterful affection."

Are you the fruit of fall, when the best flavor oozes?
A standing funeral vase that waits for mourners' tears?
A scent that makes us dream of faraway oases?
A pillow that caresses? A bouquet of flowers?

I know that there are eyes, depressive and jejune
eyes, that contain no secrets, no dear mystery,
each like an empty locket or a looted shrine,
more empty, more profound than you yourself, O sky.

But isn't it sufficient that your lovely face
reanimates a heart that runs from what is true?
Who cares about your lethargy and foolishness?
Beauty, you mask, you ornament, I worship you!

99   I still recall the little whitewashed lodging where ...°

I still recall the little whitewashed lodging where
we lived in peace, just off a major thoroughfare.
A plaster Pomona and an aging Queen of Love°
concealed their naked bodies in our garden grove,
and the august and ruddy sun, at twilight, shone
kaleidoscopic colors through the windowpane.
He seemed, a giant eye in the inquiring sky,
to watch us as we ate our long meals silently
and spread, across the worsted curtains and cut-rate
tablecloth, an effulgence fine as candlelight.

100   Think of my kind old nurse you once were jealous of ...

Think of my kind old nurse° you once were jealous of,
the one who sleeps the long sleep in a humble grave.
We two together ought to give her a bouquet.
The dead, the sorry dead, they suffer terribly.
Yes, when October cracks the boughs of trees and tosses
leaves in a sad, sad way on final resting places,
they should consider us, the living folk, ingrates
because we lie here sleeping warmly in our sheets,
while they, consumed by beasts of the imagination,
without a partner, without lively conversation,
decaying carcasses, devoured by maggots, frozen,
feel themselves filtering the snow when winter blows in.
Time passes, and no friend, no relative, comes back
to lay memorial flowers on the funeral plaque.

Sometimes at evening while the logs sing on and on,
I see her sitting calmly on the ottoman
or find her on a cold blue midnight in December
standing in a corner of my dark bedchamber.

What could I offer to this very pious shade,
this somber spirit who comes from her eternal bed
to watch once more the grown-up child she worked to raise?
I look on as the tears fall from her hollow eyes.

101   Mists and Rains

O waning autumn, winter, springtime drenched in mud,
I give you, sleepy days, love and this accolade
because, just like today, you swathe my heart and mind
in vague crepe and the odor of the funeral mound.

In that vast grassland where the cold southwester plays
and all night long the wavering wind vane makes hoarse noise,
my spirit spreads its pair of raven wings much farther
than later in the spring, when there is tepid weather.

O seasons sunk in pallor, O our climate queens,
nothing is sweeter to a gloomy heart like mine
(the sort of heart where snow has long been falling) than

your permanent and sallow dampening of light,
—unless it is two lovers deadening the pains
of living, in a chance bed, on a moonless night.

102   Parisian Dream

For Constantin Guys°

I.
The distant vision I recall
of awe-inspiring scenery
nobody ever saw for real
this morning still entrances me.

Sleep is often incredible.
I, by a singular caprice,
had banished from that spectacle
Nature's irregularities.

A painter on fire with my mastery,
I savored everywhere in the scene
the ravishing monotony
of flowing water, metal and stone.

This Babel of stairways and colonnades
was like an endless palace filled
with water basins and cascades
flowing with dull or burnished gold.

Like curtains made of precious stones,
the intimidating waterfalls
seemed to be hanging in suspense
along the murals in the walls.

Stone columns instead of trees in a wood
gathered around pools smooth as glass.
In them colossal naiads° could
bask in a self-admiring gaze.

Between the green and crimson slips
arches of indigo water came
jetting out of a million pipes
and flowed toward my creation's rim.

A tide of magical combers wore
away at unknown kinds of rock,
and massive looking-glasses there
admired the world that they gave back.

Nonchalant and taciturn,
a river Ganges in the sky
poured treasure from a bottomless urn
into a diamond-sparkling sea.

Architect of a fantastic show,
I ordered (a majestic whim)
a subjugated sea to flow
out of a gem-encrusted flume.

Everything, even the darkest hues,
seemed to be full of radiance.
The various liquids wore a glaze
because of the way that crystal shines.

No clusters of stars, no sun, no moon
appeared anywhere in that sky—
no, what lit that scene of mine
was the blazing fire inside of me.

There was, above this universe
replete with things for eyes to see,
what offered nothing to the ears—
the silence of eternity.

II.
But, open now, my eyes of fire
could see the horror of my den.
I felt my tribulations were
a needle entering my brain.

The clock announced the hour was noon—
twelve brutal strokes came, one by one.
Celestial gloom came pouring down
over this grieving world we're in.

103   Morning Twilight

Reveille sounded through the barracks' marching ground,
and lanterns flickered in the early morning wind.

It was the hour when swarms of noxious reveries
kept suntanned young men twisting on their mattresses,
when, like a bloody, bulging, palpitating eye,
the house lamp cast a tinge of crimson on the day,
when spirits, which the weight of flesh was pressing down,
mimicked the struggles of the lamplight and the dawn,
when, like a tear-stained face wiped by the breeze, the air
brimmed with the trembling of things that rise, that soar.
Man tired of writing; woman tired of making love.

Houses began to rouse; smoke rose above a roof.
Women of pleasure, still exceedingly made up,
just went on sleeping, mouths agape, a stupid sleep.
Poor women dragged along their cold and sickly dugs,
blew on their fingernails, blew on the smoldering logs.
It was the hour when, behind thin, frozen doors,
women who were in labor started suffering worse.
As if it were a blood-choked sob, a rooster's cry,
off in the distance, cut into the misty sky.
Fog bathed the buildings, even bathed the hospice house
where, room by room, the inmates, in their final throes,
rattled their lives away, consumptive, cough by cough.
Drunks stumbled home at last, scarred by the wars of love.

Aurora,° trembling in her robe of red and green,
slowly advanced along the still-deserted Seine,
and somber Paris rubbed the slumber from his eyes
and gathered up his tools, old workman that he is.

WINE

Wine's soul, from bottles, sang a song one night:
"O outcast man, for your sake, I release,
out of the wax and glass that hold me tight,
a melody of light and friendliness.

I know you need, out on a sunny hill,
to grunt and sweat beneath a brutal sun
when you conceive my life and birth my soul.
I'm grateful to you. I won't let you down,

since I feel great delight when I can dive
into the gullet of a working hand.
I'm happy with his stomach as my grave
much more than some cold cellar underground.

And do you hear the Sunday songs, the hope
forever rising from my pulsing breast?
You, elbows on the table, sleeves rolled up,
will praise me. I will put your cares to rest.

I'll light the eyes of your enraptured wife;
I'll give great health and fervor to your son
and serve, for this frail wrestler with life,
as oil that makes his muscles hot to win.

You there and I, seed of a deathless Sower,
ambrosia of the earth, will soon be one,
and poetry, conceived by our amour,
will shoot toward God like flowers on the vine."

105   The Ragpickers' Wine

Often, beneath a streetlamp's crimson glamour, as
a stiff wind skews the flame and beats against the glass,
deep in a worn-out suburb's heart, a muddy maze
where humankind is swarming, thundering en masse,

one sees a coughing ragpicker approach, unwell,
stumbling, as poets tend to do, against a wall.
Without the slightest worry about policemen's spies,
he heartily propounds some glorious enterprise.

Huffing and cussing, he proposes lofty laws,
vanquishes evildoers, saves the victims' days
and, underneath a heaven like a pulpit, grows
inebriated on his glowing righteousness.

Yes, and these men tormented by domestic strife,
racked by declining years, scarred by the cuts of life,
burdened and bowing underneath a massive load,
men who are sprawling Paris's ejected cud,

just keep on showing up, redolent of the bottle,
they and their boon companions, marked by years of battle,
mustaches drooping much like curtains turned to rags.
Triumphal arches, lovely flowers and brilliant flags,

as if invoked by magic, sprout in front of them
and, in the orgiastic pandemonium
of cris de coeur and bugles, snare drums and the sun,
they magnify a love-drunk people with renown.

And so it is throughout the fickle human race
wine flows with pure gold, like the dazzling Pactolus.
Wine sings its great adventures through our human throats
and, like a proper king, rules by its benefits.

Regretting what he had contrived, God gave us sleep
to drown out bitterness, to serve as an escape
for wretched geezers who are dying all alone.
Man added Wine, the sacred offspring of the Sun.

106   The Murderer's Wine

I'm free at last! My wife is gone.
Now I can drink to my heart's content.
When I came home without a cent,
her nagging cut me to the bone.

Now I am happy as a prince.
The sky is fair, the air is pure.
Back in the tranquil season before
the breach, my joy was this intense.

To slake the thirst consuming me,
I'd need to have my ex-wife's tomb
filled with wine up to the brim.
That was a hard, hard thing to say.

I threw my wife into a pit
and then rained down around her head
some stones stacked up around the side.
I'll try hard—maybe I'll forget.

In the name of those sentimental vows
that swear true lovers can't be split,
to make us just as when we met
in our first time of drunkenness,

I begged her for a rendezvous
one night on a forgotten road.

Since we're all crazy in the head,
she came. A crazy thing to do.

She was, I guess, still pretty enough,
though worn out with the years, and I,
I loved her way too much. That's why
I told her: "Get out of this life."

Nobody gets me. Not one sot
out of a thousand inebriates
dreams even on his maudlin nights
of making wine a winding-sheet.

That invincible company,
much like machines made out of steel,
all winter and spring, summer and fall,
have never felt what love can be:

the darkling way it entertains,
its infernal procession of commotion,
its tears on tears, its flasks of poison,
its rattlings of bones and chains.

Well, here I am—alone now, freed.
I'm going to get dead drunk tonight,
then, without pity or regret,
make my bed on the side of the road

and sleep as any mongrel might.
Some thick-wheeled chariot with a load
of broken stones and civic mud,
some random vehicle is quite

welcome to crush my guilty head,
divide me on the thoroughfare.

I care for myself as much as I care
about the Devil, Faith and God.

107   The Loner's Wine

A jolly woman's tantalizing gaze
gliding toward us like the pale-beamed moon
shimmering on a trembling lagoon
when she, remotely, bathes her gorgeousness;

the last money bag in a gambler's hand;
a wanton kiss from skinny Adeline;°
music as poignant as a man in pain
from far off wails, a warm, wearying sound—

deep bottle, none of that can match the keen
elixir that your plump and fruitful sides
offer the pious poet's ruined soul.

You give him youth, promise and life to swill
—and pride, the treasury of bankrupt men,
that makes us glorious and like the gods!

108   The Lovers' Wine

The air is dazzling today!
Let's leap on steeds of Cabernet
and, without bridles, without spurs,
ride a sublime and eccentric course.

Up in the crystal blue of dawn,
like two seraphim seized by one
relentless fever, by one vision,
let's fly toward a remote delusion!

Comfortably balanced on
the wings of a vigilant typhoon,
we'll gallop, sister, side by side,

and stop at nothing as we glide,
in parallel delirium,
beyond belief into a dream.

109 Destruction

The Fiend is always stirring here beside me.
He swims around me like the ghost of air.
I breathe him, and he lights a fire inside me
and fills me up with damnable desire.

Knowing my love of art, he sometimes uses
highly captivating female shapes
and then, with hypocritical excuses,
offers up heinous poisons to my lips.

That's how he brings me, tired, in a daze,
farther from God's gaze into desert lands—
relentless prairies subject to Ennui.

Later he holds up to my muddled eyes
contaminated garments, open wounds,
and Devastation's bloody panoply.

110 A Martyr

A Drawing by an Unknown Master°

Framed by flasks and brightly chased lamé,
by lots of sumptuous furniture,
by statues, prints and fragrant negligee
that reaches, richly, to the floor,

inside a room that, like a greenhouse, is
stuffy and warm and rank with death,
a place where fading flowers, entombed in glass,
exhale a final fragrant breath,

a headless corpse is spilling like a stream
over a pillow on a bed
vermilion blood flow, which the sheets consume
with a voracious meadow's greed.

Like pale dreams mothered by oblivion
(visions that put our eyes in chains),
the head, with its abundant jet-black mane
lit, here and there, by precious stones,

lies, like a vase stuffed full of buttercups,
on the nightstand. A thoughtless gaze
as vague and empty as the dusk, escapes
from open and contorted eyes.

The naked torso on the bed displays,
wantonly and without the blot
of shame, the hushed and fatal gorgeousness
that nature has bestowed on it.

A pink stocking adorned with golden clocks
hangs on her like a souvenir;
a garter with enkindled vision looks
outward with a diamond stare.

The curious aspect of this loneliness,
much like the portrait on the wall
with eyes just as alluring as her pose,
reveals a dark and culpable

affair, rejected wanton revelries
and kisses from satanic lips
in which those fallen angels would rejoice
from the embroidery of the drapes.

Yet, when one looks closely at the taste
of collarbone and lissome shoulder,
the pointed haunch, the swivel in the waist,
as in an aggravated adder,

how young she is! —Did her exhausted mind
and senses chewed by tedium
open her up to a corrupting band
of lusts? Did she encourage them?

Did that much cherished man, that stubborn lover
whom you could not, while living, sate,
over your passive, welcoming cadaver,
fulfill his giant appetite?

Tell me, you stinking stiff! And did he seize
your hair with trembling fingertips,
hold you aloft and plant his last goodbyes
as kisses on your frigid lips?

—Far from the loud world and insulting throng,
far from the prying of police,
sleep well in your mysterious tomb, strange thing.
I pray that you can rest in peace.

Your groom is out there, but the sight of you
haunts him wherever he lays his head.
Surely, like you yourself, he will be true
and staunch until he, too, is dead.

110x Lesbos°

Mother of Greek delights and Roman fun,
Lesbos, where kisses, sad or rapturous,
fresh as casabas, torrid as the sun,
are ornaments to nights and famous days,
mother of Greek delights and Roman fun.

Lesbos, where kisses are like waterfalls
that dash, boldly, into oblivion
and plummet, sighing, chafing with a pulse,
stormy and secret, swarming on and on;
Lesbos, where kisses are like waterfalls.

Lesbos, where prostitutes desire each other,
and every sigh is answered with the same.
Stars in the firmament adore you rather
than Paphos,° and Venus envies Sappho's fame,°
Lesbos, where prostitutes desire each other.

Lesbos, land of slow and sultry nights
which make young females with their hollow eyes
see, in their mirrors, childless delights.
They stroke the fruit of their own youthfulness,
Lesbos, land of slow and sultry nights.

Let age-old Plato° frown his grumpy face.
Your pardon is the excess of your kisses,
queen of a luscious realm, a kindly place.
Your pardon is your never-ending blisses.
Let age-old Plato frown his grumpy face.

Your pardon is the endless martyrdom
inflicted always on the amorous
who have been tempted far away from home

by radiant smiles, half glimpsed in other skies.
Your pardon is the endless martyrdom.

Lesbos, who would condemn your ways? Which god?
Who would condemn your brow, wan with travail,
because his scales had failed to weigh the flood
of tears you pour into the salt-sea swell.
Lesbos, who would condemn your ways? Which god?

What is the good of laws, unjust or just?
Virgins with holy hearts, the island's fame,
your faith, like every other, is august,
and love will laugh both Heaven and Hell to shame.
What is the good of laws, unjust or just?

Lesbos, from all the rest, selected me
to sing the secrets of her girls in bloom.
In childhood I observed their mystery—
unending laughter mixed with tears of gloom.
Lesbos, from all the rest, selected me.

Since then I look out from Leucadia's top,
a sentry with a penetrating gaze
who scans for any sort of passing ship
whose distant outline bobs against the skies.
Since then I look out from Leucadia's top

to find out if the ocean has remorse,
and if, to echoes which the rocks have kept,
it will return the night to Lesbos, which adores
the body of Sappho ever since she leapt
to find out if the ocean has remorse.

Of manly Sappho, lover, poetess,
more beautiful than Venus, though quite pale

—her blue eyes lost to Sappho's darker eyes,
eyes with dark circles, traced by the travail
of manly Sappho, lover, poetess.

—Fairer than Venus rising on the world
and spreading out a wealth of self-possession
and all the radiance of her blond hair curled
over the waters of her father Ocean;
fairer than Venus rising on the world.

—Sappho broke the rules and died the day
that, to insult her own society,
she made her flesh a pasture when she lay
beneath a brute who was the penalty
for her who broke the rules. She died that day.

Ages have passed, and still the island grieves.
Yes, though the whole world keeps on honoring her,
it still howls nightly as the tempest raves
with thunder echoed by its empty shore.
Ages have passed, and still the island grieves.

110xx   The Damned Women: Delphine and Hippolyta°

Under a fading lantern's pallid light,
on cushions drenched in scent, Hippolyta
was dreaming of the strong caresses that
had raised her curtain of naïveté.

The girl was seeking, out of storm-tossed eyes,
clear skies of innocence, now far away,
just as, at noon, a traveler reviews
the journey he has made since break of day.

Her listless manner, her lackluster tears,
her dulled delight, the stupor in her eyes,
and both her arms held out like yielded spears
only enhanced her fragile loveliness.

With eyes like fire, though calm and full of joy,
Delphine, crouching at her lover's feet,
stared at her like a lion at its prey
just after having marked it with a bite.

Strong beauty kneeled at fragile beauty's feet.
With pride and pleasure she inhaled the blood
red wine of victory and then reached out,
as if to claim the kisses she was owed.

She sought, within her pallid victim's eyes,
mute symphonies that bliss knows how to play
and looks of thanks that, like protracted sighs,
rise from the eyelids in a noble way.

"Hippolyta, what do you say to this?
What if you do not need to give your youth,
your springtime flowers, as a sacrifice
to one who wrecks them with his boisterous breath?

My kisses are as light as gnats at night
stroking the surface of a limpid pond,
but those a man gives like a chariot
or farmer's plowshare cut into your rind.

They pass across you like a heavy yoke
of cruel steeds or oxen. Hippolyta,
my sister, turn and look at me. Please look.
You are heart, soul and everything to me.

Give me your eyes, so full of stars and sky.
For just one charming glance, a holy balm,
I'd raise the veil of secret ecstasy
and lull you in a never-ending dream."

The girl, though, lifting up her head, said, "Please,
Delphine, do not think that I regret
our passion, though I suffer in distress
as if from some strange witch's feast each night.

Dismay is haunting me. I see a band
of dim ghosts beckoning me down a road
where every hazy vista seems to end
abruptly in a sky the color of blood.

What have we done here? Something reprobate?
Must I endure this turmoil and this woe?
I shudder when you call me 'angel,' yet
I feel my mouth is yearning for you. No,

Delphine, please don't stare at me like that.
I love you now and always, you alone,
even if my desire should be a net
spread for me, and my hellish pains begin."

With eyes of fire, Delphine shook her head
of tragic hair and, like the priestess of
Apollo on the sacred seat, replied:
"Why mix the word Hell with the word of Love?

My curse forever on the dizzy fool
who was the first to probe the endless maze
and tried with all his folly to enroll
love in the service of his righteousness.

Whoever hopes to bring together dusk
and daylight, utter obscurity and fire,
will never warm his vacillating husk
in that red sun our flesh knows as desire.

Go, if you want, and find some stupid man.
Give your virginity to his cruel lusts,
then, full of penitence and horror, wan,
come back to me at last with wounded breasts.

We each must choose one master here below."
The girl, though, tortured by the whole ordeal,
cried out, "There is a void inside of me,
and it is growing, and it is my soul.

It is like molten rock, like nothingness.
Nothing will satisfy the raging greed
of the fell Fury° who extinguishes
her blazing torch within my very blood.

O draw the curtains—shut the whole world out.
There must be comfort for the weary. Come,
let me snuff out my passion on your throat
and find in you the solace of a tomb."

—Descend, you melancholy casualties,
along the road to Hell. Descend, descend!
Plunge to the bottom of the pit where vice,
whipped by the gusts of no celestial wind,

roars like a tempest as it swells and surges.
Run toward desire, foolish obscurities.
You won't be able to assuage your urges.
Punishment will be born out of your bliss.

No bracing ray will ever light your damp
caverns but, once it seeps into your rooms,
feverish rot will kindle like a lamp
and pierce your flesh with frightening perfumes.

Your pleasure's bleak sterility will increase
your thirst and turn you, each, into a hag,
and the wild tempest of your lustfulness
make your flesh crackle like a threadbare flag.

Doomed women, exiled from humanity,
go wandering through desert wastes like wolves.
Dissolute souls, fulfill your destiny,
run from the infinite inside yourselves.

111   The Damned Women

Like pensive cattle lying on a beach,
they turn and gaze into the ocean swell.
Feet probe for loving female feet; hands reach
for hands with languor or a desperate chill.

Some, with hearts full of intimate confessions,
in shadowy groves where little rivers chide,
write out the love of anxious adolescence
by carving letters into fresh green wood.

Others, like sisters, stride majestically
through desertscapes where phantoms live in crags,
where rose volcanic for Saint Anthony°
his great Temptation's naked, purple dugs.

Many there are who, when the fire dies down
deep in a cave where ancient heathen met,

call you, O Bacchus,° husher of chagrin,
to cure a fever or subdue a fit.

Others, who have a taste for monkish dress
and hide a lash beneath the robe they wear,
on lonely nights out in the wilderness
mix pleasure's foam with a tormented tear.

O virgins, demons, saints, monstrosities,
spirits who scorn the actual universe
and seek the void, satyrs and devotees
as full of cries of rapture as of tears,

you whom my soul has followed to your Hell,
poor sisters, let me cherish as I mourn
all of your sorrows, all your great thirsts, all
your hearts (each one a love-tormented urn).

112   The Two Good Sisters

Orgy and Death, twin sisters giddy over
kisses, each possess a fulsome form.
Their rag-clad and immaculate haunches, ever
in labor, never bring a child to term.

To evil poets (ill-paid courtiers,
home-wreckers, the infernal certified),
grave sites and brothels show, inside their bowers,
beds where Remorse has never laid his head.

Rich in abuse, coffin and corner both
provide in turn, like those delightful twins,
terrible joys and frightening ecstasies.

Foul Orgy, when will you inter my bones?
And you, her rival, Death, when will you fuse
sad cypress to her toxic myrtle wreath?°

113   The Fountain of Blood

Sometimes it seems my blood is jetting out
rhythmically, as if from a waterspout.
I hear, clearly, the endless spurting sound
but search my skin in vain to find the wound.

A crimson tide maroons each paving stone
and makes one vast arena of the town.
Every thirsty creature bends its head
to drink it. Everything is painted red.

Sometimes I swilled subversive wine to lull
this self-destructive terror for a while,
but wine just hones my eyes and piques my ears.

I hoped that love would lead to lassitude,
but love is just a bed of needles made
to slake the bloodlust of sadistic whores!

114   Allegory

There is a fine-necked woman, an attractive one,
who lets her very long hair trail into her wine.
Love's talons and the poisons of the gambling den
approach and die upon the granite of her skin.
She thinks Death humorous and flouts Debauchery.
The gang of monstrous things that ravage and destroy
still have respect, in a flirtatious way,

for the hard, upright body of nobility.
Taut as a goddess, languid as a sultan's wife,
she cherishes, like an infidel, the joys of life.
Yes, with her open, breast-uplifting arms, she summons
the admiring eyes of all of us mere mortal humans.
This barren virgin who, for all that, makes the whole
world keep on spinning, spinning round and round, knows well,
feels well, that beauty of the flesh is a sublime
indulgence that absolves the fair of every crime.
All Hell is moot to her, all Purgatory, moot,
and, when the time arrives for her to face the Night,
she will observe Death's features like a neonate
—without revulsion and without the least regret.

115 The Beatrice°

One day while I was walking, whining, in
a landscape made of ash, a dead terrain,
and while my heart was sharpening my grief
slowly, just as the whetstone hones the knife,
I saw, at noon, descend around my head
a massive melancholy thundercloud
in which a troupe of demons had the look
of vicious dwarves—such was the form they took.
They eyed me with a great deal of disdain
and, like bystanders near a crazy man,
seemed to share jokes and murmurs, seemed to nod
and wink at one another, as they said:

"—Come, let us contemplate this travesty,
this man like Hamlet's specter in a play—
he has the tousled hair, the puzzled look.
Isn't it sad to have to watch this rake,
this empty thespian, this fraud, this fool,

since he employs some artistry in his role?
He thinks he entertains the eagles, bugs,
rivers and flowers by singing of his fugues.
He even hurls his shrill tirades at us,
who wrote the book of spite, such as it is."

I would (since my impressive pride
could easily disperse that hooting crowd)
have simply turned my lordly head, had I
not seen amid that dirty revelry
(O wrong of wrongs that should have skewed the sun!)
Her of the Gorgeous Gaze, my heart's bright queen,
titter with them at my macabre distraction
and stroke them more than once with great affection.

115x   The Metamorphoses of the Vampire

Meanwhile the woman, with her lips of strawberry,
making her breasts expand against her bustier,
twisting and writhing like a serpent in the flame,
let fall the following utterance, pregnant with perfume:

"Me, I am blessed with moist lips, and I am quite good
at killing wrinkled conscience in a spacious bed.
My all-conquering bust dries up your tears and makes
the old burst into laughter, just like little tykes.
Whenever someone sees me naked, I outshine
all the constellations and the moon and sun.
I am, dear connoisseur, so learned in my charms
that, when I crush a lover in my mighty arms,
or when I yield my breasts up to his eager bites,
when I am meek or weak or wild in my delights
atop a mattress that goes wild with ecstasy,
angels, undone, would damn themselves to lie with me."

When she had sucked the marrow from my bones, when I
had turned my body toward her in a languid way
to give her many loving kisses, nothing was
beside me but a sticky old flask full of pus.
I squeezed my eyes shut then in overwhelming fear
and, when I opened them to see the light once more,
I saw no active dead thing lying by my side,
no vampire who survived by sucking out my blood,
but what appeared a rotting, shaking skeleton
that made squeaking pronouncements like a weather vane,
or what was like a storefront's hanging signage set
atop a pole and swinging on a winter night.

116   A Voyage to Cythera°

My heart flew freely among the shrouds and gear
just as a seabird flutters joyously.
The vessel rolled beneath a cloudless sky,
much like an angel drunk on solar glare.

"What is that sad dark island?" "It's renowned
and legendary—known as Cythera.
For old-time people it's utopia.
Despite all that, it seems a wretched land."

—Island of feasting hearts and hidden joys,
like an aroma the licentious ghost
of Aphrodite flies around your coast,
inflaming souls with love and listlessness.

Island of myrtle boughs and blooming buds,
O place the whole world venerates forever,
where the sighs of the devoted lover
rise, like incense, over flower beds

or like the endless cooing of the dove
—Cythera, rather, was an arid place,
mere rocks and sand disturbed by piercing cries.
Still, there was something strange I caught sight of.

It was no temple hid in shadowy trees
where a young priestess, amorous of flowers,
her body seething with clandestine fires,
walked with her robe half-open to the breeze.

She wasn't there but, as we grazed the shore
and our bright canvas scared the gulls away,
we saw a triple-forking gallows tree,
black as a cypress, sticking in the air.

Ferocious birds were perched on what they ate—
a savaged, overripe and hanged cadaver.
Each of them used his foul beak like a lever
to pry out every little bit of rot.

The eyes were pits, and the intestines hung
the whole way from the belly to the thighs.
The birds went also for the delicacies—
they ripped the private parts out of the thing.

There were four-footed creatures. Eager maws
lifted, they padded round and round the feast.
Dead center of them moved the largest beast,
an executioner with his deputies.

Cytherean, child of so fine a view,
you silently endured humiliation
to purge your island's cultish adoration
of sins which have denied a grave to you.

Ridiculous hanged man, your grief is mine.
While looking at you hanging on display,
I felt rise to my teeth, like nausea,
a stream of bile, a flood of ancient pain.

O you fond devil of my memory,
I felt the beaks and jaws, the gaping maws,
of crows and panthers that in other days
too much enjoyed ripping my skin away.

—The sky was pleasant, and the sea was smooth.
For me, though, everything was thick black blood.
Alas! I had been wrapped up in the truth
of it as in an allegorical shroud.

O Venus, on your isle, I only found
a gallows where my form was hanging—me!
Lord, grant me strength enough to see,
without revulsion, my own body and mind!

117   Love and the Skull°

An Old Lamp Base

Poised on the skull of our race (his throne),
the God of Love,
a power both naughty and profane,
with a wicked laugh,

is blowing perfect bubbles which rise
in the atmosphere
as if to rejoin existences
at the end of the air.

Each fragile and luminescent ball,
after its bold
flight, bursts and releases its flimsy soul
like a dream of gold.

As each ascends, the skull lets out
a groaning sound:
"When will this vicious and foolish pursuit
come to an end?

What your lips, O murderous one,
make, sud by sud,
that's what I now have as my brain,
my flesh, my blood."

REVOLT

What does the Lord do with the tide of blasphemy
that rises daily toward his heavenly domain?
He, like a tyrant stuffed with rich entrées and wine,
sleeps to the sweet sound of our harsh impiety.

Martyrs' dying gasps and torture victims' sighs
compose a symphony that intoxicates his senses,
and yet the bloody scene their suffering presents is
hardly enough to sate the powers in the skies.

—Jesus, do you recall the Garden of Olives? How,
down on your knees in your naïveté, you prayed
to him who chuckled at the sound the hammers made
as villains pierced your living body blow by blow?

And when you had to see mere drunken soldiery,
mere kitchen workers, spit on your beatitude?
And when you had to feel the crown of thorns draw blood
from all around the head that meant humanity?

When your already dislocated arms stretched out
more and still more beneath your broken body's weight?
And when your pallid forehead ran with blood and sweat?
When all men saw you as the target of their spite?

Did you dream then of those fine, shining former hours
when you had come down to fulfill the oath of God?
Of how you traveled, how the gentle ass you rode
trampled on pathways strewn with tree branches and flowers?

And when, your heart brimming with hope and fortitude,
you whipped the wicked merchants in the countinghouse?°
When you had proved the master? Did remorsefulness
dig even deeper than the spear into your side?

I, for my part, would happily forsake a place
where what is done and what is dreamed do not accord.
I want to wield the sword and perish by the sword.
Peter rejected Jesus.° What he did was wise!

119   Abel and Cain°

I.
Race of Abel, sleep, drink, feed.
God smiles on you complacently.

Race of Cain, crawl in the mud.
Die in the most despairing way.

Race of Abel, your sacrifice
delights the nostrils of seraphim.

Race of Cain, will your damages
abide beyond the end of time?

Race of Abel, watch as your crops
thrive always, and your cows get fat.

Race of Cain, your stomach yaps
with hunger like a worn-out mutt.

Race of Abel, go lie down
before your forefather's hearth fire.

Race of Cain, go to your den
and, like a jackal, shiver there.

Race of Abel, love and beget.
Even your money multiplies.

Race of Cain, your heart is hot.
Beware of your licentiousness.

Race of Abel, you breed and thrive
as well as insects in the woods.

Race of Cain, you have to drive
your family over desert roads.

II.
Ah, race of Abel, your remains
will fortify the steaming soil.

Race of Cain, for all your pains,
you are condemned to further toil.

Race of Abel, here is your shame:
the hoe is stronger than the sword!

Race of Cain, go on and climb
as high as Heaven, drag down the Lord!

120   The Litanies of Satan°

O you, most wise, most gorgeous of the seraphim,
O god betrayed by fate and stripped of all your fame,

Satan, have mercy on my endless grief!

O exiled potentate, you who have been mistreated
but always come back stronger when you are defeated,

Satan, have mercy on my endless grief!

You who know all, great king of subterranean things,
eminent healer of our human sufferings,

Satan, have mercy on my endless grief!

You who instruct the lepers and anathemas
you so adore to hunger after Paradise,

Satan, have mercy on my endless grief!

You who had sex with Death, an old and potent belle,
and on her fathered Hope, that fascinating fool,

Satan, have mercy on my endless grief!

You who provide the crook with calm looks of disdain
that damn the rabble massed around the guillotine,

Satan, have mercy on my endless grief!

You who have scanned the mean earth's nooks and can disclose
the precious stones a jealous God has kept from us,

Satan, have mercy on my endless grief!

You whose keen eyes have spotted every arsenal
where multitudes of metals sleep beneath the soil,

Satan, have mercy on my endless grief!

You who with one extremely massive hand conceal
ledges from sleepwalkers out for a nightly stroll,

Satan, have mercy on my endless grief!

O you who, when some sluggish drunk gets trampled on
by horse hooves, wondrously relax the broken bone,

Satan, have mercy on my endless grief!

O you who first came up with mixing niter in
with sulfur to console the sufferings of man,

Satan, have mercy on my endless grief!

You who have set your mark on base and obdurate
Croesus's brow, you exquisite associate,

Satan, have mercy on my endless grief!

You who have put, in young girls' eyes and hearts desires
for men who dress in tatters and a cult of sores,

Satan, have mercy on my endless grief!

Lamp for the inventor, exile's walking stick,
confessor for the hanged man and the turncoat sneak,

Satan, have mercy on my endless grief!

Adoptive father of those two whom their Father God,
enraged, drove from the Paradise where they were made,

Satan, have mercy on my endless grief!

Prayer
Glory and praise to you, O Satan, both way up
in Heaven, where you once held sway, and way down deep

in Hell, where, crushed, you mutely dream the days away.
Grant that my soul may lie near you beneath the Tree
of Knowledge* in the future, when its branches spread,
like a new Temple's colonnade, above your head.

DEATH

121 The Lovers' Death

Our mattress will exude seductive scents.
Our ottoman will hold us like a tomb.
For our delight, beneath the finest suns,
flower buds on ledges will unfold and bloom.

Our hearts, two torches, two vivacious blazes,
will burn more brightly in their final hours
and twin each other in the looking-glasses
that are these corresponding souls of ours.

One night of mystic violet and rose
we shall exchange a shared and final flash
like a long sob, containing our adieus,

and, afterward, an angel will come in
with gentle steps and jubilantly shine
the tarnished mirrors and revive the ash.

122 The Death of the Poor

It's Death that makes us live, Death that consoles.
Life's ending is the only prospect that,
like an intoxicant, inspires our souls
to march, inebriated, toward the night.

Death in the distance is the living light
that guides us over frost, through snow and storm.
Death is the inn the guidebook talks about,
a place where we can eat, sleep and be warm.

Death is an angel, and his magic hand
offers, as presents, sleep and dreams of bliss.
Death makes a bed for naked homelessness.

Death is gods' glory, and the great grain-store,
the poor man's purse, the ancient fatherland.
To skies that are unknown, Death is the door.

123   The Death of Artists

How often must I jingle like a fool
and kiss your low brow, shabby caricature?
Quiver, how many arrows must I fire
before I pin all Nature to a wall?

We will exhaust our souls with slick ideas
and, over and over, trash some "grand design"
before we get to see the Wondrous One
we long for—he who fills our hearts with sighs.

Some artists never meet their heathen gods.
Some sculptors, branded with the mark of Hell,
condemned to flagellate themselves in shame,

have just one hope, the somber Capitol!°
That Death, a new day rising, soon will come
and ravel out the flowers in their heads.

124   The End of the Day

Life, saucy and intemperate,
is wildly twisting, dancing, moving
under evening's pallid light.
And later, just as pleasure-loving

night comes sweeping over us,
effacing even the disgraced

and solacing even the ravenous,
the poet tells himself: "At last!

My spine and spirit both invoke
restfulness: *Come to me, please, please, please.*
My heart rolling in reveries,

I want to lie down on my back
and wrap myself in your drapery,
replenishing obscurity."

125   The Dream of an Odd Man

For Félix Nadar°

Do you, like me, find grief delectable?
Do people say of you, "How odd he is!"?
I was near death, and in my ardent soul
desire was mixed with horror—a strange malaise:

angst and a lively lust in harmony.
The closer to the time the hourglass grew,
the more the pain tortured and pleasured me.
My heart was being torn from what it knew.

I was a child excited for the scene,
hating the drapes like something in the way.
Then came the facts, the cold truth, finally:

Dead, I was dead of course. A horrid dawn
enveloped me. And then what? Is that all?
The drapes divided. I was waiting still.

126 Voyaging

For Maxime du Camp°

I.
The world can sate the giant appetite
of children keen on stamps and atlases.
How vast it all is in the lantern's light!
How pitiful in recollection's eyes!

One dawn we ship out with our minds aflame
and hearts surcharged with raw, bitter emotions
and sail on, with the breakers keeping time,
rocking our boundlessness in finite oceans.

Many forsake the land that was their home
or a horrific birthplace. A few are like
astrologers, drowned in the eyes of some
despotic Circe who has drugs in stock.°

These men, far from becoming animals,
get drunk on fiery skies and amplitude.
The sun that tans them, the ice that gives them chills,
efface the bruising kisses from their hide.

The true voyagers, though, are those who leave
just to be leaving. Their hearts all buoyancy,
they, never fading in their fatal drive,
always say "Onward!" without knowing why.

These men are subject to a cloud-like zeal.
As soldiers dream of cannon fire, they dream
of vast delights—uncharted, changeable
locales of which we do not know the name.

II.

Gasp! We are tops and bowling balls; we bounce
and dance all over. An Inquiring Mind,
like a harsh demiurge who lashes suns,
even at night, keeps rolling us around.

How strange a game! The object of the quests
changes and could be everywhere at once.
Man, in his tireless yearning, never rests
from scrambling in circles like a dunce.

Our soul's a ship in search of Paradise.
While someone on the bridge shouts "Look alive!,"
an ardent idiot in the crow's nest cries:
"For love . . . contentment . . . glory!" Damn, a reef.

The watchman thinks that every isle they meet
is El Dorado,° their predestined goal.
Imagination, running wild all night,
finds, in the light of morning, just a shoal.

Lovers of fictive lands—they seem so sad!
Should each deranged Columbus, each drunk tar,
be clapped in chains and cast into the tide
because he makes the ocean bitterer?

So the old tramp, while slogging through a slough,
dreams of Elysium and lifts his head,
and his entranced gaze sees a Capua°
where a lone candle flickers in a shed.

III.

Astounding travelers! In your sea-deep eyes
we can decipher noble chronicles.
Show us the chest of your rich memories,
those starlight gemstones, those ethereal jewels.

We long to voyage without steam or wind.
To brighten the monotony of our cells,
let your experience, which horizons bound,
inspire our souls—souls stretched as tight as sails.

Tell us what you have seen.

IV.
                              "The constellations
and breakers; sometimes we have seen the shore.
What's more, despite disastrous situations,
we often have been bored, as we are here.

The glory of sunlight on magenta seas
and glory of cities as the sun retires
spark in our hearts an ardent restlessness
to dive into a sky of tempting fires.

The richest towns and finest countrysides
never contained the transcendental charm
of what pure chance arranges in the clouds.
Desire has always kept our passion warm.

—Enjoyment fortifies desire. Desire,
old tree manured by pleasure, even as
your bark expands and coarsens more and more,
your branches reach to see the sun up close.

Sublime tree, will you always grow more thick
and tall than cypress? —Still, we have, with care,
picked sketches for your greedy memory book,
brothers who cherish what comes from afar:

yes, there were gods with trunks like elephants,
and thrones encrusted with resplendent gems,

and palaces whose wild luxuriance
would bankrupt all your bankers in their dreams,

and clothing that intoxicates the eyes,
and womenfolk who paint their nails and teeth,
and cagey mountebanks whom snakes caress."

V.
And then? And then? What else?

VI.
                              "You childish things,

this is, for you, the most important matter:
we witnessed (without even seeking it),
the whole way up and down the fatal ladder,
immortal sin—a rather boring sight:

woman, a vile thrall, proud of her stupidity,
loves herself without being shocked or blissful;
man, obscene, of obdurate cupidity,
a greedy king, a slave of slaves, a cesspool;

jolly torturers and saints who sigh;
a finely seasoned feast of blood served up;
power's poison enervating majesty,
and common folk who love the brutal whip.

Many religions much like ours, which all
point different ways to Heaven; holy men
who dote on nails and hair shirts, as the frail
pansy luxuriates in a plush divan.

Drunk on its brilliant thoughts, Humanity,
delirious as it has ever been,

cries out to God in furious agony:
'Damn you to Hell, my overlord, my twin!'

Less foolish, though, but big on madness, some,
rather than live like cows, escape the mob
by hiding out in boundless opium.
—Such is the news of the entire globe."

VII.

Dismay is what one learns from voyaging.
Today, tomorrow, yesterday, the bland
world gives us back our own reflection: a spring
of horror rising out of boring sand!

Escape or stay? If you can do it, stay;
go if you must. One runs; another lies
low to evade the watchful enemy
named Time. Some run a never-ending race—

the Twelve Apostles and the Wandering Jew.
No means of transit, neither coach nor boat,
can help them shake that thug (though quite a few,
home in their native lands, can slit his throat).

Finally, when his boot is on our nape,
we may exult and cry out "Smartly there!"
even as, China bound, we once took ship
with giddy eyes and breezes in our hair.

Our hearts as joyous as if we were young,
we will embark upon the ghostly brine.
Now do you hear the sad entrancing song?
"Come here, come here, all you who want to dine

on Lotus flowers.° Here we gather in
the otherwordly fruit your spirits lust
after. In this unending afternoon,
come and get drunk on its seductive taste!"

We guess the ghost by her familiar voice.
Pylades° strains our way across the gulf.
The one whose knees we kissed in other days
cries, "Swim to your Electra!° Save yourself!"

VIII.
O Death, old skipper, it's time to leave the pier.
O Death, this place is boring. Let's move on.
Even if sky and sea are black as tar,
our spirits, you well know, are full of sun.

Give us your poison, and we will be well.
Our minds are burning, and we want to go
into the magnitude of Heaven or Hell,
to fathom the unknown, to find *what's new.*

AU POËTE IMPECCABLE

AU PARFAIT MAGICIEN ÈS LETTRES FRANÇAISES

À MON TRÈS-CHER ET TRÈS-VÉNÉRÉ

MAÎTRE ET AMI

THÉOPHILE GAUTIER

AVEC LES SENTIMENTS

DE LA PLUS PROFONDE HUMILITÉ

JE DÉDIE

CES FLEURS MALADIVES

C.B.

Au lecteur

La sottise, l'erreur, le péché, la lésine,
Occupent nos esprits et travaillent nos corps,
Et nous alimentons nos aimables remords,
Comme les mendiants nourrissent leur vermine.

Nos péchés sont têtus, nos repentirs sont lâches;
Nous nous faisons payer grassement nos aveux,
Et nous rentrons gaiement dans le chemin bourbeux,
Croyant par de vils pleurs laver toutes nos taches.

Sur l'oreiller du mal c'est Satan Trismégiste
Qui berce longuement notre esprit enchanté,
Et le riche métal de notre volonté
Est tout vaporisé par ce savant chimiste.

C'est le Diable qui tient les fils qui nous remuent!
Aux objets répugnants nous trouvons des appas;
Chaque jour vers l'Enfer nous descendons d'un pas,
Sans horreur, à travers des ténèbres qui puent.

Ainsi qu'un débauché pauvre qui baise et mange
Le sein martyrisé d'une antique catin,
Nous volons au passage un plaisir clandestine
Que nous pressons bien fort comme une vieille orange.

Serré, fourmillant, comme un million d'helminthes,
Dans nos cerveaux ribote un peuple de Démons,
Et, quand nous respirons, la Mort dans nos poumons
Descend, fleuve invisible, avec de sourdes plaintes.

Si le viol, le poison, le poignard, l'incendie,
N'ont pas encor brodé de leurs plaisants dessins
Le canevas banal de nos piteux destins,
C'est que notre âme, hélas! n'est pas assez hardie.

Mais parmi les chacals, les panthères, les lices,
Les singes, les scorpions, les vautours, les serpents,
Les monstres glapissants, hurlants, grognants, rampants,
Dans la ménagerie infâme de nos vices,

Il en est un plus laid, plus méchant, plus immonde!
Quoiqu'il ne pousse ni grands gestes ni grands cris,
Il ferait volontiers de la terre un débris
Et dans un bâillement avalerait le monde;

C'est l'Ennui! L'œil chargé d'un pleur involontaire,
Il rêve d'échafauds en fumant son houka.
Tu le connais, lecteur, ce monstre délicat,
— Hypocrite lecteur, — mon semblable, — mon frère!

SPLEEN
ET
IDÉAL

1 Bénédiction

Lorsque, par un décret des puissances suprêmes,
Le Poète apparaît en ce monde ennuyé,
Sa mère épouvantée et pleine de blasphèmes
Crispe ses poings vers Dieu, qui la prend en pitié:

— «Ah! que n'ai-je mis bas tout un nœud de vipères,
Plutôt que de nourrir cette dérision!
Maudite soit la nuit aux plaisirs éphémères
Où mon ventre a conçu mon expiation!

Puisque tu m'as choisie entre toutes les femmes
Pour être le dégoût de mon triste mari,
Et que je ne puis pas rejeter dans les flammes,
Comme un billet d'amour, ce monstre rabougri,

Je ferai rejaillir ta haine qui m'accable
Sur l'instrument maudit de tes méchancetés,
Et je tordrai si bien cet arbre misérable,
Qu'il ne pourra pousser ses boutons empestés!»

Elle ravale ainsi l'écume de sa haine,
Et, ne comprenant pas les desseins éternels,
Elle-même prépare au fond de la Géhenne
Les bûchers consacrés aux crimes maternels.

Pourtant, sous la tutelle invisible d'un Ange,
L'Enfant déshérité s'enivre de soleil
Et dans tout ce qu'il boit et dans tout ce qu'il mange
Retrouve l'ambroisie et le nectar vermeil.

Il joue avec le vent, cause avec le nuage,
Et s'enivre en chantant du chemin de la croix;
Et l'Esprit qui le suit dans son pèlerinage
Pleure de le voir gai comme un oiseau des bois.

Tous ceux qu'il veut aimer l'observent avec crainte,
Ou bien, s'enhardissant de sa tranquillité,
Cherchent à qui saura lui tirer une plainte,
Et font sur lui l'essai de leur férocité.

Dans le pain et le vin destinés à sa bouche
Ils mêlent de la cendre avec d'impurs crachats;
Avec hypocrisie ils jettent ce qu'il touche,
Et s'accusent d'avoir mis leurs pieds dans ses pas.

Sa femme va criant sur les places publiques:
«Puisqu'il me trouve assez belle pour m'adorer,
Je ferai le métier des idoles antiques,
Et comme elles je veux me faire redorer;

Et je me soûlerai de nard, d'encens, de myrrhe,
De génuflexions, de viandes et de vins,
Pour savoir si je puis dans un cœur qui m'admire
Usurper en riant les hommages divins!

Et, quand je m'ennuierai de ces farces impies,
Je poserai sur lui ma frêle et forte main;
Et mes ongles, pareils aux ongles des harpies,
Sauront jusqu'à son cœur se frayer un chemin.

Comme un tout jeune oiseau qui tremble et qui palpite,
J'arracherai ce cœur tout rouge de son sein,
Et, pour rassasier ma bête favorite,
Je le lui jetterai par terre avec dédain!»

Vers le Ciel, où son œil voit un trône splendide,
Le Poëte serein lève ses bras pieux
Et les vastes éclairs de son esprit lucide
Lui dérobent l'aspect des peuples furieux:

— «Soyez béni, mon Dieu, qui donnez la souffrance
Comme un divin remède à nos impuretés
Et comme la meilleure et la plus pure essence
Qui prépare les forts aux saintes voluptés!

Je sais que vous gardez une place au Poète
Dans les rangs bienheureux des saintes Légions,
Et que vous l'invitez à l'éternelle fête
Des Trônes, des Vertus, des Dominations.

Je sais que la douleur est la noblesse unique
Où ne mordront jamais la terre et les enfers,
Et qu'il faut pour tresser ma couronne mystique
Imposer tous les temps et tous les univers.

Mais les bijoux perdus de l'antique Palmyre,
Les métaux inconnus, les perles de la mer,
Par votre main montés, ne pourraient pas suffire
À ce beau diadème éblouissant et clair;

Car il ne sera fait que de pure lumière,
Puisée au foyer saint des rayons primitifs,
Et dont les yeux mortels, dans leur splendeur entière,
Ne sont que des miroirs obscurcis et plaintifs!»

2   L'Albatros

Souvent, pour s'amuser, les hommes d'équipage
Prennent des albatros, vastes oiseaux des mers,
Qui suivent, indolents compagnons de voyage,
Le navire glissant sur les gouffres amers.

À peine les ont-ils déposés sur les planches,
Que ces rois de l'azur, maladroits et honteux,

Laissent piteusement leurs grandes ailes blanches
Comme des avirons traîner à côté d'eux.

Ce voyageur ailé, comme il est gauche et veule!
Lui, naguère si beau, qu'il est comique et laid!
L'un agace son bec avec un brûle-gueule,
L'autre mime, en boitant, l'infirme qui volait!

Le Poète est semblable au prince des nuées
Qui hante la tempête et se rit de l'archer;
Exilé sur le sol au milieu des huées,
Ses ailes de géant l'empêchent de marcher.

3   Élévation

Au-dessus des étangs, au-dessus des vallées,
Des montagnes, des bois, des nuages, des mers,
Par delà le soleil, par delà les éthers,
Par delà les confins des sphères étoilées,

Mon esprit, tu te meus avec agilité,
Et, comme un bon nageur qui se pâme dans l'onde,
Tu sillonnes gaiement l'immensité profonde
Avec une indicible et mâle volupté.

Envole-toi bien loin de ces miasmes morbides;
Va te purifier dans l'air supérieur,
Et bois, comme une pure et divine liqueur,
Le feu clair qui remplit les espaces limpides.

Derrière les ennuis et les vastes chagrins
Qui chargent de leur poids l'existence brumeuse,
Heureux celui qui peut d'une aile vigoureuse
S'élancer vers les champs lumineux et sereins;

Celui dont les pensers, comme des alouettes,
Vers les cieux le matin prennent un libre essor,
— Qui plane sur la vie, et comprend sans effort
Le langage des fleurs et des choses muettes!

4   Correspondances

La Nature est un temple où de vivants piliers
Laissent parfois sortir de confuses paroles;
L'homme y passe à travers des forêts de symboles
Qui l'observent avec des regards familiers.

Comme de longs échos qui de loin se confondent
Dans une ténébreuse et profonde unité,
Vaste comme la nuit et comme la clarté,
Les parfums, les couleurs et les sons se répondent.

Il est des parfums frais comme des chairs d'enfants,
Doux comme les hautbois, verts comme les prairies,
— Et d'autres, corrompus, riches et triomphants,

Ayant l'expansion des choses infinies,
Comme l'ambre, le musc, le benjoin et l'encens,
Qui chantent les transports de l'esprit et des sens.

5   J'aime le souvenir de ces époques nues ...

J'aime le souvenir de ces époques nues,
Dont Phoebus se plaisait à dorer les statues.
Alors l'homme et la femme en leur agilité
Jouissaient sans mensonge et sans anxiété,
Et, le ciel amoureux leur caressant l'échine,
Exerçaient la santé de leur noble machine.

Cybèle alors, fertile en produits généreux,
Ne trouvait point ses fils un poids trop onéreux,
Mais, louve au cœur gonflé de tendresses communes,
Abreuvait l'univers à ses tétines brunes.
L'homme, élégant, robuste et fort, avait le droit
D'être fier des beautés qui le nommaient leur roi;
Fruits purs de tout outrage et vierges de gerçures,
Dont la chair lisse et ferme appelait les morsures!

Le Poète aujourd'hui, quand il veut concevoir
Ces natives grandeurs, aux lieux où se font voir
La nudité de l'homme et celle de la femme,
Sent un froid ténébreux envelopper son âme
Devant ce noir tableau plein d'épouvantement.
Ô monstruosités pleurant leur vêtement!
Ô ridicules troncs! torses dignes des masques!
Ô pauvres corps tordus, maigres, ventrus ou flasques,
Que le dieu de l'Utile, implacable et serein,
Enfants, emmaillota dans ses langes d'airain!
Et vous, femmes, hélas! pâles comme des cierges,
Que ronge et que nourrit la débauche, et vous, vierges,
Du vice maternel traînant l'hérédité
Et toutes les hideurs de la fécondité!

Nous avons, il est vrai, nations corrompues,
Aux peuples anciens des beautés inconnues:
Des visages rongés par les chancres du cœur,
Et comme qui dirait des beautés de langueur;
Mais ces inventions de nos muses tardives
N'empêcheront jamais les races maladives
De rendre à la jeunesse un hommage profond,
— À la sainte jeunesse, à l'air simple, au doux front,
À l'œil limpide et clair ainsi qu'une eau courante,
Et qui va répandant sur tout, insouciante
Comme l'azur du ciel, les oiseaux et les fleurs,
Ses parfums, ses chansons et ses douces chaleurs!

6 Les Phares

Rubens, fleuve d'oubli, jardin de la paresse,
Oreiller de chair fraîche où l'on ne peut aimer,
Mais où la vie afflue et s'agite sans cesse,
Comme l'air dans le ciel et la mer dans la mer;

Léonard de Vinci, miroir profond et sombre,
Où des anges charmants, avec un doux souris
Tout chargé de mystère, apparaissent à l'ombre
Des glaciers et des pins qui ferment leur pays;

Rembrandt, triste hôpital tout rempli de murmures,
Et d'un grand crucifix décoré seulement,
Où la prière en pleurs s'exhale des ordures,
Et d'un rayon d'hiver traversé brusquement;

Michel-Ange, lieu vague où l'on voit des Hercules
Se mêler à des Christs, et se lever tout droits
Des fantômes puissants qui dans les crépuscules
Déchirent leur suaire en étirant leurs doigts;

Colères de boxeur, impudences de faune,
Toi qui sus ramasser la beauté des goujats,
Grand cœur gonflé d'orgueil, homme débile et jaune,
Puget, mélancolique empereur des forçats;

Watteau, ce carnaval où bien des cœurs illustres,
Comme des papillons, errent en flamboyant,
Décors frais et légers éclairés par des lustres
Qui versent la folie à ce bal tournoyant;

Goya, cauchemar plein de choses inconnues,
De fœtus qu'on fait cuire au milieu des sabbats,
De vieilles au miroir et d'enfants toutes nues,
Pour tenter les démons ajustant bien leurs bas;

Delacroix, lac de sang hanté des mauvais anges,
Ombragé par un bois de sapins toujours vert,
Où, sous un ciel chagrin, des fanfares étranges
Passent, comme un soupir étouffé de Weber;

Ces malédictions, ces blasphèmes, ces plaintes,
Ces extases, ces cris, ces pleurs, ces Te Deum,
Sont un écho redit par mille labyrinthes;
C'est pour les cœurs mortels un divin opium!

C'est un cri répété par mille sentinelles,
Un ordre renvoyé par mille porte-voix;
C'est un phare allumé sur mille citadelles,
Un appel de chasseurs perdus dans les grands bois!

Car c'est vraiment, Seigneur, le meilleur témoignage
Que nous puissions donner de notre dignité
Que cet ardent sanglot qui roule d'âge en âge
Et vient mourir au bord de votre éternité!

7   La Muse malade

Ma pauvre muse, hélas! qu'as-tu donc ce matin?
Tes yeux creux sont peuplés de visions nocturnes,
Et je vois tour à tour réfléchis sur ton teint
La folie et l'horreur, froides et taciturnes.

Le succube verdâtre et le rose lutin
T'ont-ils versé la peur et l'amour de leurs urnes?
Le cauchemar, d'un poing despotique et mutin
T'a-t-il noyée au fond d'un fabuleux Minturnes?

Je voudrais qu'exhalant l'odeur de la santé
Ton sein de pensers forts fût toujours fréquenté,
Et que ton sang chrétien coulât à flots rythmiques,

Comme les sons nombreux des syllabes antiques,
Où règnent tour à tour le père des chansons,
Phoebus, et le grand Pan, le seigneur des moissons.

8   La Muse vénale

Ô muse de mon cœur, amante des palais,
Auras-tu, quand Janvier lâchera ses Borées,
Durant les noirs ennuis des neigeuses soirées,
Un tison pour chauffer tes deux pieds violets?

Ranimeras-tu donc tes épaules marbrées
Aux nocturnes rayons qui percent les volets?
Sentant ta bourse à sec autant que ton palais
Récolteras-tu l'or des voûtes azurées?

Il te faut, pour gagner ton pain de chaque soir,
Comme un enfant de chœur, jouer de l'encensoir,
Chanter des Te Deum auxquels tu ne crois guère,

Ou, saltimbanque à jeun, étaler tes appas
Et ton rire trempé de pleurs qu'on ne voit pas,
Pour faire épanouir la rate du vulgaire.

9   Le Mauvais Moine

Les cloîtres anciens sur leurs grandes murailles
Étalaient en tableaux la sainte Vérité,
Dont l'effet réchauffant les pieuses entrailles,
Tempérait la froideur de leur austérité.

En ces temps où du Christ florissaient les semailles,
Plus d'un illustre moine, aujourd'hui peu cité,

Prenant pour atelier le champ des funérailles,
Glorifiait la Mort avec simplicité.

— Mon âme est un tombeau que, mauvais cénobite,
Depuis l'éternité je parcours et j'habite;
Rien n'embellit les murs de ce cloître odieux.

Ô moine fainéant! quand saurai-je donc faire
Du spectacle vivant de ma triste misère
Le travail de mes mains et l'amour de mes yeux?

10   L'Ennemi

Ma jeunesse ne fut qu'un ténébreux orage,
Traversé çà et là par de brillants soleils;
Le tonnerre et la pluie ont fait un tel ravage,
Qu'il reste en mon jardin bien peu de fruits vermeils.

Voilà que j'ai touché l'automne des idées,
Et qu'il faut employer la pelle et les râteaux
Pour rassembler à neuf les terres inondées,
Où l'eau creuse des trous grands comme des tombeaux.

Et qui sait si les fleurs nouvelles que je rêve
Trouveront dans ce sol lavé comme une grève
Le mystique aliment qui ferait leur vigueur?

— Ô douleur! ô douleur! Le Temps mange la vie,
Et l'obscur Ennemi qui nous ronge le cœur
Du sang que nous perdons croît et se fortifie!

11   Le Guignon

Pour soulever un poids si lourd,
Sisyphe, il faudrait ton courage!
Bien qu'on ait du cœur à l'ouvrage,
L'Art est long et le Temps est court.

Loin des sépultures célèbres,
Vers un cimetière isolé,
Mon cœur, comme un tambour voilé,
Va battant des marches funèbres.

— Maint joyau dort enseveli
Dans les ténèbres et l'oubli,
Bien loin des pioches et des sondes;

Mainte fleur épanche à regret
Son parfum doux comme un secret
Dans les solitudes profondes.

12   La Vie antérieure

J'ai longtemps habité sous de vastes portiques
Que les soleils marins teignaient de mille feux,
Et que leurs grands piliers, droits et majestueux,
Rendaient pareils, le soir, aux grottes basaltiques.

Les houles, en roulant les images des cieux,
Mêlaient d'une façon solennelle et mystique
Les tout-puissants accords de leur riche musique
Aux couleurs du couchant reflété par mes yeux.

C'est là que j'ai vécu dans les voluptés calmes,
Au milieu de l'azur, des vagues, des splendeurs
Et des esclaves nus, tout imprégnés d'odeurs,

Qui me rafraîchissaient le front avec des palmes,
Et dont l'unique soin était d'approfondir
Le secret douloureux qui me faisait languir.

13   Bohémiens en voyage

La tribu prophétique aux prunelles ardentes
Hier s'est mise en route, emportant ses petits
Sur son dos, ou livrant à leurs fiers appétits
Le trésor toujours prêt des mamelles pendantes.

Les hommes vont à pied sous leurs armes luisantes
Le long des chariots où les leurs sont blottis,
Promenant sur le ciel des yeux appesantis
Par le morne regret des chimères absentes.

Du fond de son réduit sablonneux, le grillon,
Les regardant passer, redouble sa chanson;
Cybèle, qui les aime, augmente ses verdures,

Fait couler le rocher et fleurir le désert
Devant ces voyageurs, pour lesquels est ouvert
L'empire familier des ténèbres futures.

14   L'Homme et la Mer

Homme libre, toujours tu chériras la mer!
La mer est ton miroir; tu contemples ton âme
Dans le déroulement infini de sa lame,
Et ton esprit n'est pas un gouffre moins amer.

Tu te plais à plonger au sein de ton image;
Tu l'embrasses des yeux et des bras, et ton cœur

Se distrait quelquefois de sa propre rumeur
Au bruit de cette plainte indomptable et sauvage.

Vous êtes tous les deux ténébreux et discrets:
Homme, nul n'a sondé le fond de tes abîmes;
Ô mer, nul ne connaît tes richesses intimes,
Tant vous êtes jaloux de garder vos secrets!

Et cependant voilà des siècles innombrables
Que vous vous combattez sans pitié ni remords,
Tellement vous aimez le carnage et la mort,
Ô lutteurs éternels, ô frères implacables!

15   Don Juan aux enfers

Quand Don Juan descendit vers l'onde souterraine
Et lorsqu'il eut donné son obole à Charon,
Un sombre mendiant, l'œil fier comme Antisthène,
D'un bras vengeur et fort saisit chaque aviron.

Montrant leurs seins pendants et leurs robes ouvertes,
Des femmes se tordaient sous le noir firmament,
Et, comme un grand troupeau de victimes offertes,
Derrière lui traînaient un long mugissement.

Sganarelle en riant lui réclamait ses gages,
Tandis que Don Luis avec un doigt tremblant
Montrait à tous les morts errant sur les rivages
Le fils audacieux qui railla son front blanc.

Frissonnant sous son deuil, la chaste et maigre Elvire,
Près de l'époux perfide et qui fut son amant,
Semblait lui réclamer un suprême sourire
Où brillât la douceur de son premier serment.

Tout droit dans son armure, un grand homme de pierre
Se tenait à la barre et coupait le flot noir;
Mais le calme héros, courbé sur sa rapière,
Regardait le sillage et ne daignait rien voir.

16   Châtiment de l'orgueil

En ces temps merveilleux où la Théologie
Fleurit avec le plus de sève et d'énergie,
On raconte qu'un jour un docteur des plus grands,
— Après avoir forcé les cœurs indifférents;
Les avoir remués dans leurs profondeurs noires;
Après avoir franchi vers les célestes gloires
Des chemins singuliers à lui-même inconnus,
Où les purs Esprits seuls peut-être étaient venus, —
Comme un homme monté trop haut, pris de panique,
S'écria, transporté d'un orgueil satanique:
«Jésus, petit Jésus! je t'ai poussé bien haut!
Mais, si j'avais voulu t'attaquer au défaut
De l'armure, ta honte égalerait ta gloire,
Et tu ne serais plus qu'un fœtus dérisoire!»

Immédiatement sa raison s'en alla.
L'éclat de ce soleil d'un crêpe se voila
Tout le chaos roula dans cette intelligence,
Temple autrefois vivant, plein d'ordre et d'opulence,
Sous les plafonds duquel tant de pompe avait lui.
Le silence et la nuit s'installèrent en lui,
Comme dans un caveau dont la clef est perdue.
Dès lors il fut semblable aux bêtes de la rue,
Et, quand il s'en allait sans rien voir, à travers
Les champs, sans distinguer les étés des hivers,
Sale, inutile et laid comme une chose usée,
Il faisait des enfants la joie et la risée.

17   La Beauté

Je suis belle, ô mortels! comme un rêve de pierre,
Et mon sein, où chacun s'est meurtri tour à tour,
Est fait pour inspirer au poète un amour
Eternel et muet ainsi que la matière.

Je trône dans l'azur comme un sphinx incompris;
J'unis un cœur de neige à la blancheur des cygnes;
Je hais le mouvement qui déplace les lignes,
Et jamais je ne pleure et jamais je ne ris.

Les poètes, devant mes grandes attitudes,
Que j'ai l'air d'emprunter aux plus fiers monuments,
Consumeront leurs jours en d'austères études;

Car j'ai, pour fasciner ces dociles amants,
De purs miroirs qui font toutes choses plus belles:
Mes yeux, mes larges yeux aux clartés éternelles!

18   L'Idéal

Ce ne seront jamais ces beautés de vignettes,
Produits avariés, nés d'un siècle vaurien,
Ces pieds à brodequins, ces doigts à castagnettes,
Qui sauront satisfaire un cœur comme le mien.

Je laisse à Gavarni, poète des chloroses,
Son troupeau gazouillant de beautés d'hôpital,
Car je ne puis trouver parmi ces pâles roses
Une fleur qui ressemble à mon rouge idéal.

Ce qu'il faut à ce cœur profond comme un abîme,
C'est vous, Lady Macbeth, âme puissante au crime,
Rêve d'Eschyle éclos au climat des autans;

Ou bien toi, grande Nuit, fille de Michel-Ange,
Qui tors paisiblement dans une pose étrange
Tes appas façonnés aux bouches des Titans!

19   La Géante

Du temps que la Nature en sa verve puissante
Concevait chaque jour des enfants monstrueux,
J'eusse aimé vivre auprès d'une jeune géante,
Comme aux pieds d'une reine un chat voluptueux.

J'eusse aimé voir son corps fleurir avec son âme
Et grandir librement dans ses terribles jeux;
Deviner si son cœur couve une sombre flamme
Aux humides brouillards qui nagent dans ses yeux;

Parcourir à loisir ses magnifiques formes;
Ramper sur le versant de ses genoux énormes,
Et parfois en été, quand les soleils malsains,

Lasse, la font s'étendre à travers la campagne,
Dormir nonchalamment à l'ombre de ses seins,
Comme un hameau paisible au pied d'une montagne.

20   Le Masque

Statue allégorique dans le goût de la Renaissance
À Ernest Christophe, statuaire

Contemplons ce trésor de grâces florentines;
Dans l'ondulation de ce corps musculeux
L'Élégance et la Force abondent, sœurs divines.
Cette femme, morceau vraiment miraculeux,

Divinement robuste, adorablement mince,
Est faite pour trôner sur des lits somptueux
Et charmer les loisirs d'un pontife ou d'un prince.

— Aussi, vois ce souris fin et voluptueux
Où la Fatuité promène son extase;
Ce long regard sournois, langoureux et moqueur;
Ce visage mignard, tout encadré de gaze,
Dont chaque trait nous dit avec un air vainqueur:
«La Volupté m'appelle et l'Amour me couronne!»
À cet être doué de tant de majesté
Vois quel charme excitant la gentillesse donne!
Approchons, et tournons autour de sa beauté.

Ô blasphème de l'art! ô surprise fatale!
La femme au corps divin, promettant le bonheur,
Par le haut se termine en monstre bicéphale!

— Mais non! ce n'est qu'un masque, un décor suborneur,
Ce visage éclairé d'une exquise grimace,
Et, regarde, voici, crispée atrocement,
La véritable tête, et la sincère face
Renversée à l'abri de la face qui ment
Pauvre grande beauté! le magnifique fleuve
De tes pleurs aboutit dans mon cœur soucieux
Ton mensonge m'enivre, et mon âme s'abreuve
Aux flots que la Douleur fait jaillir de tes yeux!

— Mais pourquoi pleure-t-elle? Elle, beauté parfaite,
Qui mettrait à ses pieds le genre humain vaincu,
Quel mal mystérieux ronge son flanc d'athlète?

— Elle pleure insensé, parce qu'elle a vécu!
Et parce qu'elle vit! Mais ce qu'elle déplore
Surtout, ce qui la fait frémir jusqu'aux genoux,

C'est que demain, hélas! il faudra vivre encore!
Demain, après-demain et toujours! — comme nous!

21   Hymne à la beauté

Viens-tu du ciel profond ou sors-tu de l'abîme,
Ô Beauté? ton regard, infernal et divin,
Verse confusément le bienfait et le crime,
Et l'on peut pour cela te comparer au vin.

Tu contiens dans ton œil le couchant et l'aurore;
Tu répands des parfums comme un soir orageux;
Tes baisers sont un philtre et ta bouche une amphore
Qui font le héros lâche et l'enfant courageux.

Sors-tu du gouffre noir ou descends-tu des astres?
Le Destin charmé suit tes jupons comme un chien;
Tu sèmes au hasard la joie et les désastres,
Et tu gouvernes tout et ne réponds de rien.

Tu marches sur des morts, Beauté, dont tu te moques;
De tes bijoux l'Horreur n'est pas le moins charmant,
Et le Meurtre, parmi tes plus chères breloques,
Sur ton ventre orgueilleux danse amoureusement.

L'éphémère ébloui vole vers toi, chandelle,
Crépite, flambe et dit: Bénissons ce flambeau!
L'amoureux pantelant incliné sur sa belle
A l'air d'un moribond caressant son tombeau.

Que tu viennes du ciel ou de l'enfer, qu'importe,
Ô Beauté! monstre énorme, effrayant, ingénu!
Si ton œil, ton souris, ton pied, m'ouvrent la porte
D'un Infini que j'aime et n'ai jamais connu?

De Satan ou de Dieu, qu'importe? Ange ou Sirène,
Qu'importe, si tu rends, — fée aux yeux de velours,
Rythme, parfum, lueur, ô mon unique reine! —
L'univers moins hideux et les instants moins lourds?

21x   Les Bijoux

La très chère était nue, et, connaissant mon cœur,
Elle n'avait gardé que ses bijoux sonores,
Dont le riche attirail lui donnait l'air vainqueur
Qu'ont dans leurs jours heureux les esclaves des Mores.

Quand il jette en dansant son bruit vif et moqueur,
Ce monde rayonnant de métal et de pierre
Me ravit en extase, et j'aime à la fureur
Les choses où le son se mêle à la lumière.

Elle était donc couchée et se laissait aimer,
Et du haut du divan elle souriait d'aise
À mon amour profond et doux comme la mer,
Qui vers elle montait comme vers sa falaise.

Les yeux fixés sur moi, comme un tigre dompté,
D'un air vague et rêveur elle essayait des poses,
Et la candeur unie à la lubricité
Donnait un charme neuf à ses métamorphoses;

Et son bras et sa jambe, et sa cuisse et ses reins,
Polis comme de l'huile, onduleux comme un cygne,
Passaient devant mes yeux clairvoyants et sereins;
Et son ventre et ses seins, ces grappes de ma vigne,

S'avançaient, plus câlins que les Anges du mal,
Pour troubler le repos où mon âme était mise,

Et pour la déranger du rocher de cristal
Où, calme et solitaire, elle s'était assise.

Je croyais voir unis par un nouveau dessin
Les hanches de l'Antiope au buste d'un imberbe,
Tant sa taille faisait ressortir son bassin.
Sur ce teint fauve et brun, le fard était superbe!

— Et la lampe s'étant résignée à mourir,
Comme le foyer seul illuminait la chambre
Chaque fois qu'il poussait un flamboyant soupir,
Il inondait de sang cette peau couleur d'ambre!

22   Parfum exotique

Quand, les deux yeux fermés, en un soir chaud d'automne,
Je respire l'odeur de ton sein chaleureux,
Je vois se dérouler des rivages heureux
Qu'éblouissent les feux d'un soleil monotone;

Une île paresseuse où la nature donne
Des arbres singuliers et des fruits savoureux;
Des hommes dont le corps est mince et vigoureux,
Et des femmes dont l'œil par sa franchise étonne.

Guidé par ton odeur vers de charmants climats,
Je vois un port rempli de voiles et de mâts
Encor tout fatigués par la vague marine,

Pendant que le parfum des verts tamariniers,
Qui circule dans l'air et m'enfle la narine,
Se mêle dans mon âme au chant des mariniers.

23   La Chevelure

Ô toison, moutonnant jusque sur l'encolure!
Ô boucles! Ô parfum chargé de nonchaloir!
Extase! Pour peupler ce soir l'alcôve obscure
Des souvenirs dormant dans cette chevelure,
Je la veux agiter dans l'air comme un mouchoir!

La langoureuse Asie et la brûlante Afrique,
Tout un monde lointain, absent, presque défunt,
Vit dans tes profondeurs, forêt aromatique!
Comme d'autres esprits voguent sur la musique,
Le mien, ô mon amour! nage sur ton parfum.

J'irai là-bas où l'arbre et l'homme, pleins de sève,
Se pâment longuement sous l'ardeur des climats;
Fortes tresses, soyez la houle qui m'enlève!
Tu contiens, mer d'ébène, un éblouissant rêve
De voiles, de rameurs, de flammes et de mâts:

Un port retentissant où mon âme peut boire
À grands flots le parfum, le son et la couleur
Où les vaisseaux, glissant dans l'or et dans la moire
Ouvrent leurs vastes bras pour embrasser la gloire
D'un ciel pur où frémit l'éternelle chaleur.

Je plongerai ma tête amoureuse d'ivresse
Dans ce noir océan où l'autre est enfermé;
Et mon esprit subtil que le roulis caresse
Saura vous retrouver, ô féconde paresse,
Infinis bercements du loisir embaumé!

Cheveux bleus, pavillon de ténèbres tendues
Vous me rendez l'azur du ciel immense et rond;
Sur les bords duvetés de vos mèches tordues

Je m'enivre ardemment des senteurs confondues
De l'huile de coco, du musc et du goudron.

Longtemps! toujours! ma main dans ta crinière lourde
Sèmera le rubis, la perle et le saphir,
Afin qu'à mon désir tu ne sois jamais sourde!
N'es-tu pas l'oasis où je rêve, et la gourde
Où je hume à longs traits le vin du souvenir?

24   Je t'adore à l'égal …

Je t'adore à l'égal de la voûte nocturne,
Ô vase de tristesse, ô grande taciturne,
Et t'aime d'autant plus, belle, que tu me fuis,
Et que tu me parais, ornement de mes nuits,
Plus ironiquement accumuler les lieues
Qui séparent mes bras des immensités bleues.

Je m'avance à l'attaque, et je grimpe aux assauts,
Comme après un cadavre un chœur de vermisseaux,
Et je chéris, ô bête implacable et cruelle!
Jusqu'à cette froideur par où tu m'es plus belle!

25   Tu mettrais l'univers entier dans ta ruelle

Tu mettrais l'univers entier dans ta ruelle,
Femme impure! L'ennui rend ton âme cruelle.
Pour exercer tes dents à ce jeu singulier,
Il te faut chaque jour un cœur au râtelier.
Tes yeux, illuminés ainsi que des boutiques
Et des ifs flamboyants dans les fêtes publiques,
Usent insolemment d'un pouvoir emprunté,
Sans connaître jamais la loi de leur beauté.

Machine aveugle et sourde, en cruautés féconde!
Salutaire instrument, buveur du sang du monde,
Comment n'as-tu pas honte et comment n'as-tu pas
Devant tous les miroirs vu pâlir tes appas?
La grandeur de ce mal où tu te crois savante
Ne t'a donc jamais fait reculer d'épouvante,
Quand la nature, grande en ses desseins cachés
De toi se sert, ô femme, ô reine des péchés,
— De toi, vil animal, — pour pétrir un génie?

Ô fangeuse grandeur! sublime ignominie!

26 *Sed non satiata*

Bizarre déité, brune comme les nuits,
Au parfum mélangé de musc et de havane,
Œuvre de quelque obi, le Faust de la savane,
Sorcière au flanc d'ébène, enfant des noirs minuits,

Je préfère au constance, à l'opium, au nuits,
L'élixir de ta bouche où l'amour se pavane;
Quand vers toi mes désirs partent en caravane,
Tes yeux sont la citerne où boivent mes ennuis.

Par ces deux grands yeux noirs, soupiraux de ton âme,
Ô démon sans pitié! verse-moi moins de flamme;
Je ne suis pas le Styx pour t'embrasser neuf fois,

Hélas! et je ne puis, Mégère libertine,
Pour briser ton courage et te mettre aux abois,
Dans l'enfer de ton lit devenir Proserpine!

27   Avec ses vêtements ondoyants et nacrés...

Avec ses vêtements ondoyants et nacrés,
Même quand elle marche on croirait qu'elle danse,
Comme ces longs serpents que les jongleurs sacrés
Au bout de leurs bâtons agitent en cadence.

Comme le sable morne et l'azur des déserts,
Insensibles tous deux à l'humaine souffrance
Comme les longs réseaux de la houle des mers
Elle se développe avec indifférence.

Ses yeux polis sont faits de minéraux charmants,
Et dans cette nature étrange et symbolique
Où l'ange inviolé se mêle au sphinx antique,

Où tout n'est qu'or, acier, lumière et diamants,
Resplendit à jamais, comme un astre inutile,
La froide majesté de la femme stérile

28   Le Serpent qui danse

Que j'aime voir, chère indolente,
De ton corps si beau,
Comme une étoffe vacillante,
Miroiter la peau!

Sur ta chevelure profonde
Aux âcres parfums,
Mer odorante et vagabonde
Aux flots bleus et bruns,

Comme un navire qui s'éveille
Au vent du matin,

Mon âme rêveuse appareille
Pour un ciel lointain.

Tes yeux, où rien ne se révèle
De doux ni d'amer,
Sont deux bijoux froids où se mêle
L'or avec le fer.

À te voir marcher en cadence,
Belle d'abandon,
On dirait un serpent qui danse
Au bout d'un bâton.

Sous le fardeau de ta paresse
Ta tête d'enfant
Se balance avec la mollesse
D'un jeune éléphant,

Et ton corps se penche et s'allonge
Comme un fin vaisseau
Qui roule bord sur bord et plonge
Ses vergues dans l'eau.

Comme un flot grossi par la fonte
Des glaciers grondants,
Quand l'eau de ta bouche remonte
Au bord de tes dents,

Je crois boire un vin de Bohême,
Amer et vainqueur,
Un ciel liquide qui parsème
D'étoiles mon cœur!

29   Une Charogne

Rappelez-vous l'objet que nous vîmes, mon âme,
Ce beau matin d'été si doux:
Au détour d'un sentier une charogne infâme
Sur un lit semé de cailloux,

Les jambes en l'air, comme une femme lubrique,
Brûlante et suant les poisons,
Ouvrait d'une façon nonchalante et cynique
Son ventre plein d'exhalaisons.

Le soleil rayonnait sur cette pourriture,
Comme afin de la cuire à point,
Et de rendre au centuple à la grande Nature
Tout ce qu'ensemble elle avait joint;

Et le ciel regardait la carcasse superbe
Comme une fleur s'épanouir.
La puanteur était si forte, que sur l'herbe
Vous crûtes vous évanouir.

Les mouches bourdonnaient sur ce ventre putride,
D'où sortaient de noirs bataillons
De larves, qui coulaient comme un épais liquide
Le long de ces vivants haillons.

Tout cela descendait, montait comme une vague
Ou s'élançait en pétillant;
On eût dit que le corps, enflé d'un souffle vague,
Vivait en se multipliant.

Et ce monde rendait une étrange musique,
Comme l'eau courante et le vent,
Ou le grain qu'un vanneur d'un mouvement rythmique
Agite et tourne dans son van.

Les formes s'effaçaient et n'étaient plus qu'un rêve,
Une ébauche lente à venir
Sur la toile oubliée, et que l'artiste achève
Seulement par le souvenir.

Derrière les rochers une chienne inquiète
Nous regardait d'un œil fâché,
Épiant le moment de reprendre au squelette
Le morceau qu'elle avait lâché.

— Et pourtant vous serez semblable à cette ordure,
À cette horrible infection,
Étoile de mes yeux, soleil de ma nature,
Vous, mon ange et ma passion!

Oui! telle vous serez, ô la reine des grâces,
Après les derniers sacrements,
Quand vous irez, sous l'herbe et les floraisons grasses,
Moisir parmi les ossements.

Alors, ô ma beauté! dites à la vermine
Qui vous mangera de baisers,
Que j'ai gardé la forme et l'essence divine
De mes amours décomposés!

30 *De profundis clamavi*

J'implore ta pitié, Toi, l'unique que j'aime,
Du fond du gouffre obscur où mon cœur est tombé.
C'est un univers morne à l'horizon plombé,
Où nagent dans la nuit l'horreur et le blasphème;

Un soleil sans chaleur plane au-dessus six mois,
Et les six autres mois la nuit couvre la terre;

C'est un pays plus nu que la terre polaire
— Ni bêtes, ni ruisseaux, ni verdure, ni bois!

Or il n'est pas d'horreur au monde qui surpasse
La froide cruauté de ce soleil de glace
Et cette immense nuit semblable au vieux Chaos;

Je jalouse le sort des plus vils animaux
Qui peuvent se plonger dans un sommeil stupide,
Tant l'écheveau du temps lentement se dévide!

31   Le Vampire

Toi qui, comme un coup de couteau,
Dans mon cœur plaintif es entrée;
Toi qui, forte comme un troupeau
De démons, vins, folle et parée,

De mon esprit humilié
Faire ton lit et ton domaine;
— Infâme à qui je suis lié
Comme le forçat à la chaîne,

Comme au jeu le joueur têtu,
Comme à la bouteille l'ivrogne,
Comme aux vermines la charogne
— Maudite, maudite sois-tu!

J'ai prié le glaive rapide
De conquérir ma liberté,
Et j'ai dit au poison perfide
De secourir ma lâcheté.

Hélas! le poison et le glaive
M'ont pris en dédain et m'ont dit:
«Tu n'es pas digne qu'on t'enlève
À ton esclavage maudit,

Imbécile! — de son empire
Si nos efforts te délivraient,
Tes baisers ressusciteraient
Le cadavre de ton vampire!»

31x   Le Léthé

Viens sur mon cœur, âme cruelle et sourde,
Tigre adoré, monstre aux airs indolents;
Je veux longtemps plonger mes doigts tremblants
Dans l'épaisseur de ta crinière lourde;

Dans tes jupons remplis de ton parfum
Ensevelir ma tête endolorie,
Et respirer, comme une fleur flétrie,
Le doux relent de mon amour défunt.

Je veux dormir! dormir plutôt que vivre!
Dans un sommeil aussi doux que la mort,
J'étalerai mes baisers sans remords
Sur ton beau corps poli comme le cuivre.

Pour engloutir mes sanglots apaisés
Rien ne me vaut l'abîme de ta couche;
L'oubli puissant habite sur ta bouche,
Et le Léthé coule dans tes baisers.

À mon destin, désormais mon délice,
J'obéirai comme un prédestiné;

Martyr docile, innocent condamné,
Dont la ferveur attise le supplice,

Je sucerai, pour noyer ma rancœur,
Le népenthès et la bonne ciguë
Aux bouts charmants de cette gorge aiguë
Qui n'a jamais emprisonné de cœur.

32   Une nuit que j'étais près d'une affreuse Juive…

Une nuit que j'étais près d'une affreuse Juive,
Comme au long d'un cadavre un cadavre étendu,
Je me pris à songer près de ce corps vendu
À la triste beauté dont mon désir se prive.

Je me représentai sa majesté native,
Son regard de vigueur et de grâces armé,
Ses cheveux qui lui font un casque parfumé,
Et dont le souvenir pour l'amour me ravive.

Car j'eusse avec ferveur baisé ton noble corps,
Et depuis tes pieds frais jusqu'à tes noires tresses
Déroulé le trésor des profondes caresses,

Si, quelque soir, d'un pleur obtenu sans effort
Tu pouvais seulement, ô reine des cruelles!
Obscurcir la splendeur de tes froides prunelles.

33   Remords posthume

Lorsque tu dormiras, ma belle ténébreuse,
Au fond d'un monument construit en marbre noir,
Et lorsque tu n'auras pour alcôve et manoir
Qu'un caveau pluvieux et qu'une fosse creuse;

Quand la pierre, opprimant ta poitrine peureuse
Et tes flancs qu'assouplit un charmant nonchaloir,
Empêchera ton cœur de battre et de vouloir,
Et tes pieds de courir leur course aventureuse,

Le tombeau, confident de mon rêve infini
(Car le tombeau toujours comprendra le poète),
Durant ces grandes nuits d'où le somme est banni,

Te dira: «Que vous sert, courtisane imparfaite,
De n'avoir pas connu ce que pleurent les morts?»
— Et le ver rongera ta peau comme un remords.

34   Le Chat

Viens, mon beau chat, sur mon cœur amoureux;
Retiens les griffes de ta patte,
Et laisse-moi plonger dans tes beaux yeux,
Mêlés de métal et d'agate.

Lorsque mes doigts caressent à loisir
Ta tête et ton dos élastique,
Et que ma main s'enivre du plaisir
De palper ton corps électrique,

Je vois ma femme en esprit. Son regard,
Comme le tien, aimable bête
Profond et froid, coupe et fend comme un dard,

Et, des pieds jusques à la tête,
Un air subtil, un dangereux parfum
Nagent autour de son corps brun.

35   *Duellum*

Deux guerriers ont couru l'un sur l'autre, leurs armes
Ont éclaboussé l'air de lueurs et de sang.
Ces jeux, ces cliquetis du fer sont les vacarmes
D'une jeunesse en proie à l'amour vagissant.

Les glaives sont brisés! comme notre jeunesse,
Ma chère! Mais les dents, les ongles acérés,
Vengent bientôt l'épée et la dague traîtresse.
— Ô fureur des cœurs mûrs par l'amour ulcérés!

Dans le ravin hanté des chats-pards et des onces
Nos héros, s'étreignant méchamment, ont roulé,
Et leur peau fleurira l'aridité des ronces.

— Ce gouffre, c'est l'enfer, de nos amis peuplé!
Roulons-y sans remords, amazone inhumaine,
Afin d'éterniser l'ardeur de notre haine!

36   Le Balcon

Mère des souvenirs, maîtresse des maîtresses,
Ô toi, tous mes plaisirs! ô toi, tous mes devoirs!
Tu te rappelleras la beauté des caresses,
La douceur du foyer et le charme des soirs,
Mère des souvenirs, maîtresse des maîtresses!

Les soirs illuminés par l'ardeur du charbon,
Et les soirs au balcon, voilés de vapeurs roses.
Que ton sein m'était doux! que ton cœur m'était bon!
Nous avons dit souvent d'impérissables choses
Les soirs illuminés par l'ardeur du charbon.

Que les soleils sont beaux dans les chaudes soirées!
Que l'espace est profond! que le cœur est puissant!
En me penchant vers toi, reine des adorées,
Je croyais respirer le parfum de ton sang.
Que les soleils sont beaux dans les chaudes soirées!

La nuit s'épaississait ainsi qu'une cloison,
Et mes yeux dans le noir devinaient tes prunelles,
Et je buvais ton souffle, ô douceur! ô poison!
Et tes pieds s'endormaient dans mes mains fraternelles.
La nuit s'épaississait ainsi qu'une cloison.

Je sais l'art d'évoquer les minutes heureuses,
Et revis mon passé blotti dans tes genoux.
Car à quoi bon chercher tes beautés langoureuses
Ailleurs qu'en ton cher corps et qu'en ton cœur si doux?
Je sais l'art d'évoquer les minutes heureuses!

Ces serments, ces parfums, ces baisers infinis,
Renaîtront-ils d'un gouffre interdit à nos sondes,
Comme montent au ciel les soleils rajeunis
Après s'être lavés au fond des mers profondes?
— Ô serments! ô parfums! ô baisers infinis!

37 Le Possédé

Le soleil s'est couvert d'un crêpe. Comme lui,
Ô Lune de ma vie! emmitoufle-toi d'ombre
Dors ou fume à ton gré; sois muette, sois sombre,
Et plonge tout entière au gouffre de l'Ennui;

Je t'aime ainsi! Pourtant, si tu veux aujourd'hui,
Comme un astre éclipsé qui sort de la pénombre,
Te pavaner aux lieux que la Folie encombre
C'est bien! Charmant poignard, jaillis de ton étui!

Allume ta prunelle à la flamme des lustres!
Allume le désir dans les regards des rustres!
Tout de toi m'est plaisir, morbide ou pétulant;

Sois ce que tu voudras, nuit noire, rouge aurore;
Il n'est pas une fibre en tout mon corps tremblant
Qui ne crie: *Ô mon cher Belzébuth, je t'adore!*

38   Un Fantôme

I. Les Ténèbres

Dans les caveaux d'insondable tristesse
Où le Destin m'a déjà relégué;
Où jamais n'entre un rayon rose et gai;
Où, seul avec la Nuit, maussade hôtesse,

Je suis comme un peintre qu'un Dieu moqueur
Condamne à peindre, hélas! sur les ténèbres;
Où, cuisinier aux appétits funèbres,
Je fais bouillir et je mange mon cœur,

Par instants brille, et s'allonge, et s'étale
Un spectre fait de grâce et de splendeur.
À sa rêveuse allure orientale,
Quand il atteint sa totale grandeur,
Je reconnais ma belle visiteuse:

C'est Elle! noire et pourtant lumineuse.

II. Le Parfum

Lecteur, as-tu quelquefois respiré
Avec ivresse et lente gourmandise

Ce grain d'encens qui remplit une église,
Ou d'un sachet le musc invétéré?

Charme profond, magique, dont nous grise
Dans le présent le passé restauré!
Ainsi l'amant sur un corps adoré
Du souvenir cueille la fleur exquise.

De ses cheveux élastiques et lourds,
Vivant sachet, encensoir de l'alcôve,
Une senteur montait, sauvage et fauve,

Et des habits, mousseline ou velours,
Tout imprégnés de sa jeunesse pure,
Se dégageait un parfum de fourrure.

III. Le Cadre

Comme un beau cadre ajoute à la peinture,
Bien qu'elle soit d'un pinceau très-vanté,
Je ne sais quoi d'étrange et denchanté
En l'isolant de l'immense nature,

Ainsi bijoux, meubles, métaux, dorure,
S'adaptaient juste à sa rare beauté;
Rien n'offusquait sa parfaite clarté,
Et tout semblait lui servir de bordure.

Même on eût dit parfois qu'elle croyait
Que tout voulait l'aimer; elle noyait
Sa nudité voluptueusement

Dans les baisers du satin et du linge,
Et, lente ou brusque, à chaque mouvement
Montrait la grâce enfantine du singe.

IV. Le Portrait

La Maladie et la Mort font des cendres
De tout le feu qui pour nous flamboya.
De ces grands yeux si fervents et si tendres,
De cette bouche où mon cœur se noya,

De ces baisers puissants comme un dictame,
De ces transports plus vifs que des rayons,
Que reste-t-il? C'est affreux, ô mon âme!
Rien qu'un dessin fort pâle, aux trois crayons,

Qui, comme moi, meurt dans la solitude,
Et que le Temps, injurieux vieillard,
Chaque jour frotte avec son aile rude ...

Noir assassin de la Vie et de l'Art,
Tu ne tueras jamais dans ma mémoire
Celle qui fut mon plaisir et ma gloire!

39   Je te donne ces vers afin que si mon nom ...

Je te donne ces vers afin que si mon nom
Aborde heureusement aux époques lointaines,
Et fait rêver un soir les cervelles humaines,
Vaisseau favorisé par un grand aquilon,

Ta mémoire, pareille aux fables incertaines,
Fatigue le lecteur ainsi qu'un tympanon,
Et par un fraternel et mystique chaînon
Reste comme pendue à mes rimes hautaines;

Être maudit à qui, de l'abîme profond
Jusqu'au plus haut du ciel, rien, hors moi, ne répond!
— Ô toi qui, comme une ombre à la trace éphémère,

Foules d'un pied léger et d'un regard serein
Les stupides mortels qui t'ont jugée amère,
Statue aux yeux de jais, grand ange au front d'airain!

40 *Semper eadem*

«D'où vous vient, disiez-vous, cette tristesse étrange,
Montant comme la mer sur le roc noir et nu?»
— Quand notre cœur a fait une fois sa vendange
Vivre est un mal. C'est un secret de tous connu,

Une douleur très simple et non mystérieuse
Et, comme votre joie, éclatante pour tous.
Cessez donc de chercher, ô belle curieuse!
Et, bien que votre voix soit douce, taisez-vous!

Taisez-vous, ignorante! âme toujours ravie!
Bouche au rire enfantin! Plus encor que la Vie,
La Mort nous tient souvent par des liens subtils.

Laissez, laissez mon cœur s'enivrer d'un *mensonge*,
Plonger dans vos beaux yeux comme dans un beau songe
Et sommeiller longtemps à l'ombre de vos cils!

41 Tout entière

Le Démon, dans ma chambre haute
Ce matin est venu me voir,
Et, tâchant à me prendre en faute
Me dit: «Je voudrais bien savoir

Parmi toutes les belles choses
Dont est fait son enchantement,

Parmi les objets noirs ou roses
Qui composent son corps charmant,

Quel est le plus doux.» — Ô mon âme!
Tu répondis à l'Abhorré:
«Puisqu'en Elle tout est dictame
Rien ne peut être préféré.

Lorsque tout me ravit, j'ignore
Si quelque chose me séduit.
Elle éblouit comme l'Aurore
Et console comme la Nuit;

Et l'harmonie est trop exquise,
Qui gouverne tout son beau corps,
Pour que l'impuissante analyse
En note les nombreux accords.

Ô métamorphose mystique
De tous mes sens fondus en un!
Son haleine fait la musique,
Comme sa voix fait le parfum!»

42   Que diras-tu ce soir...

Que diras-tu ce soir, pauvre âme solitaire,
Que diras-tu, mon cœur, cœur autrefois flétri,
À la très belle, à la très bonne, à la très chère,
Dont le regard divin t'a soudain refleuri?

— Nous mettrons notre orgueil à chanter ses louanges:
Rien ne vaut la douceur de son autorité
Sa chair spirituelle a le parfum des Anges
Et son œil nous revêt d'un habit de clarté.

Que ce soit dans la nuit et dans la solitude
Que ce soit dans la rue et dans la multitude
Son fantôme dans l'air danse comme un flambeau.

Parfois il parle et dit: «Je suis belle, et j'ordonne
Que pour l'amour de moi vous n'aimiez que le Beau;
Je suis l'Ange gardien, la Muse et la Madone.»

43   Le Flambeau vivant

Ils marchent devant moi, ces Yeux pleins de lumières,
Qu'un Ange très savant a sans doute aimantés;
Ils marchent, ces divins frères qui sont mes frères,
Secouant dans mes yeux leurs feux diamantés.

Me sauvant de tout piège et de tout péché grave,
Ils conduisent mes pas dans la route du Beau;
Ils sont mes serviteurs et je suis leur esclave;
Tout mon être obéit à ce vivant flambeau.

Charmants Yeux, vous brillez de la clarté mystique
Qu'ont les cierges brûlant en plein jour; le soleil
Rougit, mais n'éteint pas leur flamme fantastique;

Ils célèbrent la Mort, vous chantez le Réveil;
Vous marchez en chantant le réveil de mon âme,
Astres dont nul soleil ne peut flétrir la flamme!

43x   À celle qui est trop gaie

Ta tête, ton geste, ton air
Sont beaux comme un beau paysage;
Le rire joue en ton visage
Comme un vent frais dans un ciel clair.

Le passant chagrin que tu frôles
Est ébloui par la santé
Qui jaillit comme une clarté
De tes bras et de tes épaules.

Les retentissantes couleurs
Dont tu parsèmes tes toilettes
Jettent dans l'esprit des poètes
L'image d'un ballet de fleurs.

Ces robes folles sont l'emblème
De ton esprit bariolé;
Folle dont je suis affolé,
Je te hais autant que je t'aime!

Quelquefois dans un beau jardin
Où je traînais mon atonie,
J'ai senti, comme une ironie,
Le soleil déchirer mon sein,

Et le printemps et la verdure
Ont tant humilié mon cœur,
Que j'ai puni sur une fleur
L'insolence de la Nature.

Ainsi je voudrais, une nuit,
Quand l'heure des voluptés sonne,
Vers les trésors de ta personne,
Comme un lâche, ramper sans bruit,

Pour châtier ta chair joyeuse,
Pour meurtrir ton sein pardonné,
Et faire à ton flanc étonné
Une blessure large et creuse,

Et, vertigineuse douceur!
À travers ces lèvres nouvelles,
Plus éclatantes et plus belles,
T'infuser mon venin, ma sœur!

44   Réversibilité

Ange plein de gaieté, connaissez-vous l'angoisse,
La honte, les remords, les sanglots, les ennuis,
Et les vagues terreurs de ces affreuses nuits
Qui compriment le cœur comme un papier qu'on froisse?
Ange plein de gaieté, connaissez-vous l'angoisse?

Ange plein de bonté, connaissez-vous la haine,
Les poings crispés dans l'ombre et les larmes de fiel,
Quand la Vengeance bat son infernal rappel,
Et de nos facultés se fait le capitaine?
Ange plein de bonté, connaissez-vous la haine?

Ange plein de santé, connaissez-vous les Fièvres,
Qui, le long des grands murs de l'hospice blafard,
Comme des exilés, s'en vont d'un pied traînard,
Cherchant le soleil rare et remuant les lèvres?
Ange plein de santé, connaissez-vous les Fièvres?

Ange plein de beauté, connaissez-vous les rides,
Et la peur de vieillir, et ce hideux tourment
De lire la secrète horreur du dévouement
Dans des yeux où longtemps burent nos yeux avide!
Ange plein de beauté, connaissez-vous les rides?

Ange plein de bonheur, de joie et de lumières,
David mourant aurait demandé la santé
Aux émanations de ton corps enchanté;

Mais de toi je n'implore, ange, que tes prières,
Ange plein de bonheur, de joie et de lumières!

45   Confession

Une fois, une seule, aimable et douce femme,
À mon bras votre bras poli
S'appuya (sur le fond ténébreux de mon âme
Ce souvenir n'est point pâli);

Il était tard; ainsi qu'une médaille neuve
La pleine lune s'étalait,
Et la solennité de la nuit, comme un fleuve,
Sur Paris dormant ruisselait.

Et le long des maisons, sous les portes cochères,
Des chats passaient furtivement
L'oreille au guet, ou bien, comme des ombres chères,
Nous accompagnaient lentement.

Tout à coup, au milieu de l'intimité libre
Éclose à la pâle clarté
De vous, riche et sonore instrument où ne vibre
Que la radieuse gaieté,

De vous, claire et joyeuse ainsi qu'une fanfare
Dans le matin étincelant
Une note plaintive, une note bizarre
S'échappa, tout en chancelant

Comme une enfant chétive, horrible, sombre, immonde,
Dont sa famille rougirait,
Et qu'elle aurait longtemps, pour la cacher au monde,
Dans un caveau mise au secret.

Pauvre ange, elle chantait, votre note criarde:
«Que rien ici-bas n'est certain,
Et que toujours, avec quelque soin qu'il se farde,
Se trahit l'égoïsme humain;

Que c'est un dur métier que d'être belle femme,
Et que c'est le travail banal
De la danseuse folle et froide qui se pâme
Dans son sourire machinal;

Que bâtir sur les cœurs est une chose sotte;
Que tout craque, amour et beauté,
Jusqu'à ce que l'Oubli les jette dans sa hotte
Pour les rendre à l'Eternité!»

J'ai souvent évoqué cette lune enchantée,
Ce silence et cette langueur,
Et cette confidence horrible chuchotée
Au confessionnal du cœur.

46   L'Aube spirituelle

Quand chez les débauchés l'aube blanche et vermeille
Entre en société de l'Idéal rongeur,
Par l'opération d'un mystère vengeur
Dans la brute assoupie un ange se réveille.

Des Cieux Spirituels l'inaccessible azur,
Pour l'homme terrassé qui rêve encore et souffre,
S'ouvre et s'enfonce avec l'attirance du gouffre.
Ainsi, chère Déesse, Être lucide et pur,

Sur les débris fumeux des stupides orgies
Ton souvenir plus clair, plus rose, plus charmant,
À mes yeux agrandis voltige incessamment.

Le soleil a noirci la flamme des bougies;
Ainsi, toujours vainqueur, ton fantôme est pareil,
Âme resplendissante, à l'immortel soleil!

47 Harmonie du soir

Voici venir les temps où vibrant sur sa tige
Chaque fleur s'évapore ainsi qu'un encensoir;
Les sons et les parfums tournent dans l'air du soir;
Valse mélancolique et langoureux vertige!

Chaque fleur s'évapore ainsi qu'un encensoir;
Le violon frémit comme un cœur qu'on afflige;
Valse mélancolique et langoureux vertige!
Le ciel est triste et beau comme un grand reposoir.

Le violon frémit comme un cœur qu'on afflige,
Un cœur tendre, qui hait le néant vaste et noir!
Le ciel est triste et beau comme un grand reposoir;
Le soleil s'est noyé dans son sang qui se fige.

Un cœur tendre, qui hait le néant vaste et noir,
Du passé lumineux recueille tout vestige!
Le soleil s'est noyé dans son sang qui se fige…
Ton souvenir en moi luit comme un ostensoir!

48 Le Flacon

Il est de forts parfums pour qui toute matière
Est poreuse. On dirait qu'ils pénètrent le verre.
En ouvrant un coffret venu de l'Orient
Dont la serrure grince et rechigne en criant,

Ou dans une maison déserte quelque armoire
Pleine de l'âcre odeur des temps, poudreuse et noire,
Parfois on trouve un vieux flacon qui se souvient,
D'où jaillit toute vive une âme qui revient.

Mille pensers dormaient, chrysalides funèbres,
Frémissant doucement dans les lourdes ténèbres,
Qui dégagent leur aile et prennent leur essor,
Teintés d'azur, glacés de rose, lamés d'or.

Voilà le souvenir enivrant qui voltige
Dans l'air troublé; les yeux se ferment; le Vertige
Saisit l'âme vaincue et la pousse à deux mains
Vers un gouffre obscurci de miasmes humains;

Il la terrasse au bord d'un gouffre séculaire,
Où, Lazare odorant déchirant son suaire,
Se meut dans son réveil le cadavre spectral
D'un vieil amour ranci, charmant et sépulcral.

Ainsi, quand je serai perdu dans la mémoire
Des hommes, dans le coin d'une sinistre armoire
Quand on m'aura jeté, vieux flacon désolé,
Décrépit, poudreux, sale, abject, visqueux, fêlé,

Je serai ton cercueil, aimable pestilence!
Le témoin de ta force et de ta virulence,
Cher poison préparé par les anges! liqueur
Qui me ronge, ô la vie et la mort de mon cœur!

49   Le Poison

Le vin sait revêtir le plus sordide bouge
D'un luxe miraculeux,
Et fait surgir plus d'un portique fabuleux
Dans l'or de sa vapeur rouge,
Comme un soleil couchant dans un ciel nébuleux.

L'opium agrandit ce qui n'a pas de bornes,
Allonge l'illimité,
Approfondit le temps, creuse la volupté,
Et de plaisirs noirs et mornes
Remplit l'âme au delà de sa capacité.

Tout cela ne vaut pas le poison qui découle
De tes yeux, de tes yeux verts,
Lacs où mon âme tremble et se voit à l'envers...
Mes songes viennent en foule
Pour se désaltérer à ces gouffres amers.

Tout cela ne vaut pas le terrible prodige
De ta salive qui mord,
Qui plonge dans l'oubli mon âme sans remords,
Et charriant le vertige,
La roule défaillante aux rives de la mort!

50   Ciel brouillé

On dirait ton regard d'une vapeur couvert;
Ton œil mystérieux (est-il bleu, gris ou vert?)
Alternativement tendre, rêveur, cruel,
Réfléchit l'indolence et la pâleur du ciel.

Tu rappelles ces jours blancs, tièdes et voilés,
Qui font se fondre en pleurs les cœurs ensorcelés,
Quand, agités d'un mal inconnu qui les tord,
Les nerfs trop éveillés raillent l'esprit qui dort.

Tu ressembles parfois à ces beaux horizons
Qu'allument les soleils des brumeuses saisons...
Comme tu resplendis, paysage mouillé
Qu'enflamment les rayons tombant d'un ciel brouillé!

Ô femme dangereuse, ô séduisants climats!
Adorerai-je aussi ta neige et vos frimas,
Et saurai-je tirer de l'implacable hiver
Des plaisirs plus aigus que la glace et le fer?

51   Le Chat

I.
Dans ma cervelle se promène,
Ainsi qu'en son appartement,
Un beau chat, fort, doux et charmant.
Quand il miaule, on l'entend à peine,

Tant son timbre est tendre et discret;
Mais que sa voix s'apaise ou gronde,
Elle est toujours riche et profonde.
C'est là son charme et son secret.

Cette voix, qui perle et qui filtre
Dans mon fonds le plus ténébreux,
Me remplit comme un vers nombreux
Et me réjouit comme un philtre.

Elle endort les plus cruels maux
Et contient toutes les extases;
Pour dire les plus longues phrases,
Elle n'a pas besoin de mots.

Non, il n'est pas d'archet qui morde
Sur mon cœur, parfait instrument,
Et fasse plus royalement
Chanter sa plus vibrante corde,

Que ta voix, chat mystérieux,
Chat séraphique, chat étrange,
En qui tout est, comme en un ange,
Aussi subtil qu'harmonieux!

II.

De sa fourrure blonde et brune
Sort un parfum si doux, qu'un soir
J'en fus embaumé, pour l'avoir
Caressée une fois, rien qu'une.

C'est l'esprit familier du lieu;
Il juge, il préside, il inspire
Toutes choses dans son empire;
Peut-être est-il fée, est-il dieu?

Quand mes yeux, vers ce chat que j'aime
Tirés comme par un aimant,
Se retournent docilement
Et que je regarde en moi-même,

Je vois avec étonnement
Le feu de ses prunelles pâles,
Clairs fanaux, vivantes opales
Qui me contemplent fixement.

52   Le Beau Navire

Je veux te raconter, ô molle enchanteresse!
Les diverses beautés qui parent ta jeunesse;
Je veux te peindre ta beauté,
Où l'enfance s'allie à la maturité.

Quand tu vas balayant l'air de ta jupe large,
Tu fais l'effet d'un beau vaisseau qui prend le large,
Chargé de toile, et va roulant
Suivant un rythme doux, et paresseux, et lent.

Sur ton cou large et rond, sur tes épaules grasses,
Ta tête se pavane avec d'étranges grâces;
D'un air placide et triomphant
Tu passes ton chemin, majestueuse enfant.

Je veux te raconter, ô molle enchanteresse!
Les diverses beautés qui parent ta jeunesse;
Je veux te peindre ta beauté,
Où l'enfance s'allie à la maturité.

Ta gorge qui s'avance et qui pousse la moire,
Ta gorge triomphante est une belle armoire
Dont les panneaux bombés et clairs
Comme les boucliers accrochent des éclairs;

Boucliers provoquants, armés de pointes roses!
Armoire à doux secrets, pleine de bonnes choses,
De vins, de parfums, de liqueurs
Qui feraient délirer les cerveaux et les cœurs!

Quand tu vas balayant l'air de ta jupe large
Tu fais l'effet d'un beau vaisseau qui prend le large,
Chargé de toile, et va roulant
Suivant un rythme doux, et paresseux, et lent.

Tes nobles jambes, sous les volants qu'elles chassent,
Tourmentent les désirs obscurs et les agacent,
Comme deux sorcières qui font
Tourner un philtre noir dans un vase profond.

Tes bras, qui se joueraient des précoces hercules,
Sont des boas luisants les solides émules,
Faits pour serrer obstinément,
Comme pour l'imprimer dans ton cœur, ton amant.

Sur ton cou large et rond, sur tes épaules grasses,
Ta tête se pavane avec d'étranges grâces;
D'un air placide et triomphant
Tu passes ton chemin, majestueuse enfant.

53   L'Invitation au voyage

Mon enfant, ma sœur,
Songe à la douceur
D'aller là-bas vivre ensemble!
Aimer à loisir,
Aimer et mourir
Au pays qui te ressemble!
Les soleils mouillés
De ces ciels brouillés
Pour mon esprit ont les charmes
Si mystérieux
De tes traîtres yeux,
Brillant à travers leurs larmes.

Là, tout n'est qu'ordre et beauté,
Luxe, calme et volupté.

Des meubles luisants,
Polis par les ans,
Décoreraient notre chambre;
Les plus rares fleurs
Mêlant leurs odeurs
Aux vagues senteurs de l'ambre,
Les riches plafonds,
Les miroirs profonds,
La splendeur orientale,
Tout y parlerait
À l'âme en secret
Sa douce langue natale.

Là, tout n'est qu'ordre et beauté,
Luxe, calme et volupté.

Vois sur ces canaux
Dormir ces vaisseaux
Dont l'humeur est vagabonde;
C'est pour assouvir
Ton moindre désir
Qu'ils viennent du bout du monde.
— Les soleils couchants
Revêtent les champs,
Les canaux, la ville entière,
D'hyacinthe et d'or;
Le monde s'endort
Dans une chaude lumière.

Là, tout n'est qu'ordre et beauté,
Luxe, calme et volupté.

54   L'Irréparable

Pouvons-nous étouffer le vieux, le long Remords,
Qui vit, s'agite et se tortille
Et se nourrit de nous comme le ver des morts,
Comme du chêne la chenille?
Pouvons-nous étouffer l'implacable Remords?

Dans quel philtre, dans quel vin, dans quelle tisane,
Noierons-nous ce vieil ennemi,
Destructeur et gourmand comme la courtisane,
Patient comme la fourmi?
Dans quel philtre? – dans quel vin? – dans quelle tisane?

Dis-le, belle sorcière, oh! dis, si tu le sais,
À cet esprit comblé d'angoisse
Et pareil au mourant qu'écrasent les blessés,
Que le sabot du cheval froisse,
Dis-le, belle sorcière, oh! dis, si tu le sais,

À cet agonisant que le loup déjà flaire
Et que surveille le corbeau,
À ce soldat brisé! s'il faut qu'il désespère
D'avoir sa croix et son tombeau;
Ce pauvre agonisant que déjà le loup flaire!

Peut-on illuminer un ciel bourbeux et noir?
Peut-on déchirer des ténèbres
Plus denses que la poix, sans matin et sans soir,
Sans astres, sans éclairs funèbres?
Peut-on illuminer un ciel bourbeux et noir?

L'Espérance qui brille aux carreaux de l'Auberge
Est soufflée, est morte à jamais!
Sans lune et sans rayons, trouver où l'on héberge

Les martyrs d'un chemin mauvais!
Le Diable a tout éteint aux carreaux de l'Auberge!

Adorable sorcière, aimes-tu les damnés?
Dis, connais-tu l'irrémissible?
Connais-tu le Remords, aux traits empoisonnés,
À qui notre cœur sert de cible?
Adorable sorcière, aimes-tu les damnés?

L'Irréparable ronge avec sa dent maudite
Notre âme, piteux monument,
Et souvent il attaque ainsi que le termite,
Par la base le bâtiment.
L'Irréparable ronge avec sa dent maudite!

— J'ai vu parfois, au fond d'un théâtre banal
Qu'enflammait l'orchestre sonore,
Une fée allumer dans un ciel infernal
Une miraculeuse aurore;
J'ai vu parfois au fond d'un théâtre banal

Un être, qui n'était que lumière, or et gaze,
Terrasser l'énorme Satan;
Mais mon cœur, que jamais ne visite l'extase,
Est un théâtre où l'on attend
Toujours, toujours en vain, l'Être aux ailes de gaze!

55   Causerie

Vous êtes un beau ciel d'automne, clair et rose!
Mais la tristesse en moi monte comme la mer,
Et laisse, en refluant, sur ma lèvre morose
Le souvenir cuisant de son limon amer.

— Ta main se glisse en vain sur mon sein qui se pâme;
Ce qu'elle cherche, amie, est un lieu saccagé
Par la griffe et la dent féroce de la femme.
Ne cherchez plus mon cœur; les bêtes l'ont mangé.

Mon cœur est un palais flétri par la cohue;
On s'y soûle, on s'y tue, on s'y prend aux cheveux!
— Un parfum nage autour de votre gorge nue!…

Ô Beauté, dur fléau des âmes, tu le veux!
Avec tes yeux de feu, brillants comme des fêtes,
Calcine ces lambeaux qu'ont épargnés les bêtes!

56   Chant d'automne

I.

Bientôt nous plongerons dans les froides ténèbres;
Adieu, vive clarté de nos étés trop courts!
J'entends déjà tomber avec des chocs funèbres
Le bois retentissant sur le pavé des cours.

Tout l'hiver va rentrer dans mon être: colère,
Haine, frissons, horreur, labeur dur et forcé,
Et, comme le soleil dans son enfer polaire,
Mon cœur ne sera plus qu'un bloc rouge et glacé.

J'écoute en frémissant chaque bûche qui tombe;
L'échafaud qu'on bâtit n'a pas d'écho plus sourd.
Mon esprit est pareil à la tour qui succombe
Sous les coups du bélier infatigable et lourd.

Il me semble, bercé par ce choc monotone,
Qu'on cloue en grande hâte un cercueil quelque part.
Pour qui? — C'était hier l'été; voici l'automne!
Ce bruit mystérieux sonne comme un départ.

II.

J'aime de vos longs yeux la lumière verdâtre,
Douce beauté, mais tout aujourd'hui m'est amer,
Et rien, ni votre amour, ni le boudoir, ni l'âtre,
Ne me vaut le soleil rayonnant sur la mer.

Et pourtant aimez-moi, tendre cœur! soyez mère,
Même pour un ingrat, même pour un méchant;
Amante ou sœur, soyez la douceur éphémère
D'un glorieux automne ou d'un soleil couchant.

Courte tâche! La tombe attend; elle est avide!
Ah! laissez-moi, mon front posé sur vos genoux,
Goûter, en regrettant l'été blanc et torride,
De l'arrière-saison le rayon jaune et doux!

57   À une madone

Ex-voto dans le goût espagnol

Je veux bâtir pour toi, Madone, ma maîtresse,
Un autel souterrain au fond de ma détresse,
Et creuser dans le coin le plus noir de mon cœur,
Loin du désir mondain et du regard moqueur,
Une niche, d'azur et d'or tout émaillée,
Où tu te dresseras, Statue émerveillée.
Avec mes Vers polis, treillis d'un pur métal
Savamment constellé de rimes de cristal,
Je ferai pour ta tête une énorme Couronne;
Et dans ma Jalousie, ô mortelle Madone
Je saurai te tailler un Manteau, de façon
Barbare, roide et lourd, et doublé de soupçon,
Qui, comme une guérite, enfermera tes charmes,
Non de Perles brodé, mais de toutes mes Larmes!

Ta Robe, ce sera mon Désir, frémissant,
Onduleux, mon Désir qui monte et qui descend,
Aux pointes se balance, aux vallons se repose,
Et revêt d'un baiser tout ton corps blanc et rose.

Je te ferai de mon Respect de beaux Souliers
De satin, par tes pieds divins humiliés,
Qui, les emprisonnant dans une molle étreinte
Comme un moule fidèle en garderont l'empreinte.

Si je ne puis, malgré tout mon art diligent
Pour Marchepied tailler une Lune d'argent
Je mettrai le Serpent qui me mord les entrailles
Sous tes talons, afin que tu foules et railles
Reine victorieuse et féconde en rachats
Ce monstre tout gonflé de haine et de crachats.

Tu verras mes Pensers, rangés comme les Cierges
Devant l'autel fleuri de la Reine des Vierges
Etoilant de reflets le plafond peint en bleu,
Te regarder toujours avec des yeux de feu;
Et comme tout en moi te chérit et t'admire,
Tout se fera Benjoin, Encens, Oliban, Myrrhe,
Et sans cesse vers toi, sommet blanc et neigeux,
En Vapeurs montera mon Esprit orageux.

Enfin, pour compléter ton rôle de Marie,
Et pour mêler l'amour avec la barbarie,
Volupté noire! des sept Péchés capitaux,
Bourreau plein de remords, je ferai sept Couteaux
Bien affilés, et comme un jongleur insensible,
Prenant le plus profond de ton amour pour cible,
Je les planterai tous dans ton Cœur pantelant,
Dans ton Cœur sanglotant, dans ton Cœur ruisselant!

58   Chanson d'après-midi

Quoique tes sourcils méchants
Te donnent un air étrange
Qui n'est pas celui d'un ange,
Sorcière aux yeux alléchants,

Je t'adore, ô ma frivole,
Ma terrible passion!
Avec la dévotion
Du prêtre pour son idole.

Le désert et la forêt
Embaument tes tresses rudes,
Ta tête a les attitudes
De l'énigme et du secret.

Sur ta chair le parfum rôde
Comme autour d'un encensoir;
Tu charmes comme le soir,
Nymphe ténébreuse et chaude.

Ah! les philtres les plus forts
Ne valent pas ta paresse,
Et tu connais la caresse
Qui fait revivre les morts!

Tes hanches sont amoureuses
De ton dos et de tes seins,
Et tu ravis les coussins
Par tes poses langoureuses.

Quelquefois, pour apaiser
Ta rage mystérieuse,
Tu prodigues, sérieuse,
La morsure et le baiser;

Tu me déchires, ma brune,
Avec un rire moqueur,
Et puis tu mets sur mon cœur
Ton œil doux comme la lune.

Sous tes souliers de satin,
Sous tes charmants pieds de soie,
Moi, je mets ma grande joie,
Mon génie et mon destin,

Mon âme par toi guérie,
Par toi, lumière et couleur!
Explosion de chaleur
Dans ma noire Sibérie!

59   Sisina

Imaginez Diane en galant équipage,
Parcourant les forêts ou battant les halliers,
Cheveux et gorge au vent, s'enivrant de tapage,
Superbe et défiant les meilleurs cavaliers!

Avez-vous vu Théroigne, amante du carnage,
Excitant à l'assaut un peuple sans souliers,
La joue et l'œil en feu, jouant son personnage,
Et montant, sabre au poing, les royaux escaliers?

Telle la Sisina! Mais la douce guerrière
À l'âme charitable autant que meurtrière;
Son courage, affolé de poudre et de tambours,

Devant les suppliants sait mettre bas les armes,
Et son cœur, ravagé par la flamme, a toujours,
Pour qui s'en montre digne, un réservoir de larmes.

60   *Franciscae meae laudes*

Novis te cantabo chordis,
O novelletum quod ludis
In solitudine cordis.

Esto sertis implicata,
O femina delicata
Per quam solvuntur peccata!

Sicut beneficum Lethe,
Hauriam oscula de te,
Quae imbuta es magnete.

Quum vitiorum tempegtas
Turbabat omnes semitas,
Apparuisti, Deitas,

Velut stella salutaris
In naufragiis amaris ...
Suspendam cor tuis aris!

Piscina plena virtutis,
Fons aeternae juventutis
Labris vocem redde mutis!

Quod erat spurcum, cremasti;
Quod rudius, exaequasti;
Quod debile, confirmasti.

In fame mea taberna
In nocte mea lucerna,
Recte me semper guberna.

Adde nunc vires viribus,
Dulce balneum suavibus
Unguentatum odoribus!

Meos circa lumbos mica,
O castitatis lorica,
Aqua tincta seraphica;

Patera gemmis corusca,
Panis salsus, mollis esca,
Divinum vinum, Francisca!

61   À une dame créole

Au pays parfumé que le soleil caresse,
J'ai connu, sous un dais d'arbres tout empourprés
Et de palmiers d'où pleut sur les yeux la paresse,
Une dame créole aux charmes ignorés.

Son teint est pâle et chaud; la brune enchanteresse
A dans le cou des airs noblement maniérés;
Grande et svelte en marchant comme une chasseresse,
Son sourire est tranquille et ses yeux assurés.

Si vous alliez, Madame, au vrai pays de gloire,
Sur les bords de la Seine ou de la verte Loire,
Belle digne d'orner les antiques manoirs,

Vous feriez, à l'abri des ombreuses retraites
Germer mille sonnets dans le cœur des poètes,
Que vos grands yeux rendraient plus soumis que vos noirs.

62   *Moesta et errabunda*

Dis-moi, ton cœur parfois s'envole-t-il, Agathe,
Loin du noir océan de l'immonde cité,
Vers un autre océan où la splendeur éclate,
Bleu, clair, profond, ainsi que la virginité?
Dis-moi, ton cœur parfois s'envole-t-il, Agathe?

La mer, la vaste mer, console nos labeurs!
Quel démon a doté la mer, rauque chanteuse
Qu'accompagne l'immense orgue des vents grondeurs,
De cette fonction sublime de berceuse?
La mer, la vaste mer, console nos labeurs!

Emporte-moi wagon! enlève-moi, frégate!
Loin! loin! ici la boue est faite de nos pleurs!
— Est-il vrai que parfois le triste cœur d'Agathe
Dise: Loin des remords, des crimes, des douleurs,
Emporte-moi, wagon, enlève-moi, frégate?

Comme vous êtes loin, paradis parfumé,
Où sous un clair azur tout n'est qu'amour et joie,
Où tout ce que l'on aime est digne d'être aimé,
Où dans la volupté pure le cœur se noie!
Comme vous êtes loin, paradis parfumé!

Mais le vert paradis des amours enfantines,
Les courses, les chansons, les baisers, les bouquets,
Les violons vibrant derrière les collines,
Avec les brocs de vin, le soir, dans les bosquets,
— Mais le vert paradis des amours enfantines,

L'innocent paradis, plein de plaisirs furtifs,
Est-il déjà plus loin que l'Inde et que la Chine?
Peut-on le rappeler avec des cris plaintifs,

Et l'animer encor d'une voix argentine,
L'innocent paradis plein de plaisirs furtifs?

63   Le Revenant

Comme les anges à l'œil fauve,
Je reviendrai dans ton alcôve
Et vers toi glisserai sans bruit
Avec les ombres de la nuit;

Et je te donnerai, ma brune,
Des baisers froids comme la lune
Et des caresses de serpent
Autour d'une fosse rampant.

Quand viendra le matin livide,
Tu trouveras ma place vide,
Où jusqu'au soir il fera froid.

Comme d'autres par la tendresse,
Sur ta vie et sur ta jeunesse,
Moi, je veux régner par l'effroi.

64   Sonnet d'automne

Ils me disent, tes yeux, clairs comme le cristal:
«Pour toi, bizarre amant, quel est donc mon mérite?»
— Sois charmante et tais-toi! Mon cœur, que tout irrite,
Excepté la candeur de l'antique animal,

Ne veut pas te montrer son secret infernal,
Berceuse dont la main aux longs sommeils m'invite,
Ni sa noire légende avec la flamme écrite.
Je hais la passion et l'esprit me fait mal!

Aimons-nous doucement. L'Amour dans sa guérite,
Ténébreux, embusqué, bande son arc fatal.
Je connais les engins de son vieil arsenal:

Crime, horreur et folie! — Ô pâle marguerite!
Comme moi n'es-tu pas un soleil automnal,
Ô ma si blanche, ô ma si froide Marguerite?

65 Tristesses de la lune

Ce soir, la lune rêve avec plus de paresse;
Ainsi qu'une beauté, sur de nombreux coussins,
Qui d'une main distraite et légère caresse
Avant de s'endormir le contour de ses seins,

Sur le dos satiné des molles avalanches,
Mourante, elle se livre aux longues pâmoisons,
Et promène ses yeux sur les visions blanches
Qui montent dans l'azur comme des floraisons.

Quand parfois sur ce globe, en sa langueur oisive,
Elle laisse filer une larme furtive,
Un poète pieux, ennemi du sommeil,

Dans le creux de sa main prend cette larme pâle,
Aux reflets irisés comme un fragment d'opale,
Et la met dans son cœur loin des yeux du soleil.

66   Les Chats

Les amoureux fervents et les savants austères
Aiment également, dans leur mûre saison,
Les chats puissants et doux, orgueil de la maison,
Qui comme eux sont frileux et comme eux sédentaires.

Amis de la science et de la volupté,
Ils cherchent le silence et l'horreur des ténèbres;
L'Erèbe les eût pris pour ses coursiers funèbres,
S'ils pouvaient au servage incliner leur fierté.

Ils prennent en songeant les nobles attitudes
Des grands sphinx allongés au fond des solitudes,
Qui semblent s'endormir dans un rêve sans fin;

Leurs reins féconds sont pleins d'étincelles magiques,
Et des parcelles d'or, ainsi qu'un sable fin,
Étoilent vaguement leurs prunelles mystiques.

67   Les Hiboux

Sous les ifs noirs qui les abritent
Les hiboux se tiennent rangés
Ainsi que des dieux étrangers
Dardant leur œil rouge. Ils méditent.

Sans remuer ils se tiendront
Jusqu'à l'heure mélancolique
Où, poussant le soleil oblique,
Les ténèbres s'établiront.

Leur attitude au sage enseigne
Qu'il faut en ce monde qu'il craigne
Le tumulte et le mouvement;

L'homme ivre d'une ombre qui passe
Porte toujours le châtiment
D'avoir voulu changer de place.

68   La Pipe

Je suis la pipe d'un auteur;
On voit, à contempler ma mine
D'Abyssinienne ou de Cafrine,
Que mon maître est un grand fumeur.

Quand il est comblé de douleur,
Je fume comme la chaumine
Où se prépare la cuisine
Pour le retour du laboureur.

J'enlace et je berce son âme
Dans le réseau mobile et bleu
Qui monte de ma bouche en feu,

Et je roule un puissant dictame
Qui charme son cœur et guérit
De ses fatigues son esprit.

69   La Musique

La musique souvent me prend comme une mer!
Vers ma pâle étoile,
Sous un plafond de brume ou dans un vaste éther,
Je mets à la voile;

La poitrine en avant et les poumons gonflés
Comme de la toile

J'escalade le dos des flots amoncelés
Que la nuit me voile;

Je sens vibrer en moi toutes les passions
D'un vaisseau qui souffre;
Le bon vent, la tempête et ses convulsions

Sur l'immense gouffre
Me bercent. D'autres fois, calme plat, grand miroir
De mon désespoir!

70   Sépulture

Si par une nuit lourde et sombre
Un bon chrétien, par charité,
Derrière quelque vieux décombre
Enterre votre corps vanté,

À l'heure où les chastes étoiles
Ferment leurs yeux appesantis,
L'araignée y fera ses toiles,
Et la vipère ses petits;

Vous entendrez toute l'année
Sur votre tête condamnée
Les cris lamentables des loups

Et des sorcières faméliques,
Les ébats des vieillards lubriques
Et les complots des noirs filous.

71   Une Gravure fantastique

Ce spectre singulier n'a pour toute toilette,
Grotesquement campé sur son front de squelette,
Qu'un diadème affreux sentant le carnaval.
Sans éperons, sans fouet, il essouffle un cheval,
Fantôme comme lui, rosse apocalyptique,
Qui bave des naseaux comme un épileptique.
Au travers de l'espace ils s'enfoncent tous deux,
Et foulent l'infini d'un sabot hasardeux.
Le cavalier promène un sabre qui flamboie
Sur les foules sans nom que sa monture broie,
Et parcourt, comme un prince inspectant sa maison,
Le cimetière immense et froid, sans horizon,
Où gisent, aux lueurs d'un soleil blanc et terne,
Les peuples de l'histoire ancienne et moderne.

72   Le Mort joyeux

Dans une terre grasse et pleine d'escargots
Je veux creuser moi-même une fosse profonde,
Où je puisse à loisir étaler mes vieux os
Et dormir dans l'oubli comme un requin dans l'onde.

Je hais les testaments et je hais les tombeaux;
Plutôt que d'implorer une larme du monde,
Vivant, j'aimerais mieux inviter les corbeaux
À saigner tous les bouts de ma carcasse immonde.

Ô vers! noirs compagnons sans oreille et sans yeux,
Voyez venir à vous un mort libre et joyeux;
Philosophes viveurs, fils de la pourriture,

À travers ma ruine allez donc sans remords,
Et dites-moi s'il est encor quelque torture
Pour ce vieux corps sans âme et mort parmi les morts!

73   Le Tonneau de la haine

La Haine est le tonneau des pâles Danaïdes;
La Vengeance éperdue aux bras rouges et forts
À beau précipiter dans ses ténèbres vides
De grands seaux pleins du sang et des larmes des morts,

Le Démon fait des trous secrets à ces abîmes,
Par où fuiraient mille ans de sueurs et d'efforts,
Quand même elle saurait ranimer ses victimes,
Et pour les pressurer ressusciter leurs corps.

La Haine est un ivrogne au fond d'une taverne,
Qui sent toujours la soif naître de la liqueur
Et se multiplier comme l'hydre de Lerne.

— Mais les buveurs heureux connaissent leur vainqueur,
Et la Haine est vouée à ce sort lamentable
De ne pouvoir jamais s'endormir sous la table.

74   La Cloche fêlée

Il est amer et doux, pendant les nuits d'hiver,
D'écouter, près du feu qui palpite et qui fume,
Les souvenirs lointains lentement s'élever
Au bruit des carillons qui chantent dans la brume.

Bienheureuse la cloche au gosier vigoureux
Qui, malgré sa vieillesse, alerte et bien portante,

Jette fidèlement son cri religieux,
Ainsi qu'un vieux soldat qui veille sous la tente!

Moi, mon âme est fêlée, et lorsqu'en ses ennuis
Elle veut de ses chants peupler l'air froid des nuits,
Il arrive souvent que sa voix affaiblie

Semble le râle épais d'un blessé qu'on oublie
Au bord d'un lac de sang, sous un grand tas de morts
Et qui meurt, sans bouger, dans d'immenses efforts.

75 Spleen (I)

Pluviôse, irrité contre la ville entière,
De son urne à grands flots verse un froid ténébreux
Aux pâles habitants du voisin cimetière
Et la mortalité sur les faubourgs brumeux.

Mon chat sur le carreau cherchant une litière
Agite sans repos son corps maigre et galeux;
L'âme d'un vieux poète erre dans la gouttière
Avec la triste voix d'un fantôme frileux.

Le bourdon se lamente, et la bûche enfumée
Accompagne en fausset la pendule enrhumée
Cependant qu'en un jeu plein de sales parfums,

Héritage fatal d'une vieille hydropique,
Le beau valet de cœur et la dame de pique
Causent sinistrement de leurs amours défunts.

76   Spleen (II)

J'ai plus de souvenirs que si j'avais mille ans.

Un gros meuble à tiroirs encombré de bilans,
De vers, de billets doux, de procès, de romances,
Avec de lourds cheveux roulés dans des quittances,
Cache moins de secrets que mon triste cerveau.
C'est une pyramide, un immense caveau,
Qui contient plus de morts que la fosse commune.
— Je suis un cimetière abhorré de la lune,
Où comme des remords se traînent de longs vers
Qui s'acharnent toujours sur mes morts les plus chers.
Je suis un vieux boudoir plein de roses fanées,
Où gît tout un fouillis de modes surannées,
Où les pastels plaintifs et les pâles Boucher
Seuls, respirent l'odeur d'un flacon débouché.

Rien n'égale en longueur les boiteuses journées,
Quand sous les lourds flocons des neigeuses années
L'ennui, fruit de la morne incuriosité,
Prend les proportions de l'immortalité.
— Désormais tu n'es plus, ô matière vivante!
Qu'un granit entouré d'une vague épouvante,
Assoupi dans le fond d'un Sahara brumeux;
Un vieux sphinx ignoré du monde insoucieux,
Oublié sur la carte, et dont l'humeur farouche
Ne chante qu'aux rayons du soleil qui se couche.

77   Spleen (III)

Je suis comme le roi d'un pays pluvieux,
Riche, mais impuissant, jeune et pourtant très vieux,
Qui, de ses précepteurs méprisant les courbettes,

S'ennuie avec ses chiens comme avec d'autres bêtes.
Rien ne peut l'égayer, ni gibier, ni faucon,
Ni son peuple mourant en face du balcon.
Du bouffon favori la grotesque ballade
Ne distrait plus le front de ce cruel malade;
Son lit fleurdelisé se transforme en tombeau,
Et les dames d'atour, pour qui tout prince est beau,
Ne savent plus trouver d'impudique toilette
Pour tirer un souris de ce jeune squelette.
Le savant qui lui fait de l'or n'a jamais pu
De son être extirper l'élément corrompu,
Et dans ces bains de sang qui des Romains nous viennent,
Et dont sur leurs vieux jours les puissants se souviennent,
Il n'a su réchauffer ce cadavre hébété
Où coule au lieu de sang l'eau verte du Léthé.

78   Spleen (IV)

Quand le ciel bas et lourd pèse comme un couvercle
Sur l'esprit gémissant en proie aux longs ennuis,
Et que de l'horizon embrassant tout le cercle
Il nous verse un jour noir plus triste que les nuits;

Quand la terre est changée en un cachot humide,
Où l'Espérance, comme une chauve-souris,
S'en va battant les murs de son aile timide
Et se cognant la tête à des plafonds pourris;

Quand la pluie étalant ses immenses traînées
D'une vaste prison imite les barreaux,
Et qu'un peuple muet d'infâmes araignées
Vient tendre ses filets au fond de nos cerveaux,

Des cloches tout à coup sautent avec furie
Et lancent vers le ciel un affreux hurlement,
Ainsi que des esprits errants et sans patrie
Qui se mettent à geindre opiniâtrement.

— Et de longs corbillards, sans tambours ni musique,
Défilent lentement dans mon âme; l'Espoir,
Vaincu, pleure, et l'Angoisse atroce, despotique,
Sur mon crâne incliné plante son drapeau noir.

79   Obsession

Grands bois, vous m'effrayez comme des cathédrales;
Vous hurlez comme l'orgue; et dans nos cœurs maudits,
Chambres d'éternel deuil où vibrent de vieux râles,
Répondent les échos de vos *De profundis.*

Je te hais, Océan! tes bonds et tes tumultes,
Mon esprit les retrouve en lui; ce rire amer
De l'homme vaincu, plein de sanglots et d'insultes,
Je l'entends dans le rire énorme de la mer

Comme tu me plairais, ô nuit! sans ces étoiles
Dont la lumière parle un langage connu!
Car je cherche le vide, et le noir, et le nu!

Mais les ténèbres sont elles-mêmes des toiles
Où vivent, jaillissant de mon œil par milliers,
Des êtres disparus aux regards familiers.

80   Le Goût du néant

Morne esprit, autrefois amoureux de la lutte,
L'Espoir, dont l'éperon attisait ton ardeur,
Ne veut plus t'enfourcher! Couche-toi sans pudeur,
Vieux cheval dont le pied à chaque obstacle butte.

Résigne-toi, mon cœur; dors ton sommeil de brute.

Esprit vaincu, fourbu! Pour toi, vieux maraudeur,
L'amour n'a plus de goût, non plus que la dispute;
Adieu donc, chants du cuivre et soupirs de la flûte!
Plaisirs, ne tentez plus un cœur sombre et boudeur!

Le Printemps adorable a perdu son odeur!

Et le Temps m'engloutit minute par minute,
Comme la neige immense un corps pris de roideur;
— Je contemple d'en haut le globe en sa rondeur
Et je n'y cherche plus l'abri d'une cahute.

Avalanche, veux-tu m'emporter dans ta chute?

81   Alchimie de la douleur

L'un t'éclaire avec son ardeur,
L'autre en toi met son deuil, Nature!
Ce qui dit à l'un: Sépulture!
Dit à l'autre: Vie et splendeur!

Hermès inconnu qui m'assistes
Et qui toujours m'intimidas,
Tu me rends l'égal de Midas,
Le plus triste des alchimistes;

Par toi je change l'or en fer
Et le paradis en enfer;
Dans le suaire des nuages

Je découvre un cadavre cher,
Et sur les célestes rivages
Je bâtis de grands sarcophages.

82   Horreur sympathique

De ce ciel bizarre et livide,
Tourmenté comme ton destin,
Quels pensers dans ton âme vide
Descendent? réponds, libertin.

— Insatiablement avide
De l'obscur et de l'incertain,
Je ne geindrai pas comme Ovide
Chassé du paradis latin.

Cieux déchirés comme des grèves
En vous se mire mon orgueil;
Vos vastes nuages en deuil

Sont les corbillards de mes rêves,
Et vos lueurs sont le reflet
De l'Enfer où mon cœur se plaît.

83   L'Héautontimorouménos

À J.G.F.

Je te frapperai sans colère
Et sans haine, comme un boucher,
Comme Moïse le rocher
Et je ferai de ta paupière,

Pour abreuver mon Saharah
Jaillir les eaux de la souffrance.
Mon désir gonflé d'espérance
Sur tes pleurs salés nagera

Comme un vaisseau qui prend le large,
Et dans mon cœur qu'ils soûleront
Tes chers sanglots retentiront
Comme un tambour qui bat la charge!

Ne suis-je pas un faux accord
Dans la divine symphonie,
Grâce à la vorace Ironie
Qui me secoue et qui me mord?

Elle est dans ma voix, la criarde!
C'est tout mon sang ce poison noir!
Je suis le sinistre miroir
Où la mégère se regarde.

Je suis la plaie et le couteau!
Je suis le soufflet et la joue!
Je suis les membres et la roue,
Et la victime et le bourreau!

Je suis de mon cœur le vampire,
— Un de ces grands abandonnés
Au rire éternel condamnés
Et qui ne peuvent plus sourire!

84   L'Irrémédiable

I.
Une Idée, une Forme, un Être
Parti de l'azur et tombé
Dans un Styx bourbeux et plombé
Où nul œil du Ciel ne pénètre;

Un Ange, imprudent voyageur
Qu'a tenté l'amour du difforme,
Au fond d'un cauchemar énorme
Se débattant comme un nageur,

Et luttant, angoisses funèbres!
Contre un gigantesque remous
Qui va chantant comme les fous
Et pirouettant dans les ténèbres;

Un malheureux ensorcelé
Dans ses tâtonnements futiles
Pour fuir d'un lieu plein de reptiles,
Cherchant la lumière et la clé;

Un damné descendant sans lampe
Au bord d'un gouffre dont l'odeur
Trahit l'humide profondeur
D'éternels escaliers sans rampe,

Où veillent des monstres visqueux
Dont les larges yeux de phosphore
Font une nuit plus noire encore
Et ne rendent visibles qu'eux;

Un navire pris dans le pôle
Comme en un piège de cristal,
Cherchant par quel détroit fatal
Il est tombé dans cette geôle;

— Emblèmes nets, tableau parfait
D'une fortune irrémédiable
Qui donne à penser que le Diable
Fait toujours bien tout ce qu'il fait!

II.
Tête-à-tête sombre et limpide
Qu'un cœur devenu son miroir!
Puits de Vérité, clair et noir
Où tremble une étoile livide,

Un phare ironique, infernal
Flambeau des grâces sataniques,
Soulagement et gloire uniques,
— La conscience dans le Mal!

85   L'Horloge

Horloge! dieu sinistre, effrayant, impassible,
Dont le doigt nous menace et nous dit: *«Souviens-toi!*
Les vibrantes Douleurs dans ton cœur plein d'effroi
Se planteront bientôt comme dans une cible;

Le Plaisir vaporeux fuira vers l'horizon
Ainsi qu'une sylphide au fond de la coulisse;
Chaque instant te dévore un morceau du délice
À chaque homme accordé pour toute sa saison.

Trois mille six cents fois par heure, la Seconde
Chuchote: *Souviens-toi!* — Rapide, avec sa voix
D'insecte, Maintenant dit: Je suis Autrefois,
Et j'ai pompé ta vie avec ma trompe immonde!

Remember! Souviens-toi! prodigue! *Esto memor!*
(Mon gosier de métal parle toutes les langues.)
Les minutes, mortel folâtre, sont des gangues
Qu'il ne faut pas lâcher sans en extraire l'or!

Souviens-toi que le Temps est un joueur avide
Qui gagne sans tricher, à tout coup! c'est la loi.
Le jour décroît; la nuit augmente; *souviens-toi!*
Le gouffre a toujours soif; la clepsydre se vide.

Tantôt sonnera l'heure où le divin Hasard,
Où l'auguste Vertu, ton épouse encor vierge,
Où le Repentir même (oh! la dernière auberge!),
Où tout te dira Meurs, vieux lâche! il est trop tard!»

TABLEAUX
PARISIENS

Je veux, pour composer chastement mes églogues,
Coucher auprès du ciel, comme les astrologues,
Et, voisin des clochers écouter en rêvant
Leurs hymnes solennels emportés par le vent.
Les deux mains au menton, du haut de ma mansarde,
Je verrai l'atelier qui chante et qui bavarde;
Les tuyaux, les clochers, ces mâts de la cité,
Et les grands ciels qui font rêver d'éternité.

Il est doux, à travers les brumes, de voir naître
L'étoile dans l'azur, la lampe à la fenêtre
Les fleuves de charbon monter au firmament
Et la lune verser son pâle enchantement.
Je verrai les printemps, les étés, les automnes;
Et quand viendra l'hiver aux neiges monotones,
Je fermerai partout portières et volets
Pour bâtir dans la nuit mes féeriques palais.
Alors je rêverai des horizons bleuâtres,
Des jardins, des jets d'eau pleurant dans les albâtres,
Des baisers, des oiseaux chantant soir et matin,
Et tout ce que l'Idylle a de plus enfantin.
L'Émeute, tempêtant vainement à ma vitre,
Ne fera pas lever mon front de mon pupitre;
Car je serai plongé dans cette volupté
D'évoquer le Printemps avec ma volonté,
De tirer un soleil de mon cœur, et de faire
De mes pensers brûlants une tiède atmosphère.

87   Le Soleil

Le long du vieux faubourg, où pendent aux masures
Les persiennes, abri des secrètes luxures,
Quand le soleil cruel frappe à traits redoublés
Sur la ville et les champs, sur les toits et les blés,
Je vais m'exercer seul à ma fantasque escrime,
Flairant dans tous les coins les hasards de la rime,
Trébuchant sur les mots comme sur les pavés
Heurtant parfois des vers depuis longtemps rêvés.

Ce père nourricier, ennemi des chloroses,
Éveille dans les champs les vers comme les roses;
Il fait s'évaporer les soucis vers le ciel,
Et remplit les cerveaux et les ruches de miel.
C'est lui qui rajeunit les porteurs de béquilles
Et les rend gais et doux comme des jeunes filles,
Et commande aux moissons de croître et de mûrir
Dans le cœur immortel qui toujours veut fleurir!

Quand, ainsi qu'un poète, il descend dans les villes,
Il ennoblit le sort des choses les plus viles,
Et s'introduit en roi, sans bruit et sans valets,
Dans tous les hôpitaux et dans tous les palais.

88   À une mendiante rousse

Blanche fille aux cheveux roux,
Dont la robe par ses trous
Laisse voir la pauvreté
Et la beauté,

Pour moi, poète chétif,
Ton jeune corps maladif,

Plein de taches de rousseur,
A sa douceur.

Tu portes plus galamment
Qu'une reine de roman
Ses cothurnes de velours
Tes sabots lourds.

Au lieu d'un haillon trop court,
Qu'un superbe habit de cour
Traîne à plis bruyants et longs
Sur tes talons;

En place de bas troués
Que pour les yeux des roués
Sur ta jambe un poignard d'or
Reluise encor;

Que des nœuds mal attachés
Dévoilent pour nos péchés
Tes deux beaux seins, radieux
Comme des yeux;

Que pour te déshabiller
Tes bras se fassent prier
Et chassent à coups mutins
Les doigts lutins,

Perles de la plus belle eau,
Sonnets de maître Belleau
Par tes galants mis aux fers
Sans cesse offerts,

Valetaille de rimeurs
Te dédiant leurs primeurs

Et contemplant ton soulier
Sous l'escalier,

Maint page épris du hasard,
Maint seigneur et maint Ronsard
Épieraient pour le déduit
Ton frais réduit!

Tu compterais dans tes lits
Plus de baisers que de lis
Et rangerais sous tes lois
Plus d'un Valois!

— Cependant tu vas gueusant
Quelque vieux débris gisant
Au seuil de quelque Véfour
De carrefour;

Tu vas lorgnant en dessous
Des bijoux de vingt-neuf sous
Dont je ne puis, oh! Pardon!
Te faire don.

Va donc, sans autre ornement,
Parfum, perles, diamant,
Que ta maigre nudité,
Ô ma beauté!

89 Le Cygne

À Victor Hugo

I.

Andromaque, je pense à vous! Ce petit fleuve,
Pauvre et triste miroir où jadis resplendit
L'immense majesté de vos douleurs de veuve,
Ce Simoïs menteur qui par vos pleurs grandit,

A fécondé soudain ma mémoire fertile,
Comme je traversais le nouveau Carrousel.
Le vieux Paris n'est plus (la forme d'une ville
Change plus vite, hélas! que le cœur d'un mortel);

Je ne vois qu'en esprit tout ce camp de baraques,
Ces tas de chapiteaux ébauchés et de fûts,
Les herbes, les gros blocs verdis par l'eau des flaques,
Et, brillant aux carreaux, le bric-à-brac confus.

Là s'étalait jadis une ménagerie;
Là je vis, un matin, à l'heure où sous les cieux
Froids et clairs le Travail s'éveille, où la voirie
Pousse un sombre ouragan dans l'air silencieux,

Un cygne qui s'était évadé de sa cage,
Et, de ses pieds palmés frottant le pavé sec,
Sur le sol raboteux traînait son blanc plumage.
Près d'un ruisseau sans eau la bête ouvrant le bec

Baignait nerveusement ses ailes dans la poudre,
Et disait, le cœur plein de son beau lac natal:
«Eau, quand donc pleuvras-tu? quand tonneras-tu, foudre?»
Je vois ce malheureux, mythe étrange et fatal,

Vers le ciel quelquefois, comme l'homme d'Ovide,
Vers le ciel ironique et cruellement bleu,
Sur son cou convulsif tendant sa tête avide
Comme s'il adressait des reproches à Dieu!

II.

Paris change! mais rien dans ma mélancolie
N'a bougé! palais neufs, échafaudages, blocs,
Vieux faubourgs, tout pour moi devient allégorie,
Et mes chers souvenirs sont plus lourds que des rocs.

Aussi devant ce Louvre une image m'opprime:
Je pense à mon grand cygne, avec ses gestes fous,
Comme les exilés, ridicule et sublime
Et rongé d'un désir sans trêve! et puis à vous,

Andromaque, des bras d'un grand époux tombée,
Vil bétail, sous la main du superbe Pyrrhus,
Auprès d'un tombeau vide en extase courbée
Veuve d'Hector, hélas! et femme d'Hélénus!

Je pense à la négresse, amaigrie et phtisique
Piétinant dans la boue, et cherchant, l'œil hagard,
Les cocotiers absents de la superbe Afrique
Derrière la muraille immense du brouillard;

À quiconque a perdu ce qui ne se retrouve
Jamais, jamais! à ceux qui s'abreuvent de pleurs
Et tètent la Douleur comme une bonne louve!
Aux maigres orphelins séchant comme des fleurs!

Ainsi dans la forêt où mon esprit s'exile
Un vieux Souvenir sonne à plein souffle du cor!
Je pense aux matelots oubliés dans une île,
Aux captifs, aux vaincus! . . . à bien d'autres encor!

90   Les Sept Vieillards

À Victor Hugo

Fourmillante cité, cité pleine de rêves,
Où le spectre en plein jour raccroche le passant!
Les mystères partout coulent comme des sèves
Dans les canaux étroits du colosse puissant.

Un matin, cependant que dans la triste rue
Les maisons, dont la brume allongeait la hauteur,
Simulaient les deux quais d'une rivière accrue,
Et que, décor semblable à l'âme de l'acteur,

Un brouillard sale et jaune inondait tout l'espace,
Je suivais, roidissant mes nerfs comme un héros
Et discutant avec mon âme déjà lasse,
Le faubourg secoué par les lourds tombereaux.

Tout à coup, un vieillard dont les guenilles jaunes
Imitaient la couleur de ce ciel pluvieux,
Et dont l'aspect aurait fait pleuvoir les aumônes,
Sans la méchanceté qui luisait dans ses yeux,

M'apparut. On eût dit sa prunelle trempée
Dans le fiel; son regard aiguisait les frimas,
Et sa barbe à longs poils, roide comme une épée,
Se projetait, pareille à celle de Judas.

Il n'était pas voûté, mais cassé, son échine
Faisant avec sa jambe un parfait angle droit,
Si bien que son bâton, parachevant sa mine,
Lui donnait la tournure et le pas maladroit

D'un quadrupède infirme ou d'un juif à trois pattes.
Dans la neige et la boue il allait s'empêtrant,
Comme s'il écrasait des morts sous ses savates,
Hostile à l'univers plutôt qu'indifférent.

Son pareil le suivait: barbe, œil, dos, bâton, loques,
Nul trait ne distinguait, du même enfer venu,
Ce jumeau centenaire, et ces spectres baroques
Marchaient du même pas vers un but inconnu.

À quel complot infâme étais-je donc en butte,
Ou quel méchant hasard ainsi m'humiliait?
Car je comptai sept fois, de minute en minute,
Ce sinistre vieillard qui se multipliait!

Que celui-là qui rit de mon inquiétude,
Et qui n'est pas saisi d'un frisson fraternel,
Songe bien que malgré tant de décrépitude
Ces sept monstres hideux avaient l'air éternel!

Aurais-je, sans mourir, contemplé le huitième,
Sosie inexorable, ironique et fatal
Dégoûtant Phénix, fils et père de lui-même?
— Mais je tournai le dos au cortège infernal.

Exaspéré comme un ivrogne qui voit double,
Je rentrai, je fermai ma porte, épouvanté,
Malade et morfondu, l'esprit fiévreux et trouble,
Blessé par le mystère et par l'absurdité!

Vainement ma raison voulait prendre la barre;
La tempête en jouant déroutait ses efforts,
Et mon âme dansait, dansait, vieille gabarre
Sans mâts, sur une mer monstrueuse et sans bords!

91   Les Petites Vieilles

À Victor Hugo

I.
Dans les plis sinueux des vieilles capitales,
Où tout, même l'horreur, tourne aux enchantements,
Je guette, obéissant à mes humeurs fatales,
Des êtres singuliers, décrépits et charmants.

Ces monstres disloqués furent jadis des femmes,
Éponine ou Laïs! Monstres brisés, bossus
Ou tordus, aimons-les! ce sont encor des âmes.
Sous des jupons troués et sous de froids tissus

Ils rampent, flagellés par les bises iniques,
Frémissant au fracas roulant des omnibus,
Et serrant sur leur flanc, ainsi que des reliques,
Un petit sac brodé de fleurs ou de rébus;

Ils trottent, tout pareils à des marionnettes;
Se traînent, comme font les animaux blessés,
Ou dansent, sans vouloir danser, pauvres sonnettes
Où se pend un Démon sans pitié! Tout cassés

Qu'ils sont, ils ont des yeux perçants comme une vrille,
Luisants comme ces trous où l'eau dort dans la nuit;
Ils ont les yeux divins de la petite fille
Qui s'étonne et qui rit à tout ce qui reluit.

— Avez-vous observé que maints cercueils de vieilles
Sont presque aussi petits que celui d'un enfant?
La Mort savante met dans ces bières pareilles
Un symbole d'un goût bizarre et captivant,

Et lorsque j'entrevois un fantôme débile
Traversant de Paris le fourmillant tableau,
Il me semble toujours que cet être fragile
S'en va tout doucement vers un nouveau berceau;

À moins que, méditant sur la géométrie,
Je ne cherche, à l'aspect de ces membres discords,
Combien de fois il faut que l'ouvrier varie
La forme de la boîte où l'on met tous ces corps.

— Ces yeux sont des puits faits d'un million de larmes,
Des creusets qu'un métal refroidi pailleta...
Ces yeux mystérieux ont d'invincibles charmes
Pour celui que l'austère Infortune allaita!

II.

De Frascati défunt Vestale enamourée;
Prêtresse de Thalie, hélas! dont le souffleur
Enterré sait le nom; célèbre évaporée
Que Tivoli jadis ombragea dans sa fleur,

Toutes m'enivrent; mais parmi ces êtres frêles
Il en est qui, faisant de la douleur un miel,
Ont dit au Dévouement qui leur prêtait ses ailes:
Hippogriffe puissant, mène-moi jusqu'au ciel!

L'une, par sa patrie au malheur exercée,
L'autre, que son époux surchargea de douleurs,
L'autre, par son enfant Madone transpercée,
Toutes auraient pu faire un fleuve avec leurs pleurs!

III.

Ah! que j'en ai suivi de ces petites vieilles!
Une, entre autres, à l'heure où le soleil tombant
Ensanglante le ciel de blessures vermeilles,
Pensive, s'asseyait à l'écart sur un banc,

Pour entendre un de ces concerts, riches de cuivre,
Dont les soldats parfois inondent nos jardins,
Et qui, dans ces soirs d'or où l'on se sent revivre,
Versent quelque héroïsme au cœur des citadins.

Celle-là, droite encor, fière et sentant la règle,
Humait avidement ce chant vif et guerrier;
Son œil parfois s'ouvrait comme l'œil d'un vieil aigle;
Son front de marbre avait l'air fait pour le laurier!

IV.

Telles vous cheminez, stoïques et sans plaintes,
À travers le chaos des vivantes cités,
Mères au cœur saignant, courtisanes ou saintes,
Dont autrefois les noms par tous étaient cités.

Vous qui fûtes la grâce ou qui fûtes la gloires,
Nul ne vous reconnaît! un ivrogne incivil
Vous insulte en passant d'un amour dérisoire;
Sur vos talons gambade un enfant lâche et vil.

Honteuses d'exister, ombres ratatinées,
Peureuses, le dos bas, vous côtoyez les murs;
Et nul ne vous salue, étranges destinées!
Débris d'humanité pour l'éternité mûrs!

Mais moi, moi qui de loin tendrement vous surveille,
L'œil inquiet, fixé sur vos pas incertains,
Tout comme si j'étais votre père, ô merveille!
Je goûte à votre insu des plaisirs clandestins:

Je vois s'épanouir vos passions novices;
Sombres ou lumineux, je vis vos jours perdus;
Mon cœur multiplié jouit de tous vos vices!
Mon âme resplendit de toutes vos vertus!

Ruines! ma famille! ô cerveaux congénères!
Je vous fais chaque soir un solennel adieu!
Où serez-vous demain, Èves octogénaires,
Sur qui pèse la griffe effroyable de Dieu?

92   Les Aveugles

Contemple-les, mon âme; ils sont vraiment affreux!
Pareils aux mannequins; vaguement ridicules;
Terribles, singuliers comme les somnambules;
Dardant on ne sait où leurs globes ténébreux.

Leurs yeux, d'où la divine étincelle est partie,
Comme s'ils regardaient au loin, restent levés
Au ciel; on ne les voit jamais vers les pavés
Pencher rêveusement leur tête appesantie.

Ils traversent ainsi le noir illimité,
Ce frère du silence éternel. Ô cité!
Pendant qu'autour de nous tu chantes, ris et beugles,

Éprise du plaisir jusqu'à l'atrocité,
Vois! je me traîne aussi! mais, plus qu'eux hébété,
Je dis: Que cherchent-ils au Ciel, tous ces aveugles?

93   À une passante

La rue assourdissante autour de moi hurlait.
Longue, mince, en grand deuil, douleur majestueuse,
Une femme passa, d'une main fastueuse
Soulevant, balançant le feston et l'ourlet;

Agile et noble, avec sa jambe de statue.
Moi, je buvais, crispé comme un extravagant,
Dans son œil, ciel livide où germe l'ouragan,
La douceur qui fascine et le plaisir qui tue.

Un éclair... puis la nuit! — Fugitive beauté
Dont le regard m'a fait soudainement renaître,
Ne te verrai-je plus que dans l'éternité?

Ailleurs, bien loin d'ici! trop tard! *jamais* peut-être!
Car j'ignore où tu fuis, tu ne sais où je vais,
Ô toi que j'eusse aimée, ô toi qui le savais!

94   Le Squelette laboureur

I.

Dans les planches d'anatomie
Qui traînent sur ces quais poudreux
Où maint livre cadavéreux
Dort comme une antique momie,

Dessins auxquels la gravité
Et le savoir d'un vieil artiste,
Bien que le sujet en soit triste,
Ont communiqué la Beauté,

On voit, ce qui rend plus complètes
Ces mystérieuses horreurs,
Bêchant comme des laboureurs,
Des Écorchés et des Squelettes.

II.

De ce terrain que vous fouillez,
Manants résignés et funèbres

De tout l'effort de vos vertèbres,
Ou de vos muscles dépouillés,

Dites, quelle moisson étrange,
Forçats arrachés au charnier,
Tirez-vous, et de quel fermier
Avez-vous à remplir la grange?

Voulez-vous (d'un destin trop dur
Épouvantable et clair emblème!)
Montrer que dans la fosse même
Le sommeil promis n'est pas sûr;

Qu'envers nous le Néant est traître;
Que tout, même la Mort, nous ment,
Et que sempiternellement
Hélas! il nous faudra peut-être

Dans quelque pays inconnu
Écorcher la terre revêche
Et pousser une lourde bêche
Sous notre pied sanglant et nu?

95   Le Crépuscule du soir

Voici le soir charmant, ami du criminel;
Il vient comme un complice, à pas de loup; le ciel
Se ferme lentement comme une grande alcôve,
Et l'homme impatient se change en bête fauve.

Ô soir, aimable soir, désiré par celui
Dont les bras, sans mentir, peuvent dire: Aujourd'hui
Nous avons travaillé! — C'est le soir qui soulage
Les esprits que dévore une douleur sauvage,

Le savant obstiné dont le front s'alourdit,
Et l'ouvrier courbé qui regagne son lit.

Cependant des démons malsains dans l'atmosphère
S'éveillent lourdement, comme des gens d'affaire,
Et cognent en volant les volets et l'auvent.
À travers les lueurs que tourmente le vent
La Prostitution s'allume dans les rues;
Comme une fourmilière elle ouvre ses issues;
Partout elle se fraye un occulte chemin,
Ainsi que l'ennemi qui tente un coup de main;
Elle remue au sein de la cité de fange
Comme un ver qui dérobe à l'Homme ce qu'il mange.
On entend çà et là les cuisines siffler,
Les théâtres glapir, les orchestres ronfler;
Les tables d'hôte, dont le jeu fait les délices,
S'emplissent de catins et d'escrocs, leurs complices,
Et les voleurs, qui n'ont ni trêve ni merci,
Vont bientôt commencer leur travail, eux aussi,
Et forcer doucement les portes et les caisses
Pour vivre quelques jours et vêtir leurs maîtresses.

Recueille-toi, mon âme, en ce grave moment,
Et ferme ton oreille à ce rugissement.
C'est l'heure où les douleurs des malades s'aigrissent!
La sombre Nuit les prend à la gorge; ils finissent
Leur destinée et vont vers le gouffre commun;
L'hôpital se remplit de leurs soupirs. — Plus d'un
Ne viendra plus chercher la soupe parfumée,
Au coin du feu, le soir, auprès d'une âme aimée.

Encore la plupart n'ont-ils jamais connu
La douceur du foyer et n'ont jamais vécu!

96   Le Jeu

Dans des fauteuils fanés des courtisanes vieilles,
Pâles, le sourcil peint, l'œil câlin et fatal,
Minaudant, et faisant de leurs maigres oreilles
Tomber un cliquetis de pierre et de métal;

Autour des verts tapis des visages sans lèvre,
Des lèvres sans couleur, des mâchoires sans dent,
Et des doigts convulsés d'une infernale fièvre,
Fouillant la poche vide ou le sein palpitant;

Sous de sales plafonds un rang de pâles lustres
Et d'énormes quinquets projetant leurs lueurs
Sur des fronts ténébreux de poètes illustres
Qui viennent gaspiller leurs sanglantes sueurs;

Voilà le noir tableau qu'en un rêve nocturne
Je vis se dérouler sous mon œil clairvoyant.
Moi-même, dans un coin de l'antre taciturne,
Je me vis accoudé, froid, muet, enviant,

Enviant de ces gens la passion tenace,
De ces vieilles putains la funèbre gaieté,
Et tous gaillardement trafiquant à ma face,
L'un de son vieil honneur, l'autre de sa beauté!

Et mon cœur s'effraya d'envier maint pauvre homme
Courant avec ferveur à l'abîme béant,
Et qui, soûl de son sang, préférerait en somme
La douleur à la mort et l'enfer au néant!

97   Danse macabre

À Ernest Christophe

Fière, autant qu'un vivant, de sa noble stature
Avec son gros bouquet, son mouchoir et ses gants
Elle a la nonchalance et la désinvolture
D'une coquette maigre aux airs extravagants.

Vit-on jamais au bal une taille plus mince?
Sa robe exagérée, en sa royale ampleur,
S'écroule abondamment sur un pied sec que pince
Un soulier pomponné, joli comme une fleur.

La ruche qui se joue au bord des clavicules,
Comme un ruisseau lascif qui se frotte au rocher,
Défend pudiquement des lazzi ridicules
Les funèbres appas qu'elle tient à cacher.

Ses yeux profonds sont faits de vide et de ténèbres,
Et son crâne, de fleurs artistement coiffé,
Oscille mollement sur ses frêles vertèbres.
Ô charme d'un néant follement attifé.

Aucuns t'appelleront une caricature,
Qui ne comprennent pas, amants ivres de chair,
L'élégance sans nom de l'humaine armature.
Tu réponds, grand squelette, à mon goût le plus cher!

Viens-tu troubler, avec ta puissante grimace,
La fête de la Vie? ou quelque vieux désir,
Éperonnant encor ta vivante carcasse,
Te pousse-t-il, crédule, au sabbat du Plaisir?

Au chant des violons, aux flammes des bougies,
Espères-tu chasser ton cauchemar moqueur,
Et viens-tu demander au torrent des orgies
De rafraîchir l'enfer allumé dans ton cœur?

Inépuisable puits de sottise et de fautes!
De l'antique douleur éternel alambic!
À travers le treillis recourbé de tes côtes
Je vois, errant encor, l'insatiable aspic.

Pour dire vrai, je crains que ta coquetterie
Ne trouve pas un prix digne de ses efforts
Qui, de ces cœurs mortels, entend la raillerie?
Les charmes de l'horreur n'enivrent que les forts!

Le gouffre de tes yeux, plein d'horribles pensées,
Exhale le vertige, et les danseurs prudents
Ne contempleront pas sans d'amères nausées
Le sourire éternel de tes trente-deux dents.

Pourtant, qui n'a serré dans ses bras un squelette,
Et qui ne s'est nourri des choses du tombeau?
Qu'importe le parfum, l'habit ou la toilette?
Qui fait le dégoûté montre qu'il se croit beau.

Bayadère sans nez, irrésistible gouge,
Dis donc à ces danseurs qui font les offusqués:
«Fiers mignons, malgré l'art des poudres et du rouge
Vous sentez tous la mort! Ô squelettes musqués,

Antinoüs flétris, dandys à face glabre,
Cadavres vernissés, lovelaces chenus,
Le branle universel de la danse macabre
Vous entraîne en des lieux qui ne sont pas connus!

Des quais froids de la Seine aux bords brûlants du Gange,
Le troupeau mortel saute et se pâme, sans voir
Dans un trou du plafond la trompette de l'Ange
Sinistrement béante ainsi qu'un tromblon noir.

En tout climat, sous tout soleil, la Mort t'admire
En tes contorsions, risible Humanité
Et souvent, comme toi, se parfumant de myrrhe,
Mêle son ironie à ton insanité!»

98 L'Amour du mensonge

Quand je te vois passer, ô ma chère indolente,
Au chant des instruments qui se brise au plafond
Suspendant ton allure harmonieuse et lente,
Et promenant l'ennui de ton regard profond;

Quand je contemple, aux feux du gaz qui le colore,
Ton front pâle, embelli par un morbide attrait,
Où les torches du soir allument une aurore,
Et tes yeux attirants comme ceux d'un portrait,

Je me dis: Qu'elle est belle! et bizarrement fraîche!
Le souvenir massif, royale et lourde tour,
La couronne, et son cœur, meurtri comme une pêche,
Est mûr, comme son corps, pour le savant amour.

Es-tu le fruit d'automne aux saveurs souveraines?
Es-tu vase funèbre attendant quelques pleurs,
Parfum qui fait rêver aux oasis lointaines,
Oreiller caressant, ou corbeille de fleurs?

Je sais qu'il est des yeux, des plus mélancoliques,
Qui ne recèlent point de secrets précieux;

Beaux écrins sans joyaux, médaillons sans reliques,
Plus vides, plus profonds que vous-mêmes, ô Cieux!

Mais ne suffit-il pas que tu sois l'apparence,
Pour réjouir un cœur qui fuit la vérité?
Qu'importe ta bêtise ou ton indifférence?
Masque ou décor, salut! J'adore ta beauté.

99   Je n'ai pas oublié, voisine de la ville...

Je n'ai pas oublié, voisine de la ville,
Notre blanche maison, petite mais tranquille;
Sa Pomone de plâtre et sa vieille Vénus
Dans un bosquet chétif cachant leurs membres nus,
Et le soleil, le soir, ruisselant et superbe,
Qui, derrière la vitre où se brisait sa gerbe
Semblait, grand œil ouvert dans le ciel curieux,
Contempler nos dîners longs et silencieux,
Répandant largement ses beaux reflets de cierge
Sur la nappe frugale et les rideaux de serge.

100   La servante au grand cœur dont vous étiez jalouse...

La servante au grand cœur dont vous étiez jalouse,
Et qui dort son sommeil sous une humble pelouse,
Nous devrions pourtant lui porter quelques fleurs.
Les morts, les pauvres morts, ont de grandes douleurs,
Et quand Octobre souffle, émondeur des vieux arbres,
Son vent mélancolique à l'entour de leurs marbres,
Certe, ils doivent trouver les vivants bien ingrats,
À dormir, comme ils font, chaudement dans leurs draps,
Tandis que, dévorés de noires songeries,
Sans compagnon de lit, sans bonnes causeries,

Vieux squelettes gelés travaillés par le ver,
Ils sentent s'égoutter les neiges de l'hiver
Et le siècle couler, sans qu'amis ni famille
Remplacent les lambeaux qui pendent à leur grille.

Lorsque la bûche siffle et chante, si le soir
Calme, dans le fauteuil je la voyais s'asseoir,
Si, par une nuit bleue et froide de décembre,
Je la trouvais tapie en un coin de ma chambre,
Grave, et venant du fond de son lit éternel
Couver l'enfant grandi de son œil maternel,
Que pourrais-je répondre à cette âme pieuse,
Voyant tomber des pleurs de sa paupière creuse?

101   Brumes et Pluies

Ô fins d'automne, hivers, printemps trempés de boue,
Endormeuses saisons! je vous aime et vous loue
D'envelopper ainsi mon cœur et mon cerveau
D'un linceul vaporeux et d'un vague tombeau.

Dans cette grande plaine où l'autan froid se joue,
Où par les longues nuits la girouette s'enroue,
Mon âme mieux qu'au temps du tiède renouveau
Ouvrira largement ses ailes de corbeau.

Rien n'est plus doux au cœur plein de choses funèbres,
Et sur qui dès longtemps descendent les frimas,
Ô blafardes saisons, reines de nos climats,

Que l'aspect permanent de vos pâles ténèbres,
— Si ce n'est, par un soir sans lune, deux à deux,
D'endormir la douleur sur un lit hasardeux.

102   Rêve parisien

À Constantin Guys

I.
De ce terrible paysage,
Tel que jamais mortel n'en vit,
Ce matin encore l'image,
Vague et lointaine, me ravit.

Le sommeil est plein de miracles!
Par un caprice singulier
J'avais banni de ces spectacles
Le végétal irrégulier,

Et, peintre fier de mon génie,
Je savourais dans mon tableau
L'enivrante monotonie
Du métal, du marbre et de l'eau.

Babel d'escaliers et d'arcades,
C'était un palais infini
Plein de bassins et de cascades
Tombant dans l'or mat ou bruni;

Et des cataractes pesantes,
Comme des rideaux de cristal
Se suspendaient, éblouissantes,
À des murailles de métal.

Non d'arbres, mais de colonnades
Les étangs dormants s'entouraient
Où de gigantesques naïades,
Comme des femmes, se miraient.

Des nappes d'eau s'épanchaient, bleues,
Entre des quais roses et verts,
Pendant des millions de lieues,
Vers les confins de l'univers:

C'étaient des pierres inouïes
Et des flots magiques; c'étaient
D'immenses glaces éblouies
Par tout ce qu'elles reflétaient!

Insouciants et taciturnes,
Des Ganges, dans le firmament,
Versaient le trésor de leurs urnes
Dans des gouffres de diamant.

Architecte de mes féeries,
Je faisais, à ma volonté,
Sous un tunnel de pierreries
Passer un océan dompté;

Et tout, même la couleur noire,
Semblait fourbi, clair, irisé;
Le liquide enchâssait sa gloire
Dans le rayon cristallisé.

Nul astre d'ailleurs, nuls vestiges
De soleil, même au bas du ciel,
Pour illuminer ces prodiges,
Qui brillaient d'un feu personnel!

Et sur ces mouvantes merveilles
Planait (terrible nouveauté!
Tout pour l'œil, rien pour les oreilles!)
Un silence d'éternité.

II.

En rouvrant mes yeux pleins de flamme
J'ai vu l'horreur de mon taudis,
Et senti, rentrant dans mon âme,
La pointe des soucis maudits;

La pendule aux accents funèbres
Sonnait brutalement midi,
Et le ciel versait des ténèbres
Sur le triste monde engourdi.

103   Le Crépuscule du matin

La diane chantait dans les cours des casernes,
Et le vent du matin soufflait sur les lanternes.

C'était l'heure où l'essaim des rêves malfaisants
Tord sur leurs oreillers les bruns adolescents;
Où, comme un œil sanglant qui palpite et qui bouge,
La lampe sur le jour fait une tache rouge;
Où l'âme, sous le poids du corps revêche et lourd,
Imite les combats de la lampe et du jour.
Comme un visage en pleurs que les brises essuient,
L'air est plein du frisson des choses qui s'enfuient,
Et l'homme est las d'écrire et la femme d'aimer.

Les maisons çà et là commençaient à fumer.
Les femmes de plaisir, la paupière livide,
Bouche ouverte, dormaient de leur sommeil stupide;
Les pauvresses, traînant leurs seins maigres et froids,
Soufflaient sur leurs tisons et soufflaient sur leurs doigts.
C'était l'heure où parmi le froid et la lésine
S'aggravent les douleurs des femmes en gésine;
Comme un sanglot coupé par un sang écumeux

Le chant du coq au loin déchirait l'air brumeux;
Une mer de brouillards baignait les édifices,
Et les agonisants dans le fond des hospices
Poussaient leur dernier râle en hoquets inégaux.
Les débauchés rentraient, brisés par leurs travaux.

L'aurore grelottante en robe rose et verte
S'avançait lentement sur la Seine déserte,
Et le sombre Paris, en se frottant les yeux
Empoignait ses outils, vieillard laborieux.

LE VIN

Un soir, l'âme du vin chantait dans les bouteilles:
«Homme, vers toi je pousse, ô cher déshérité,
Sous ma prison de verre et mes cires vermeilles,
Un chant plein de lumière et de fraternité!

Je sais combien il faut, sur la colline en flamme,
De peine, de sueur et de soleil cuisant
Pour engendrer ma vie et pour me donner l'âme;
Mais je ne serai point ingrat ni malfaisant,

Car j'éprouve une joie immense quand je tombe
Dans le gosier d'un homme usé par ses travaux,
Et sa chaude poitrine est une douce tombe
Où je me plais bien mieux que dans mes froids caveaux.

Entends-tu retentir les refrains des dimanches
Et l'espoir qui gazouille en mon sein palpitant?
Les coudes sur la table et retroussant tes manches,
Tu me glorifieras et tu seras content;

J'allumerai les yeux de ta femme ravie;
À ton fils je rendrai sa force et ses couleurs
Et serai pour ce frêle athlète de la vie
L'huile qui raffermit les muscles des lutteurs.

En toi je tomberai, végétale ambroisie,
Grain précieux jeté par l'éternel Semeur,
Pour que de notre amour naisse la poésie
Qui jaillira vers Dieu comme une rare fleur!»

105   Le Vin des chiffonniers

Souvent à la clarté rouge d'un réverbère
Dont le vent bat la flamme et tourmente le verre,
Au cœur d'un vieux faubourg, labyrinthe fangeux
Où l'humanité grouille en ferments orageux,

On voit un chiffonnier qui vient, hochant la tête,
Butant, et se cognant aux murs comme un poète,
Et, sans prendre souci des mouchards, ses sujets,
Épanche tout son cœur en glorieux projets.

Il prête des serments, dicte des lois sublimes,
Terrasse les méchants, relève les victimes,
Et sous le firmament comme un dais suspendu
S'enivre des splendeurs de sa propre vertu.

Oui, ces gens harcelés de chagrins de ménage,
Moulus par le travail et tourmentés par l'âge,
Ereintés et pliant sous un tas de débris,
Vomissement confus de l'énorme Paris,

Reviennent, parfumés d'une odeur de futailles,
Suivis de compagnons, blanchis dans les batailles,
Dont la moustache pend comme les vieux drapeaux.
Les bannières, les fleurs et les arcs triomphaux

Se dressent devant eux, solennelle magie!
Et dans l'étourdissante et lumineuse orgie
Des clairons, du soleil, des cris et du tambour,
Ils apportent la gloire au peuple ivre d'amour!

C'est ainsi qu'à travers l'Humanité frivole
Le vin roule de l'or, éblouissant Pactole;
Par le gosier de l'homme il chante ses exploits
Et règne par ses dons ainsi que les vrais rois.

Pour noyer la rancœur et bercer l'indolence
De tous ces vieux maudits qui meurent en silence,
Dieu, touché de remords, avait fait le sommeil;
L'Homme ajouta le Vin, fils sacré du Soleil!

106   Le Vin de l'assassin

Ma femme est morte, je suis libre!
Je puis donc boire tout mon soûl.
Lorsque je rentrais sans un sou,
Ses cris me déchiraient la fibre.

Autant qu'un roi je suis heureux;
L'air est pur, le ciel admirable...
Nous avions un été semblable
Lorsque j'en devins amoureux!

L'horrible soif qui me déchire
Aurait besoin pour s'assouvir
D'autant de vin qu'en peut tenir
Son tombeau; — ce n'est pas peu dire:

Je l'ai jetée au fond d'un puits,
Et j'ai même poussé sur elle
Tous les pavés de la margelle.
— Je l'oublierai si je le puis!

Au nom des serments de tendresse,
Dont rien ne peut nous délier,
Et pour nous réconcilier
Comme au beau temps de notre ivresse,

J'implorai d'elle un rendez-vous,
Le soir, sur une route obscure.

Elle y vint — folle créature!
Nous sommes tous plus ou moins fous!

Elle était encore jolie,
Quoique bien fatiguée! et moi,
Je l'aimais trop! voilà pourquoi
Je lui dis: Sors de cette vie!

Nul ne peut me comprendre. Un seul
Parmi ces ivrognes stupides
Songea-t-il dans ses nuits morbides
À faire du vin un linceul?

Cette crapule invulnérable
Comme les machines de fer
Jamais, ni l'été ni l'hiver,
N'a connu l'amour véritable,

Avec ses noirs enchantements,
Son cortège infernal d'alarmes,
Ses fioles de poison, ses larmes,
Ses bruits de chaîne et d'ossements!

— Me voilà libre et solitaire!
Je serai ce soir ivre mort;
Alors, sans peur et sans remords,
Je me coucherai sur la terre,

Et je dormirai comme un chien!
Le chariot aux lourdes roues
Chargé de pierres et de boues,
Le wagon enragé peut bien

Ecraser ma tête coupable
Ou me couper par le milieu,

Je m'en moque comme de Dieu,
Du Diable ou de la Sainte Table!

107   Le Vin du solitaire

Le regard singulier d'une femme galante
Qui se glisse vers nous comme le rayon blanc
Que la lune onduleuse envoie au lac tremblant,
Quand elle y veut baigner sa beauté nonchalante;

Le dernier sac d'écus dans les doigts d'un joueur;
Un baiser libertin de la maigre Adeline;
Les sons d'une musique énervante et câline,
Semblable au cri lointain de l'humaine douleur,

Tout cela ne vaut pas, ô bouteille profonde,
Les baumes pénétrants que ta panse féconde
Garde au cœur altéré du poète pieux;

Tu lui verses l'espoir, la jeunesse et la vie,
— Et l'orgueil, ce trésor de toute gueuserie,
Qui nous rend triomphants et semblables aux Dieux!

108   Le Vin des amants

Aujourd'hui l'espace est splendide!
Sans mors, sans éperons, sans bride,
Partons à cheval sur le vin
Pour un ciel féerique et divin!

Comme deux anges que torture
Une implacable calenture,
Dans le bleu cristal du matin
Suivons le mirage lointain!

Mollement balancés sur l'aile
Du tourbillon intelligent,
Dans un délire parallèle,

Ma sœur, côte à côte nageant,
Nous fuirons sans repos ni trêves
Vers le paradis de mes rêves!

FLEURS

DU

MAL

109 La Destruction

Sans cesse à mes côtés s'agite le Démon;
Il nage autour de moi comme un air impalpable;
Je l'avale et le sens qui brûle mon poumon
Et l'emplit d'un désir éternel et coupable.

Parfois il prend, sachant mon grand amour de l'Art,
La forme de la plus séduisante des femmes,
Et, sous de spécieux prétextes de cafard,
Accoutume ma lèvre à des philtres infâmes.

Il me conduit ainsi, loin du regard de Dieu,
Haletant et brisé de fatigue, au milieu
Des plaines de l'Ennui, profondes et désertes,

Et jette dans mes yeux pleins de confusion
Des vêtements souillés, des blessures ouvertes,
Et l'appareil sanglant de la Destruction!

110 Une Martyre

Dessin d'un maître inconnu

Au milieu des flacons, des étoffes lamées
Et des meubles voluptueux,
Des marbres, des tableaux, des robes parfumées
Qui traînent à plis somptueux,

Dans une chambre tiède où, comme en une serre,
L'air est dangereux et fatal,
Où des bouquets mourants dans leurs cercueils de verre
Exhalent leur soupir final,

Un cadavre sans tête épanche, comme un fleuve,
Sur l'oreiller désaltéré
Un sang rouge et vivant, dont la toile s'abreuve
Avec l'avidité d'un pré.

Semblable aux visions pâles qu'enfante l'ombre
Et qui nous enchaînent les yeux,
La tête, avec l'amas de sa crinière sombre
Et de ses bijoux précieux,

Sur la table de nuit, comme une renoncule,
Repose; et, vide de pensers,
Un regard vague et blanc comme le crépuscule
S'échappe des yeux révulsés.

Sur le lit, le tronc nu sans scrupules étale
Dans le plus complet abandon
La secrète splendeur et la beauté fatale
Dont la nature lui fit don;

Un bas rosâtre, orné de coins d'or, à la jambe,
Comme un souvenir est resté;
La jarretière, ainsi qu'un œil secret qui flambe,
Darde un regard diamanté.

Le singulier aspect de cette solitude
Et d'un grand portrait langoureux,
Aux yeux provocateurs comme son attitude,
Révèle un amour ténébreux,

Une coupable joie et des fêtes étranges
Pleines de baisers infernaux,
Dont se réjouissait l'essaim des mauvais anges
Nageant dans les plis des rideaux;

Et cependant, à voir la maigreur élégante
De l'épaule au contour heurté,
La hanche un peu pointue et la taille fringante
Ainsi qu'un reptile irrité,

Elle est bien jeune encor! — Son âme exaspérée
Et ses sens par l'ennui mordus
S'étaient-ils entr'ouverts à la meute altérée
Des désirs errants et perdus?

L'homme vindicatif que tu n'as pu, vivante,
Malgré tant d'amour, assouvir,
Combla-t-il sur ta chair inerte et complaisante
L'immensité de son désir?

Réponds, cadavre impur! et par tes tresses roides
Te soulevant d'un bras fiévreux,
Dis-moi, tête effrayante, a-t-il sur tes dents froides
Collé les suprêmes adieux?

— Loin du monde railleur, loin de la foule impure,
Loin des magistrats curieux,
Dors en paix, dors en paix, étrange créature,
Dans ton tombeau mystérieux;

Ton époux court le monde, et ta forme immortelle
Veille près de lui quand il dort;
Autant que toi sans doute il te sera fidèle,
Et constant jusques à la mort.

110x   Lesbos

Mère des jeux latins et des voluptés grecques,
Lesbos, où les baisers, languissants ou joyeux,
Chauds comme les soleils, frais comme les pastèques,

Font l'ornement des nuits et des jours glorieux,
Mère des jeux latins et des voluptés grecques,

Lesbos, où les baisers sont comme les cascades
Qui se jettent sans peur dans les gouffres sans fonds,
Et courent, sanglotant et gloussant par saccades,
Orageux et secrets, fourmillants et profonds;
Lesbos, où les baisers sont comme les cascades!

Lesbos, où les Phrynés l'une l'autre s'attirent,
Où jamais un soupir ne resta sans écho,
À l'égal de Paphos les étoiles t'admirent,
Et Vénus à bon droit peut jalouser Sapho!
Lesbos, où les Phrynés l'une l'autre s'attirent,

Lesbos, terre des nuits chaudes et langoureuses,
Qui font qu'à leurs miroirs, stérile volupté!
Les filles aux yeux creux, de leur corps amoureuses,
Caressent les fruits mûrs de leur nubilité;
Lesbos, terre des nuits chaudes et langoureuses,

Laisse du vieux Platon se froncer l'œil austère;
Tu tires ton pardon de l'excès des baisers,
Reine du doux empire, aimable et noble terre,
Et des raffinements toujours inépuisés.
Laisse du vieux Platon se froncer l'œil austère.

Tu tires ton pardon de l'éternel martyre,
Infligé sans relâche aux cœurs ambitieux,
Qu'attire loin de nous le radieux sourire
Entrevu vaguement au bord des autres cieux!
Tu tires ton pardon de l'éternel martyre!

Qui des Dieux osera, Lesbos, être ton juge
Et condamner ton front pâli dans les travaux,

Si ses balances d'or n'ont pesé le déluge
De larmes qu'à la mer ont versé tes ruisseaux?
Qui des Dieux osera, Lesbos, être ton juge?

Que nous veulent les lois du juste et de l'injuste?
Vierges au cœur sublime, honneur de l'archipel,
Votre religion comme une autre est auguste,
Et l'amour se rira de l'Enfer et du Ciel!
Que nous veulent les lois du juste et de l'injuste?

Car Lesbos entre tous m'a choisi sur la terre
Pour chanter le secret de ses vierges en fleurs,
Et je fus dès l'enfance admis au noir mystère
Des rires effrénés mêlés aux sombres pleurs;
Car Lesbos entre tous m'a choisi sur la terre.

Et depuis lors je veille au sommet de Leucate,
Comme une sentinelle à l'œil perçant et sûr,
Qui guette nuit et jour brick, tartane ou frégate,
Dont les formes au loin frissonnent dans l'azur;
Et depuis lors je veille au sommet de Leucate,

Pour savoir si la mer est indulgente et bonne,
Et parmi les sanglots dont le roc retentit
Un soir ramènera vers Lesbos, qui pardonne,
Le cadavre adoré de Sapho, qui partit
Pour savoir si la mer est indulgente et bonne!

De la mâle Sapho, l'amante et le poète,
Plus belle que Vénus par ses mornes pâleurs!
— L'œil d'azur est vaincu par l'œil noir que tachète
Le cercle ténébreux tracé par les douleurs
De la mâle Sapho, l'amante et le poète!

— Plus belle que Vénus se dressant sur le monde
Et versant les trésors de sa sérénité
Et le rayonnement de sa jeunesse blonde
Sur le vieil Océan de sa fille enchanté;
Plus belle que Vénus se dressant sur le monde!

— De Sapho qui mourut le jour de son blasphème,
Quand, insultant le rite et le culte inventé,
Elle fit son beau corps la pâture suprême
D'un brutal dont l'orgueil punit l'impiété
De celle qui mourut le jour de son blasphème.

Et c'est depuis ce temps que Lesbos se lamente,
Et, malgré les honneurs que lui rend l'univers,
S'enivre chaque nuit du cri de la tourmente
Que poussent vers les cieux ses rivages déserts.
Et c'est depuis ce temps que Lesbos se lamente!

110xx   Femmes damnées (Delphine et Hippolyte)

À la pâle clarté des lampes languissantes,
Sur de profonds coussins tout imprégnés d'odeur,
Hippolyte rêvait aux caresses puissantes
Qui levaient le rideau de sa jeune candeur.

Elle cherchait, d'un œil troublé par la tempête,
De sa naïveté le ciel déjà lointain,
Ainsi qu'un voyageur qui retourne la tête
Vers les horizons bleus dépassés le matin.

De ses yeux amortis les paresseuses larmes,
L'air brisé, la stupeur, la morne volupté,
Ses bras vaincus, jetés comme de vaines armes,
Tout servait, tout parait sa fragile beauté.

Étendue à ses pieds, calme et pleine de joie,
Delphine la couvait avec des yeux ardents,
Comme un animal fort qui surveille une proie,
Après l'avoir d'abord marquée avec les dents.

Beauté forte à genoux devant la beauté frêle,
Superbe, elle humait voluptueusement
Le vin de son triomphe, et s'allongeait vers elle,
Comme pour recueillir un doux remerciement.

Elle cherchait dans l'œil de sa pâle victime
Le cantique muet que chante le plaisir,
Et cette gratitude infinie et sublime
Qui sort de la paupière ainsi qu'un long soupir.

— «Hippolyte, cher cœur, que dis-tu de ces choses?
Comprends-tu maintenant qu'il ne faut pas offrir
L'holocauste sacré de tes premières roses
Aux souffles violents qui pourraient les flétrir?

Mes baisers sont légers comme ces éphémères
Qui caressent le soir les grands lacs transparents,
Et ceux de ton amant creuseront leurs ornières
Comme des chariots ou des socs déchirants;

Ils passeront sur toi comme un lourd attelage
De chevaux et de bœufs aux sabots sans pitié…
Hippolyte, ô ma sœur! tourne donc ton visage,
Toi, mon âme et mon cœur, mon tout et ma moitié,

Tourne vers moi tes yeux pleins d'azur et d'étoiles!
Pour un de ces regards charmants, baume divin,
Des plaisirs plus obscurs je lèverai les voiles,
Et je t'endormirai dans un rêve sans fin!»

Mais Hippolyte alors, levant sa jeune tête:
— «Je ne suis point ingrate et ne me repens pas,
Ma Delphine, je souffre et je suis inquiète,
Comme après un nocturne et terrible repas.

Je sens fondre sur moi de lourdes épouvantes
Et de noirs bataillons de fantômes épars,
Qui veulent me conduire en des routes mouvantes
Qu'un horizon sanglant ferme de toutes parts.

Avons-nous donc commis une action étrange?
Explique, si tu peux, mon trouble et mon effroi:
Je frissonne de peur quand tu me dis: 'Mon ange!'
Et cependant je sens ma bouche aller vers toi.

Ne me regarde pas ainsi, toi, ma pensée!
Toi que j'aime à jamais, ma sœur d'élection,
Quand même tu serais une embûche dressée
Et le commencement de ma perdition!»

Delphine secouant sa crinière tragique,
Et comme trépignant sur le trépied de fer,
L'œil fatal, répondit d'une voix despotique:
— «Qui donc devant l'amour ose parler d'enfer?

Maudit soit à jamais le rêveur inutile
Qui voulut le premier, dans sa stupidité,
S'éprenant d'un problème insoluble et stérile,
Aux choses de l'amour mêler l'honnêteté!

Celui qui veut unir dans un accord mystique
L'ombre avec la chaleur, la nuit avec le jour,
Ne chauffera jamais son corps paralytique
À ce rouge soleil que l'on nomme l'amour!

Va, si tu veux, chercher un fiancé stupide;
Cours offrir un cœur vierge à ses cruels baisers;
Et, pleine de remords et d'horreur, et livide,
Tu me rapporteras tes seins stigmatisés...

On ne peut ici-bas contenter qu'un seul maître!»
Mais l'enfant, épanchant une immense douleur,
Cria soudain: — «Je sens s'élargir dans mon être
Un abîme béant; cet abîme est mon cœur!

Brûlant comme un volcan, profond comme le vide!
Rien ne rassasiera ce monstre gémissant
Et ne rafraîchira la soif de l'Euménide
Qui, la torche à la main, le brûle jusqu'au sang.

Que nos rideaux fermés nous séparent du monde,
Et que la lassitude amène le repos!
Je veux m'anéantir dans ta gorge profonde,
Et trouver sur ton sein la fraîcheur des tombeaux!»

— Descendez, descendez, lamentables victimes,
Descendez le chemin de l'enfer éternel!
Plongez au plus profond du gouffre, où tous les crimes
Flagellés par un vent qui ne vient pas du ciel,

Bouillonnent pêle-mêle avec un bruit d'orage.
Ombres folles, courez au but de vos désirs;
Jamais vous ne pourrez assouvir votre rage,
Et votre châtiment naîtra de vos plaisirs.

Jamais un rayon frais n'éclaira vos cavernes;
Par les fentes des murs des miasmes fiévreux
Filtrent en s'enflammant ainsi que des lanternes
Et pénètrent vos corps de leurs parfums affreux.

L'âpre stérilité de votre jouissance
Altère votre soif et roidit votre peau,
Et le vent furibond de la concupiscence
Fait claquer votre chair ainsi qu'un vieux drapeau.

Loin des peuples vivants, errantes, condamnées,
À travers les déserts courez comme les loups;
Faites votre destin, âmes désordonnées,
Et fuyez l'infini que vous portez en vous!

111   Femmes damnées

Comme un bétail pensif sur le sable couchées,
Elles tournent leurs yeux vers l'horizon des mers,
Et leurs pieds se cherchant et leurs mains rapprochées
Ont de douces langueurs et des frissons amers.

Les unes, cœurs épris des longues confidences,
Dans le fond des bosquets où jasent les ruisseaux,
Vont épelant l'amour des craintives enfances
Et creusent le bois vert des jeunes arbrisseaux;

D'autres, comme des sœurs, marchent lentes et graves
À travers les rochers pleins d'apparitions,
Où saint Antoine a vu surgir comme des laves
Les seins nus et pourprés de ses tentations;

Il en est, aux lueurs des résines croulantes,
Qui dans le creux muet des vieux antres païens
T'appellent au secours de leurs fièvres hurlantes,
Ô Bacchus, endormeur des remords anciens!

Et d'autres, dont la gorge aime les scapulaires,
Qui, recélant un fouet sous leurs longs vêtements,

Mêlent, dans le bois sombre et les nuits solitaires,
L'écume du plaisir aux larmes des tourments.

Ô vierges, ô démons, ô monstres, ô martyres,
De la réalité grands esprits contempteurs,
Chercheuses d'infini, dévotes et satyres,
Tantôt pleines de cris, tantôt pleines de pleurs,

Vous que dans votre enfer mon âme a poursuivies,
Pauvres sœurs, je vous aime autant que je vous plains,
Pour vos mornes douleurs, vos soifs inassouvies,
Et les urnes d'amour dont vos grands cœurs sont pleins.

112 Les Deux Bonnes Sœurs

La Débauche et la Mort sont deux aimables filles,
Prodigues de baisers et riches de santé,
Dont le flanc toujours vierge et drapé de guenilles
Sous l'éternel labeur n'a jamais enfanté.

Au poète sinistre, ennemi des familles,
Favori de l'enfer, courtisan mal renté,
Tombeaux et lupanars montrent sous leurs charmilles
Un lit que le remords n'a jamais fréquenté.

Et la bière et l'alcôve en blasphèmes fécondes
Nous offrent tour à tour, comme deux bonnes sœurs,
De terribles plaisirs et d'affreuses douceurs.

Quand veux-tu m'enterrer, Débauche aux bras immondes?
Ô Mort, quand viendras-tu, sa rivale en attraits,
Sur ses myrtes infects enter tes noirs cyprès?

113   La Fontaine de sang

Il me semble parfois que mon sang coule à flots,
Ainsi qu'une fontaine aux rythmiques sanglots.
Je l'entends bien qui coule avec un long murmure,
Mais je me tâte en vain pour trouver la blessure.

À travers la cité, comme dans un champ clos,
Il s'en va, transformant les pavés en îlots,
Désaltérant la soif de chaque créature,
Et partout colorant en rouge la nature.

J'ai demandé souvent à des vins captieux
D'endormir pour un jour la terreur qui me mine;
Le vin rend l'œil plus clair et l'oreille plus fine!

J'ai cherché dans l'amour un sommeil oublieux;
Mais l'amour n'est pour moi qu'un matelas d'aiguilles
Fait pour donner à boire à ces cruelles filles!

114   Allégorie

C'est une femme belle et de riche encolure,
Qui laisse dans son vin traîner sa chevelure.
Les griffes de l'amour, les poisons du tripot,
Tout glisse et tout s'émousse au granit de sa peau.
Elle rit à la Mort et nargue la Débauche,
Ces monstres dont la main, qui toujours gratte et fauche,
Dans ses jeux destructeurs a pourtant respecté
De ce corps ferme et droit la rude majesté.
Elle marche en déesse et repose en sultane;
Elle a dans le plaisir la foi mahométane,
Et dans ses bras ouverts, que remplissent ses seins,
Elle appelle des yeux la race des humains.
Elle croit, elle sait, cette vierge inféconde

Et pourtant nécessaire à la marche du monde,
Que la beauté du corps est un sublime don
Qui de toute infamie arrache le pardon.
Elle ignore l'Enfer comme le Purgatoire,
Et quand l'heure viendra d'entrer dans la Nuit noire
Elle regardera la face de la Mort,
Ainsi qu'un nouveau-né, — sans haine et sans remords.

115 La Béatrice

Dans des terrains cendreux, calcinés, sans verdure,
Comme je me plaignais un jour à la nature,
Et que de ma pensée, en vaguant au hasard,
J'aiguisais lentement sur mon cœur le poignard,
Je vis en plein midi descendre sur ma tête
Un nuage funèbre et gros d'une tempête,
Qui portait un troupeau de démons vicieux,
Semblables à des nains cruels et curieux.
À me considérer froidement ils se mirent,
Et, comme des passants sur un fou qu'ils admirent,
Je les entendis rire et chuchoter entre eux,
En échangeant maint signe et maint clignement d'yeux:

— «Contemplons à loisir cette caricature
Et cette ombre d'Hamlet imitant sa posture,
Le regard indécis et les cheveux au vent.
N'est-ce pas grand'pitié de voir ce bon vivant,
Ce gueux, cet histrion en vacances, ce drôle,
Parce qu'il sait jouer artistement son rôle,
Vouloir intéresser au chant de ses douleurs
Les aigles, les grillons, les ruisseaux et les fleurs,
Et même à nous, auteurs de ces vieilles rubriques,
Réciter en hurlant ses tirades publiques?»

J'aurais pu (mon orgueil aussi haut que les monts
Domine la nuée et le cri des démons)
Détourner simplement ma tête souveraine,
Si je n'eusse pas vu parmi leur troupe obscène,
Crime qui n'a pas fait chanceler le soleil!
La reine de mon cœur au regard nonpareil
Qui riait avec eux de ma sombre détresse
Et leur versait parfois quelque sale caresse.

115x   Les Métamorphoses du vampire

La femme cependant, de sa bouche de fraise,
En se tordant ainsi qu'un serpent sur la braise,
Et pétrissant ses seins sur le fer de son busc,
Laissait couler ces mots tout imprégnés de musc:
— «Moi, j'ai la lèvre humide, et je sais la science
De perdre au fond d'un lit l'antique conscience.
Je sèche tous les pleurs sur mes seins triomphants,
Et fais rire les vieux du rire des enfants.
Je remplace, pour qui me voit nue et sans voiles,
La lune, le soleil, le ciel et les étoiles!
Je suis, mon cher savant, si docte aux voluptés,
Lorsque j'étouffe un homme en mes bras redoutés,
Ou lorsque j'abandonne aux morsures mon buste,
Timide et libertine, et fragile et robuste,
Que sur ces matelas qui se pâment d'émoi,
Les anges impuissants se damneraient pour moi!»

Quand elle eut de mes os sucé toute la moelle,
Et que languissamment je me tournai vers elle
Pour lui rendre un baiser d'amour, je ne vis plus
Qu'une outre aux flancs gluants, toute pleine de pus!
Je fermai les deux yeux, dans ma froide épouvante,
Et quand je les rouvris à la clarté vivante,

À mes côtés, au lieu du mannequin puissant
Qui semblait avoir fait provision de sang,
Tremblaient confusément des débris de squelette,
Qui d'eux-mêmes rendaient le cri d'une girouette
Ou d'une enseigne, au bout d'une tringle de fer,
Que balance le vent pendant les nuits d'hiver.

116   Un Voyage à Cythère

Mon cœur, comme un oiseau, voltigeait tout joyeux
Et planait librement à l'entour des cordages;
Le navire roulait sous un ciel sans nuages;
Comme un ange enivré d'un soleil radieux.

Quelle est cette île triste et noire? — C'est Cythère,
Nous dit-on, un pays fameux dans les chansons,
Eldorado banal de tous les vieux garçons.
Regardez, après tout, c'est une pauvre terre.

— Île des doux secrets et des fêtes du cœur!
De l'antique Vénus le superbe fantôme
Au-dessus de tes mers plane comme un arôme
Et charge les esprits d'amour et de langueur.

Belle île aux myrtes verts, pleine de fleurs écloses,
Vénérée à jamais par toute nation,
Où les soupirs des cœurs en adoration
Roulent comme l'encens sur un jardin de roses

Ou le roucoulement éternel d'un ramier!
— Cythère n'était plus qu'un terrain des plus maigres,
Un désert rocailleux troublé par des cris aigres.
J'entrevoyais pourtant un objet singulier!

Ce n'était pas un temple aux ombres bocagères,
Où la jeune prêtresse, amoureuse des fleurs,
Allait, le corps brûlé de secrètes chaleurs,
Entrebâillant sa robe aux brises passagères;

Mais voilà qu'en rasant la côte d'assez près
Pour troubler les oiseaux avec nos voiles blanches,
Nous vîmes que c'était un gibet à trois branches,
Du ciel se détachant en noir, comme un cyprès.

De féroces oiseaux perchés sur leur pâture
Détruisaient avec rage un pendu déjà mûr,
Chacun plantant, comme un outil, son bec impur
Dans tous les coins saignants de cette pourriture;

Les yeux étaient deux trous, et du ventre effondré
Les intestins pesants lui coulaient sur les cuisses,
Et ses bourreaux, gorgés de hideuses délices,
L'avaient à coups de bec absolument châtré.

Sous les pieds, un troupeau de jaloux quadrupèdes,
Le museau relevé, tournoyait et rôdait;
Une plus grande bête au milieu s'agitait
Comme un exécuteur entouré de ses aides.

Habitant de Cythère, enfant d'un ciel si beau,
Silencieusement tu souffrais ces insultes
En expiation de tes infâmes cultes
Et des péchés qui t'ont interdit le tombeau.

Ridicule pendu, tes douleurs sont les miennes!
Je sentis, à l'aspect de tes membres flottants,
Comme un vomissement, remonter vers mes dents
Le long fleuve de fiel des douleurs anciennes;

Devant toi, pauvre diable au souvenir si cher,
J'ai senti tous les becs et toutes les mâchoires
Des corbeaux lancinants et des panthères noires
Qui jadis aimaient tant à triturer ma chair.

— Le ciel était charmant, la mer était unie;
Pour moi tout était noir et sanglant désormais,
Hélas! et j'avais, comme en un suaire épais,
Le cœur enseveli dans cette allégorie.

Dans ton île, ô Vénus! je n'ai trouvé debout
Qu'un gibet symbolique où pendait mon image...
— Ah! Seigneur! donnez-moi la force et le courage
De contempler mon cœur et mon corps sans dégoût!

117   L'Amour et le Crâne

Vieux cul-de-lampe

L'Amour est assis sur le crâne
De l'Humanité,
Et sur ce trône le profane,
Au rire effronté,

Souffle gaiement des bulles rondes
Qui montent dans l'air,
Comme pour rejoindre les mondes
Au fond de l'éther.

Le globe lumineux et frêle
Prend un grand essor,
Crève et crache son âme grêle
Comme un songe d'or.

J'entends le crâne à chaque bulle
Prier et gémir:
— «Ce jeu féroce et ridicule,
Quand doit-il finir?

Car ce que ta bouche cruelle
Éparpille en l'air,
Monstre assassin, c'est ma cervelle,
Mon sang et ma chair!»

RÉVOLTE

Qu'est-ce que Dieu fait donc de ce flot d'anathèmes
Qui monte tous les jours vers ses chers Séraphins?
Comme un tyran gorgé de viande et de vins,
Il s'endort au doux bruit de nos affreux blasphèmes.

Les sanglots des martyrs et des suppliciés
Sont une symphonie enivrante sans doute,
Puisque, malgré le sang que leur volupté coûte,
Les cieux ne s'en sont point encore rassasiés!

— Ah! Jésus, souviens-toi du Jardin des Olives!
Dans ta simplicité tu priais à genoux
Celui qui dans son ciel riait au bruit des clous
Que d'ignobles bourreaux plantaient dans tes chairs vives,

Lorsque tu vis cracher sur ta divinité
La crapule du corps de garde et des cuisines,
Et lorsque tu sentis s'enfoncer les épines
Dans ton crâne où vivait l'immense Humanité;

Quand de ton corps brisé la pesanteur horrible
Allongeait tes deux bras distendus, que ton sang
Et ta sueur coulaient de ton front pâlissant,
Quand tu fus devant tous posé comme une cible,

Rêvais-tu de ces jours si brillants et si beaux
Où tu vins pour remplir l'éternelle promesse,
Où tu foulais, monté sur une douce ânesse,
Des chemins tout jonchés de fleurs et de rameaux,

Où, le cœur tout gonflé d'espoir et de vaillance,
Tu fouettais tous ces vils marchands à tour de bras,

Où tu fus maître enfin? Le remords n'a-t-il pas
Pénétré dans ton flanc plus avant que la lance?

— Certes, je sortirai, quant à moi, satisfait
D'un monde où l'action n'est pas la sœur du rêve;
Puissé-je user du glaive et périr par le glaive!
Saint Pierre a renié Jésus ... il a bien fait!

119   Abel et Caïn

I.
Race d'Abel, dors, bois et mange;
Dieu te sourit complaisamment.

Race de Caïn, dans la fange
Rampe et meurs misérablement.

Race d'Abel, ton sacrifice
Flatte le nez du Séraphin!

Race de Caïn, ton supplice
Aura-t-il jamais une fin?

Race d'Abel, vois tes semailles
Et ton bétail venir à bien;

Race de Caïn, tes entrailles
Hurlent la faim comme un vieux chien.

Race d'Abel, chauffe ton ventre
À ton foyer patriarcal;

Race de Caïn, dans ton antre
Tremble de froid, pauvre chacal!

Race d'Abel, aime et pullule!
Ton or fait aussi des petits.

Race de Caïn, cœur qui brûle,
Prends garde à ces grands appétits.

Race d'Abel, tu croîs et broutes
Comme les punaises des bois!

Race de Caïn, sur les routes
Traîne ta famille aux abois.

II.
Ah! race d'Abel, ta charogne
Engraissera le sol fumant!

Race de Caïn, ta besogne
N'est pas faite suffisamment;

Race d'Abel, voici ta honte:
Le fer est vaincu par l'épieu!

Race de Caïn, au ciel monte,
Et sur la terre jette Dieu!

120   Les Litanies de Satan

Ô toi, le plus savant et le plus beau des Anges,
Dieu trahi par le sort et privé de louanges,

Ô Satan, prends pitié de ma longue misère!

Ô Prince de l'exil, à qui l'on a fait tort
Et qui, vaincu, toujours te redresses plus fort,

Ô Satan, prends pitié de ma longue misère!

Toi qui sais tout, grand roi des choses souterraines,
Guérisseur familier des angoisses humaines,

Ô Satan, prends pitié de ma longue misère!

Toi qui, même aux lépreux, aux parias maudits,
Enseignes par l'amour le goût du Paradis,

Ô Satan, prends pitié de ma longue misère!

Ô toi qui de la Mort, ta vieille et forte amante,
Engendras l'Espérance, — une folle charmante!

Ô Satan, prends pitié de ma longue misère!

Toi qui fais au proscrit ce regard calme et haut
Qui damne tout un peuple autour d'un échafaud.

Ô Satan, prends pitié de ma longue misère!

Toi qui sais en quels coins des terres envieuses
Le Dieu jaloux cacha les pierres précieuses,

Ô Satan, prends pitié de ma longue misère!

Toi dont l'œil clair connaît les profonds arsenaux
Où dort enseveli le peuple des métaux,

Ô Satan, prends pitié de ma longue misère!

Toi dont la large main cache les précipices
Au somnambule errant au bord des édifices,

Ô Satan, pitié de ma longue misère!

Toi qui, magiquement, assouplis les vieux os
De l'ivrogne attardé foulé par les chevaux,

Ô Satan, prends pitié de ma longue misère!

Toi qui, pour consoler l'homme frêle qui souffre,
Nous appris à mêler le salpêtre et le soufre,

Ô Satan, prends pitié de ma longue misère!

Toi qui poses ta marque, ô complice subtil,
Sur le front du Crésus impitoyable et vil,

Ô Satan, prends pitié de ma longue misère!

Toi qui mets dans les yeux et dans le cœur des filles
Le culte de la plaie et l'amour des guenilles,

Ô Satan, prends pitié de ma longue misère!

Bâton des exilés, lampe des inventeurs,
Confesseur des pendus et des conspirateurs,

Ô Satan, prends pitié de ma longue misère!

Père adoptif de ceux qu'en sa noire colère
Du paradis terrestre a chassés Dieu le Père,

Ô Satan, prends pitié de ma longue misère!

Prière
Gloire et louange à toi, Satan, dans les hauteurs
Du Ciel, où tu régnas, et dans les profondeurs

De l'Enfer, où, vaincu, tu rêves en silence!
Fais que mon âme un jour, sous l'Arbre de Science,
Près de toi se repose, à l'heure où sur ton front
Comme un Temple nouveau ses rameaux s'épandront!

LA MORT

121   La Mort des amants

Nous aurons des lits pleins d'odeurs légères,
Des divans profonds comme des tombeaux,
Et d'étranges fleurs sur des étagères,
Écloses pour nous sous des cieux plus beaux.

Usant à l'envi leurs chaleurs dernières,
Nos deux cœurs seront deux vastes flambeaux,
Qui réfléchiront leurs doubles lumières
Dans nos deux esprits, ces miroirs jumeaux.

Un soir fait de rose et de bleu mystique,
Nous échangerons un éclair unique,
Comme un long sanglot, tout chargé d'adieux;

Et plus tard un Ange, entr'ouvrant les portes,
Viendra ranimer, fidèle et joyeux,
Les miroirs ternis et les flammes mortes.

122   La Mort des pauvres

C'est la Mort qui console, hélas! et qui fait vivre;
C'est le but de la vie, et c'est le seul espoir
Qui, comme un élixir, nous monte et nous enivre,
Et nous donne le cœur de marcher jusqu'au soir;

À travers la tempête, et la neige, et le givre,
C'est la clarté vibrante à notre horizon noir;
C'est l'auberge fameuse inscrite sur le livre,
Où l'on pourra manger, et dormir, et s'asseoir;

C'est un Ange qui tient dans ses doigts magnétiques
Le sommeil et le don des rêves extatiques,
Et qui refait le lit des gens pauvres et nus;

C'est la gloire des Dieux, c'est le grenier mystique,
C'est la bourse du pauvre et sa patrie antique,
C'est le portique ouvert sur les Cieux inconnus!

123   La Mort des artistes

Combien faut-il de fois secouer mes grelots
Et baiser ton front bas, morne caricature?
Pour piquer dans le but, de mystique nature,
Combien, ô mon carquois, perdre de javelots?

Nous userons notre âme en de subtils complots,
Et nous démolirons mainte lourde armature,
Avant de contempler la grande Créature
Dont l'infernal désir nous remplit de sanglots!

Il en est qui jamais n'ont connu leur Idole,
Et ces sculpteurs damnés et marqués d'un affront,
Qui vont se martelant la poitrine et le front,

N'ont qu'un espoir, étrange et sombre Capitole!
C'est que la Mort, planant comme un soleil nouveau,
Fera s'épanouir les fleurs de leur cerveau!

124   La Fin de la journée

Sous une lumière blafarde
Court, danse et se tord sans raison
La Vie, impudente et criarde.
Aussi, sitôt qu'à l'horizon

La nuit voluptueuse monte,
Apaisant tout, même la faim,

Effaçant tout, même la honte,
Le Poète se dit: «Enfin!

Mon esprit, comme mes vertèbres,
Invoque ardemment le repos;
Le cœur plein de songes funèbres,

Je vais me coucher sur le dos
Et me rouler dans vos rideaux,
Ô rafraîchissantes ténèbres!»

125   Le Rêve d'un curieux

À Félix Nadar

Connais-tu, comme moi, la douleur savoureuse,
Et de toi fais-tu dire: «Oh! l'homme singulier!»
— J'allais mourir. C'était dans mon âme amoureuse
Désir mêlé d'horreur, un mal particulier;

Angoisse et vif espoir, sans humeur factieuse.
Plus allait se vidant le fatal sablier,
Plus ma torture était âpre et délicieuse;
Tout mon cœur s'arrachait au monde familier.

J'étais comme l'enfant avide du spectacle,
Haïssant le rideau comme on hait un obstacle...
Enfin la vérité froide se révéla:

J'étais mort sans surprise, et la terrible aurore
M'enveloppait. — Eh quoi! n'est-ce donc que cela?
La toile était levée et j'attendais encore.

126   Le Voyage

À Maxime du Camp

I.

Pour l'enfant, amoureux de cartes et d'estampes,
L'univers est égal à son vaste appétit.
Ah! que le monde est grand à la clarté des lampes!
Aux yeux du souvenir que le monde est petit!

Un matin nous partons, le cerveau plein de flamme,
Le cœur gros de rancune et de désirs amers,
Et nous allons, suivant le rythme de la lame,
Berçant notre infini sur le fini des mers:

Les uns, joyeux de fuir une patrie infâme;
D'autres, l'horreur de leurs berceaux, et quelques-uns,
Astrologues noyés dans les yeux d'une femme,
La Circé tyrannique aux dangereux parfums.

Pour n'être pas changés en bêtes, ils s'enivrent
D'espace et de lumière et de cieux embrasés;
La glace qui les mord, les soleils qui les cuivrent,
Effacent lentement la marque des baisers.

Mais les vrais voyageurs sont ceux-là seuls qui partent
Pour partir; cœurs légers, semblables aux ballons,
De leur fatalité jamais ils ne s'écartent,
Et, sans savoir pourquoi, disent toujours: Allons!

Ceux-là dont les désirs ont la forme des nues,
Et qui rêvent, ainsi qu'un conscrit le canon,
De vastes voluptés, changeantes, inconnues,
Et dont l'esprit humain n'a jamais su le nom!

II.

Nous imitons, horreur! la toupie et la boule
Dans leur valse et leurs bonds; même dans nos sommeils
La Curiosité nous tourmente et nous roule
Comme un Ange cruel qui fouette des soleils.

Singulière fortune où le but se déplace,
Et, n'étant nulle part, peut être n'importe où!
Où l'Homme, dont jamais l'espérance n'est lasse,
Pour trouver le repos court toujours comme un fou!

Notre âme est un trois-mâts cherchant son Icarie;
Une voix retentit sur le pont: «Ouvre l'œil!»
Une voix de la hune, ardente et folle, crie:
«Amour... gloire... bonheur!» Enfer! c'est un écueil!

Chaque îlot signalé par l'homme de vigie
Est un Eldorado promis par le Destin;
L'Imagination qui dresse son orgie
Ne trouve qu'un récif aux clartés du matin.

Ô le pauvre amoureux des pays chimériques!
Faut-il le mettre aux fers, le jeter à la mer,
Ce matelot ivrogne, inventeur d'Amériques
Dont le mirage rend le gouffre plus amer?

Tel le vieux vagabond, piétinant dans la boue,
Rêve, le nez en l'air, de brillants paradis;
Son œil ensorcelé découvre une Capoue
Partout où la chandelle illumine un taudis.

III.

Étonnants voyageurs! quelles nobles histoires
Nous lisons dans vos yeux profonds comme les mers!
Montrez-nous les écrins de vos riches mémoires,
Ces bijoux merveilleux, faits d'astres et d'éthers.

Nous voulons voyager sans vapeur et sans voile!
Faites, pour égayer l'ennui de nos prisons,
Passer sur nos esprits, tendus comme une toile,
Vos souvenirs avec leurs cadres d'horizons.

Dites, qu'avez-vous vu?

IV.

«Nous avons vu des astres
Et des flots, nous avons vu des sables aussi;
Et, malgré bien des chocs et d'imprévus désastres,
Nous nous sommes souvent ennuyés, comme ici.

La gloire du soleil sur la mer violette,
La gloire des cités dans le soleil couchant,
Allumaient dans nos cœurs une ardeur inquiète
De plonger dans un ciel au reflet alléchant.

Les plus riches cités, les plus grands paysages,
Jamais ne contenaient l'attrait mystérieux
De ceux que le hasard fait avec les nuages.
Et toujours le désir nous rendait soucieux!

— La jouissance ajoute au désir de la force.
Désir, vieil arbre à qui le plaisir sert d'engrais,
Cependant que grossit et durcit ton écorce,
Tes branches veulent voir le soleil de plus près!

Grandiras-tu toujours, grand arbre plus vivace
Que le cyprès? — Pourtant nous avons, avec soin,
Cueilli quelques croquis pour votre album vorace,
Frères qui trouvez beau tout ce qui vient de loin!

Nous avons salué des idoles à trompe;
Des trônes constellés de joyaux lumineux;

Des palais ouvragés dont la féerique pompe
Serait pour vos banquiers un rêve ruineux;

Des costumes qui sont pour les yeux une ivresse;
Des femmes dont les dents et les ongles sont teints,
Et des jongleurs savants que le serpent caresse.»

V.
Et puis, et puis encore?

VI.
            «Ô cerveaux enfantins!

Pour ne pas oublier la chose capitale,
Nous avons vu partout, et sans l'avoir cherché,
Du haut jusques en bas de l'échelle fatale,
Le spectacle ennuyeux de l'immortel péché:

La femme, esclave vile, orgueilleuse et stupide,
Sans rire s'adorant et s'aimant sans dégoût;
L'homme, tyran goulu, paillard, dur et cupide,
Esclave de l'esclave et ruisseau dans l'égout;

Le bourreau qui jouit, le martyr qui sanglote;
La fête qu'assaisonne et parfume le sang;
Le poison du pouvoir énervant le despote,
Et le peuple amoureux du fouet abrutissant;

Plusieurs religions semblables à la nôtre,
Toutes escaladant le ciel; la Sainteté,
Comme en un lit de plume un délicat se vautre,
Dans les clous et le crin cherchant la volupté;

L'Humanité bavarde, ivre de son génie,
Et, folle maintenant comme elle était jadis,

Criant à Dieu, dans sa furibonde agonie:
'Ô mon semblable, mon maître, je te maudis!'

Et les moins sots, hardis amants de la Démence,
Fuyant le grand troupeau parqué par le Destin,
Et se réfugiant dans l'opium immense!
— Tel est du globe entier l'éternel bulletin.»

VII.
Amer savoir, celui qu'on tire du voyage!
Le monde, monotone et petit, aujourd'hui,
Hier, demain, toujours, nous fait voir notre image:
Une oasis d'horreur dans un désert d'ennui!

Faut-il partir? rester? Si tu peux rester, reste;
Pars, s'il le faut. L'un court, et l'autre se tapit
Pour tromper l'ennemi vigilant et funeste,
Le Temps! Il est, hélas! des coureurs sans répit,

Comme le Juif errant et comme les apôtres,
À qui rien ne suffit, ni wagon ni vaisseau,
Pour fuir ce rétiaire infâme; il en est d'autres
Qui savent le tuer sans quitter leur berceau.

Lorsque enfin il mettra le pied sur notre échine,
Nous pourrons espérer et crier: En avant!
De même qu'autrefois nous partions pour la Chine,
Les yeux fixés au large et les cheveux au vent,

Nous nous embarquerons sur la mer des Ténèbres
Avec le cœur joyeux d'un jeune passager.
Entendez-vous ces voix charmantes et funèbres,
Qui chantent: «Par ici vous qui voulez manger

Le Lotus parfumé! c'est ici qu'on vendange
Les fruits miraculeux dont votre cœur a faim;
Venez vous enivrer de la douceur étrange
De cette après-midi qui n'a jamais de fin!»

À l'accent familier nous devinons le spectre;
Nos Pylades là-bas tendent leurs bras vers nous.
«Pour rafraîchir ton cœur nage vers ton Electre!»
Dit celle dont jadis nous baisions les genoux.

VIII.
Ô Mort, vieux capitaine, il est temps! levons l'ancre!
Ce pays nous ennuie, ô Mort! Appareillons!
Si le ciel et la mer sont noirs comme de l'encre,
Nos cœurs que tu connais sont remplis de rayons!

Verse-nous ton poison pour qu'il nous réconforte!
Nous voulons, tant ce feu nous brûle le cerveau,
Plonger au fond du gouffre, Enfer ou Ciel, qu'importe?
Au fond de l'Inconnu pour trouver du *nouveau*!

AFTERWORD

I first read *The Flowers of Evil* when I was twelve years old, the perfect age to be really thinking about wickedness. In childhood, wickedness is an anomalous injustice, something that, if not already fixed, has been momentarily overlooked and will be attended to eventually in one way or another. School bullies, we're told, will be apprehended and punished, even if the authorities don't seem to be paying attention while you're being kicked. People living on the streets, or afflicted with a dread disease, or being subjected to violence, are part of a story in which help is on the way—which is why nobody appears to be doing much about it just then, whether it is happening onscreen someplace, or just outside your window, or in your bedroom. Indeed, particularly and perhaps especially in America, whole swaths of wickedness—genocide and slavery and institutionalized violence—are presented to young people as things contrary to our principles of fairness that have stopped happening, or, if they have not stopped, are lingering only as a brief echo soon to be corrected, the way you are still cold for a little bit after you put on a sweater. In early childhood, the story is that everything is OK; later on, it's that everything will be, should be, OK, if we'll just give the world a minute or two to right itself.

Irony, like any other manifestation of puberty, doesn't arrive uniformly across the population, and indeed it never drops for a significant number of people. But twelve is about right. You begin to look askance at the world, to understand that the narratives in front of your eyes are just shiny surfaces. The world is something else, beneath or beyond—it's more complicated than what you've been told, or maybe just worse. The giddy chirps of beginner's culture lose their appeal, and you begin to consume things that parents find not just grating but worrisome. Not that it matters: all your authority figures begin to seem quite full of shit, and their inspirational nonsense and stale assurances begin to feel not just hollow but part of a larger hollowness, a static performance that you suspect, not incorrectly, of spreading out over everything. You begin to sense the instinctive appeal to stories which acknowledge that wickedness is much, much more widespread than promised. *The Flowers of Evil* sounded about right.

I thought it was a horror novel, of course. My local public library—West Portal Branch, San Francisco—had it on the shelf of new arrivals. The French title had been taped over by some helpful librarian, so *The Flowers of Evil* in handwritten block print looked a little disreputable and thus more alluring. Menacing plants, I thought, the work of a mad scientist or ancient curse or radiation from a passing comet, growing at an exponential, horrific rate, like ivy spreading on an outside wall, but faster, fiercer, engulfing its helpless human prey in its thorns and brambles and flytrap mouths. It sounded perfect. At twelve, I was largely ignorant of the haphazard hierarchies by which pedants try to regulate art, and I read without regard to reputation or cultural stamp. I read Kafka's short book about becoming an insect and Stephen King's long one about becoming a vampire. I tried both Nabokov and V. C. Andrews's tales of inappropriate sexual obsession. I remember putting down James Joyce's *Ulysses* because Ulysses wasn't in it, picking up *Dune* because I'd seen *Lawrence of Arabia* and figured it was about the same thing. I remember making it all the way to the end of *Gone with the Wind* and thinking, Wait a minute, this endless chronicle of a selfish woman's reckless love affairs on the wrong side of the Civil War—is this trashy?

I'm sure I picked up *The Flowers of Evil* with the same careless innocence. In my mind's eye, the copy I found at the library—a translation first published in 1982, which is how I know I was twelve—had an utterly blank cover, with no other information except the title. I know that isn't the case—I have long since purchased a duplicate copy—and yet it must have been a surprise when I found that it was in fact a collection of poetry.

> For all of us, greed, folly, error, vice
> exhaust the body and obsess the soul,
> and we keep feeding our congenial
> remorse the same way vagrants nurse their lice.

I have no clear memory of the first time I read this first stanza of *The Flowers of Evil*'s first poem. I don't know if these lines produced some epiphanic moment. In my mind they did not. It was something slower than that, I think. The poems nagged me, and I went back to the library and found the book again—soon afterward, and over and over. I wish I could remember if I flipped through the card catalog to find it again—what title would be right before, or right after, *The Flowers of Evil?*—as I likely wouldn't have remembered the poet's name, and poetry is filed, irrationally, in an outdated corner of Dewey decimals. I could make it up, some early reading narrative, but really I can only guess that what struck me about these lines then is what strikes me now: the way they invite a grotesque culpability, that you cannot read *The Flowers of Evil* without being a participant in it. So much poetry makes the case that the world is beautiful, and seeks to remind us that we're connected to this beauty. That was likely the poetry I was encountering in school at the time. I don't remember any of that poetry, not even hating it—it failed to register with me at all. Age twelve puts me in sixth or seventh grade, at a large public middle school, ugly and underfunded—the school, I mean, although like anyone that age I was uncomfortable in my own skin, and so unlikely to be persuaded by claims of truth and beauty. This startling rejoinder, that instead we were exhausted by greed, folly, error, and vice, must have struck me then, and struck me forever; it is no exaggeration to say that this book has cast a shadow over my entire life.

In some ways, this is a familiar shadow. Baudelaire strikes quite the pose in the literary landscape. Elegantly debauched, romantic in a nihilistic way and vice versa, drunk on absinthe and moonlight, Baudelaire is adored by people all over the world who have not really read him, but get the gist. "Spleen and Ideal,"* the name of the largest section of *The*

---

* "Spleen and the Ideal" in this edition.

Flowers of Evil, is perhaps better known as the title of an album by the arty music group Dead Can Dance, who combine music from disparate cultures and eras into long, drony pieces perfect for making out in a dorm room, and that's just about perfect. For years Baudelaire stayed with me as this kind of talisman, in which the image fed the poetry feeding the image, and although I never quite went full Baudelaire—fountain pen yes, velvet jacket no—I kept coming back to *The Flowers of Evil*. As I grew older and read more books, I realized that Baudelaire's brand of wickedness was considered a little immature, that you really weren't supposed to read him past a certain age, the way you weren't supposed to listen to heavy metal or play Dungeons & Dragons. Baudelaire's rage and loneliness weren't rooted in relevant history or politics, just in the horror of being alive. Of all the figures in the canon, Baudelaire was the one easiest to discard, reviled by all would-be gatekeepers of every persuasion, perhaps because he never really belonged there. He was a weirdo, a perv, a lush. Serious readers were supposed to avert their eyes, and step over him as he lay muttering in the gutter.

I couldn't give him up, though. My own copy of *The Flowers of Evil* got battered as it moved from apartment to apartment, its coffee and cocktail stains competing with its lurid metaphors and rash interjections. I kept catching myself staring again at its misty ruins, its desperate shipwrecks, its shabby murders under gossamer moonlight, and while his pleasures still feel adolescent, what sticks with us more, from pop song to romantic snapshot, than the pleasures of adolescence? My comrade-in-arms Dana Gioia, three hundred pages back, takes the oft-repeated stance that Baudelaire is the first Modernist, a claim that makes the most sense if you regard Modernism as the arrival of irony, of looking askance at the patrician tropes of traditional Western literature. Baudelaire was one of the first Western poets to show us injustice and ignorance, ugly tumult and fervent wickedness, as the truest state of the world—the first pangs of Modernism's adolescence, that is—the way you feel when you are about twelve years old. When I started to write for children approaching this age, a story in which young orphans wade deeper and deeper into a wicked world only to find themselves getting wickeder and wickeder, I didn't think long about what they ought to be called. A shadowy, ever-growing evil, engulfing everyone in its shadowy stems: I wasn't so wrong about *The Flowers of Evil* after all.

Young readers still show me Baudelaire at libraries and bookstores where I go to talk about Lemony Snicket and the Baudelaire orphans. One way or another they've picked up a volume, the way I hope you've picked up this one: just because it sounds like something they've been looking for. Look, they say to me, standing in the same shadow that first found me at twelve. Baudelaire! Is he a relative of—is he related to—?

Yes, I always say. Of course he is.

Daniel Handler
San Francisco, California
January 2021

NOTES

Annotations are preceded by the poem number (or, if no number applies, to the title of the poem), the line number ("0" denotes a poem's title, or any description or dedication under the title), and an italicized quotation of the text being annotated.

Dedication.5 *Teacher and Friend, Théophile Gautier*: The poet, novelist, and journalist Théophile Gautier (1811–1872) was an elder contemporary of Baudelaire. His career traces the transition of taste from Romanticism to Aestheticism and Naturalism.

To the Reader.9 *Thrice-potent Satan*: Satan is here given the epithet ("Thrice-potent") of Hermes Trismegistus, a legendary alchemist associated with the Egyptian god Thoth.

1.25 *He sings ecstatically from Calvary*: Calvary, also known as Golgotha, was a place just outside the walls of Jerusalem where Jesus was crucified.

1.64 *Dominations, Virtues, Thrones*: Baudelaire here refers to three of the nine orders of the angels in the medieval hierarchy. They are, in ascending order: Angels, Archangels, Principalities, Powers, Virtues, Dominations, Thrones, Cherubim, Seraphim.

1.69 *Palmyra's lost antiquities*: Now an archaeological site, Palmyra was an ancient Semitic city that became a regional center under the Romans in the first centuries CE.

5.2 *Phoebus*: An epithet of the Greco-Roman god Apollo, who was a sun god.

5.7 *prolific Cybele*: Cybele was a Phrygian fertility goddess who, in classical mythology, became identified with the Titan Rhea.

5.9 *like a she-wolf brimming with compassion*: Baudelaire is likely thinking here of the Roman foundation myth in which a she-wolf nurses the infants Romulus and Remus, who would go on to build the walls of Rome.

6.1 *Rubens*: Peter Paul Rubens (1577–1640), in addition to being a diplomat, was an influential artist in the Baroque Flemish tradition.

6.5 *Leonardo*: Leonardo da Vinci (1452–1519), an Italian polymath, is generally considered one of the greatest painters of all time.

6.9   *Rembrandt*:   Rembrandt van Rijn (1606–1669) was a Dutch draftsman, printmaker, and painter. The most eminent of Dutch artists, he is regarded as one of the greatest artists of all time.

6.13   *Michelangelo*:   Michelangelo Buonarotti (1475–1564) was an Italian poet, architect, painter, and sculptor. He, too, is considered one of the greatest artists of all time.

6.20   *Puget*:   Pierre Puget (1620–1694) was an engineer, architect, sculptor, and painter in the French Baroque period.

6.21   *Watteau*:   Antoine Watteau (1684–1721) was a French painter who revitalized the Baroque style.

6.25   *Goya*:   Francisco Goya (1746–1828) was a Spanish printmaker and painter of the Romantic period.

6.29   *Delacroix*:   Eugène Delacroix (1798–1863) was a painter considered the leader of the French Romantic school.

6.32   *like one of Weber's stifled sighs*:   Carl Maria von Weber (1786–1826) was a German guitarist, composer, conductor, and pianist of the Romantic period.

8.8   *Minturnae's famous mud*:   Minturnae was a city in a swampy part of Latium. Marius, a politician and general in the Roman Republic, fled there for refuge in the first century BCE.

8.13   *Phoebus, lord of melody*:   The god Apollo, whom the epithet "Phoebus" refers to, presided over music, among other things.

8.14   *Pan, the harvest god*:   Pan, who was half human and half goat, was a god of animal husbandry and fertility in general. His instrument was panpipes, which he made from reeds.

11.2   *lift that great weight, Sisyphus*:   One of those eternally punished in the classical underworld, Sisyphus, for the crime of temporarily outwitting Death, is condemned to roll, forever, a rock up a hill only to have it roll back down again.

11.4   *Art takes time and Life is brief*:   Baudelaire here translates into French the famous aphorism *Ars longa, vita brevis* (Art is long, life brief), which is itself a translation from ancient Greek of one of the *Aphorismoi* of the physician Hippocrates.

13.0   *Traveling Gypsies*:   A print with the same title by Jacques Callot was the inspiration for this poem.

13.11   *Cybele*:   See note on poem 5, line 7.

15.0   *Don Juan in Hell*:   The archetypal seducer of women, the legendary Don Juan, in many accounts, ends up condemned to Hell.

15.2   *Charon the ferryman*:   In classical mythology, Charon is the ferryman who conveys the souls of the dead over the Acheron into the underworld.

15.3 *a man fierce as Antisthenes*:   Antisthenes (circa 446–366 BCE) was a student of Socrates. He was regarded as the founder of the Cynic school of philosophy.

15.9 *Sganarelle*:   Don Juan's servant in Molière's comedy *Don Juan* (1665).

15.10 *with a trembling finger, Don Luis*:   Don Juan's father in Molière's *Don Juan*.

15.14 *Elvira*:   Don Juan's wife in Molière's *Don Juan*.

16.3 *a famous doctor of religion*:   A reference to Simon of Tournai, who was a professor at the University of Paris in the late twelfth century CE. He taught philosophy and, later, theology, based on the writings of Aristotle.

17.5 *Like an unfathomed sphinx*:   In classical mythology, the sphinx is a creature with a woman's head, lion's body, and bird's wings. In Thebes she asks a riddle of those who approach her and eats those who answer incorrectly. Eventually, when Oedipus solves the riddle, she throws herself to her death.

18.2 *worn vignettes*:   Baudelaire is referring to decorative illustrations in books.

18.5 *Paul Gavarni, artist of chlorosis*:   Chlorosis is a type of anemia; Paul Gavarni was the nom de plume of Sulpice Guillaume Chevalier (1804–1866), a famous French illustrator whose later work took a dark and grotesque turn.

18.10 *It's you, Lady Macbeth*:   In Shakespeare's *Macbeth*, Lady Macbeth plots with her husband to kill the king of Scotland so that they can become king and queen.

18.11 *a storm-born dream of Aeschylus*:   Baudelaire is referring to Clytemnestra, a character in Aeschylus's *Oresteia*, who kills her husband Agamemnon.

18.12 *offspring of Michelangelo*:   Baudelaire is referring to Michelangelo's statue of Night, a female goddess, in the chapel of the Medicis.

18.14 *to be fed to Titans' maws*:   In classical mythology, the Titan Cronus devours his own children as they emerge from the womb of his wife Rhea.

20.0 *For Ernest Christophe, Sculptor*:   Ernest Christophe (1827–1892), who was a friend of Baudelaire's, made the statue that Baudelaire describes in this poem. Though he originally titled the piece *The Human Comedy*, Christophe changed its name to *The Mask* to honor Baudelaire's poem. This piece is now in the Musée d'Orsay in Paris.

21.25 *Angel or Siren*:   In Homer's *Odyssey*, the Sirens, half bird, half woman, sing irresistibly beautiful songs that tempt sailors to their death.

21x.20 *grape clusters on my vine*:   This is an allusion to the Song of Solomon 7.8.

24.2 *O tear-filled vase*:   This vase is a lachrymal, common in Roman tombs and once regarded as being a vessel for the tears of mourners.

26.0 *Sed non satiata*:   This Latin phrase (meaning "but not sated") originated in line 130 of the Sixth Satire of the Roman poet Juvenal (active in the late first and early second centuries CE). It refers to the wife of the

Emperor Claudius, Messalina, who allegedly would sneak out of the palace to work as a prostitute.

26.3   *work of an obeah, Faust*: The legendary student who turned to magic and sold his soul to the Devil. He is best known from Goethe's *Faust* (Part I, 1808; Part II, 1833).

26.11   *I am no river Styx*: In classical mythology, Styx, the river of hate, is said to be so convoluted as to wrap the underworld nine times.

26.14   *on your infernal mattress play Persephone*: Carried off by her uncle Hades, Persephone becomes his bride in the underworld.

27.11   *classical sphinxes*: See note on poem 17, line 5.

30.0   *De profundis clamavi*: This phrase comes from Psalm 130. It was used as a part of the Catholic funeral liturgy.

31x.0   *Lethe*: In classical mythology, Lethe is the river of forgetfulness in the underworld.

31x.22   *I'll suck in drugs / of oblivion*: Baudelaire is here referring to nepenthe, a legendary drug that cures grief with oblivion.

35.0   *Duellum*: an archaic form of the Latin word *bellum* (war) that here refers to a duel.

35.12   *Savage Amazon*: In classical mythology, the Amazons were warrior women. The heroes Hercules and Theseus defeat them in battle.

36.0   *The Balcony*: This poem employs the *strophe encadrée*, in which the first and final lines of each stanza are identical. Baudelaire also uses this type of stanza in poems 44, 54, 62, and 110x.

37.14   *My dear Beelzebub*: Meaning "Lord of the Flies" in Hebrew, Beelzebub is another name for Satan.

40.0   *Semper eadem*: This Latin phrase means "always the same woman."

44.23   *that radiates from your tantalizing prime*: In the Bible (1 Kings 1–4), the aged King David is given the maiden Abishag to keep him warm.

47.0   *The Harmony of Evening*: This poem is a variation on the Malayan form the pantoum, which involves lines repeated in a fixed pattern.

47.16   *You, like a monstrance*: A monstrance is a display case for the sacred host in the Roman Catholic Church.

48.18   *just as Lazarus once tore his winding-sheet*: Jesus raises Lazarus from the dead in John 11:38–44.

54.47   *swoop down and drive great Satan out*: The actress Marie Daubrun was briefly Baudelaire's mistress and muse. In 1847 she played the lead in a play called *The Girl with the Golden Hair* in which a fairy (played by a different actor) overcomes evil powers. This poem was originally entitled "The Girl with the Golden Hair."

57.0   *A Votive in the Spanish Style*: In this poem Baudelaire imagines a Spanish Baroque art object that is a votive ("dedicated with a vow"). This imagined object blends representations of the Immaculate Virgin (standing atop a moon and serpent) and of the Virgin of Sorrows (whose flesh was pierced by seven swords).

58.40   *my long Siberian night*:   Siberia is an Arctic region of Russia where, in winter, there is almost constant darkness.

59.0   *Sisina*:   "Sisina" is what Baudelaire called his acquaintance the Italian Elisa Nieri, who was sympathetic to the Italian rebels who attempted to kill Napoleon III, the last French monarch, in 1858.

59.1   *Picture Diana*:   Diana is the Roman name for the Greek goddess Artemis, who presides over hunting and female adolescence.

59.5   *What of Théroigne*:   A heroine of the French Revolution, Théroigne de Méricourt stormed the staircase at Versailles.

60.0   *Franciscae meae laudes*:   This is the only poem in *Les Fleurs du mal* written in Latin instead of French. Baudelaire won awards for Latin composition in his youth.

61.0   *To a Creole Lady*:   This poem is addressed to Emmeline de Carcenac, whom Baudelaire met in Mauritius.

62.0   *Moesta et errabunda*:   The title means "Sorrowful and Wandering" in Latin.

62.1   *Agatha*:   Biographers have been unable to identify the Agatha addressed here.

64.10   *dark Cupid pulls his lethal longbow tight*:   Cupid here is the traditional classical god of love. He shoots people with arrows to make them fall in love.

64.14   *my oh-so-white, so frigid Marguerite*:   There is a pun on "Marguerite" that is impossible to translate. The word means both (1) a daisy and (2) the character Marguerite in Goethe's *Faust*, who dies at the end of Part I.

66.7   *Darkness*:   My translation of Erebus, the god of the darkness of the underworld, who is mentioned by name here in the original.

71.0   *A Fantastical Engraving*:   This poem is an ekphrasis of the image *Death on a Pale Horse* (1784), designed by John Mortimer and engraved by Joseph Haynes.

73.1   *Hatred is the Danaïdes' wine cask*:   The Danaïdes are the forty-nine daughters of Danaus in classical mythology. Compelled to marry their cousins, they kill them on the wedding night. Their punishment in the underworld is forever to try to fetch water in jugs with a sieve for a bottom. Baudelaire uses them to suggest that Hatred's wine cask is never filled to the brim.

73.11   *like the Lernaen Hydra's heads in fable*:   Hercules's second labor involves defeating, in Lerna, a hydra (water snake) that regenerates two heads for each one that is lopped off.

75.1   *Pluvius*:   Pluvius (meaning "rainy") refers (1) to the month Pluviôse in the French Republican calendar (January 21–February 19) and (2), as an epithet, to the Roman weather god Jupiter.

76.13   *sad pastels and pale Bouchers*: "Bouchers" refers to paintings by François Boucher (1703–1770), who belongs to the Rococo period.

76.22   *a primeval sphinx*: Baudelaire is here referring not to the sphinx of classical mythology but to the Egyptian statue of Memnon, which, according to legend, sings in the light of the setting sun.

77.15   *baths of blood in which the Romans used to lie*: The Romans believed that bathing in blood would restore bodily vitality.

77.18   *veins, instead of blood, pump green Lethean ooze*: See note on poem 31x, the title.

79.4   *De profundis*: See note on poem 30, the title.

81.5   *You, secret Hermes*: See note on "To the Reader," line 9.

81.8   *King Midas*: In classical mythology, Midas, a king of Phrygia in Asia Minor, asks the god Dionysus to make it so that everything he touches turned to gold. Unable to eat and drink because of this boon, he, on Dionysus's advice, cures himself by bathing in the river Pactolus.

82.8   *like Ovid / chased from the Roman paradise*: Exiled by the Emperor Augustus from Rome to Scythia, Ovid laments his expulsion in the *Tristia*.

83.0   *Heautontimoroumenos*: Ancient Greek: "he who torments himself."

83.0   *To J.G.F.*: Though also the dedicatee of Baudelaire's study of opium, J.G.F. remains unidentified by biographers.

83.3   *the way that Moses hit the rock*: At the direction of God, Moses strikes a rock with his staff to provide water for his people (Numbers 20).

84.3   *the river Styx*: See note on poem 26, line 11.

85.6   *much like a sylphid*: The ballet *La Syphide* debuted in 1832. It is regarded as the first "Romantic" ballet.

85.13   *Remember! Souviens-toi! Esto memor!*: *Souviens-toi* and *Esto memor* are, respectively, French and Latin for "Remember." Baudelaire also uses the English word "Remember" in this list of imperatives.

86.1   *So as to write my eclogues*: Eclogues are pastoral poems. The genre was originated by the ancient Greeks. Baudelaire's "eclogues" are entirely urban.

86.20   *Idylls*: An idyll is a description of a picturesque scene, especially in rural life.

87.9   *the destroyer of chlorosis*: See note on poem 18, line 5.

88.0   *To a Red-Haired Beggar Girl*: Baudelaire's friend Émile Deroy painted a picture of the same girl. She was a street performer in Paris's Latin Quarter.

88.32   *Belleau the Bard*: The love poet Rémi Belleau (1528–1577).

88.38   *one page boy and Ronsard*: The poet Pierre Ronsard (1524–1585). Ronsard wrote in the form Baudelaire uses here. This poem also contains archaisms evocative of earlier French poetry.

88.48   *run-down Véfour:*   Baudelaire here refers to an esteemed and expensive restaurant of his own time. Today it is known as Le Grand Véfour.

89.0   *For Victor Hugo:*   An eminent French novelist and poet (1802–1885).

89.1   *Andromache:*   The wife of the Trojan hero Hector. Though she appears in Homer's *Iliad*, Baudelaire is here referring to the "toy Troy" episode in book 3 of Virgil's *Aeneid*. The Greek Pyrrhus, son of Achilles, claims Andromache as his wife after the Trojan War. Later, after wedding another, he hands Andromache off to the Greek prophet Helenus, brother of Hector, to marry.

89.4   *the tears you shed to feed that "Simoïs":*   In book 3 of Virgil's *Aeneid*, Andromache looks at a little stream that suggests the Trojan river Simoïs to her.

89.6   *as I walked through the modern Carrousel:*   This is the area between the Louvre and the Carrousel Arch. An open square at the time Baudelaire composed this poem, it had previously been densely populated.

89.26   *Ovid:*   Such laments are common in Ovid's *Metamorphoses*. Baudelaire may be alluding to *Metamorphoses*, book 1, lines 84–85.

89.47   *who suck a grief milk from the she-wolf's tit:*   See note on poem 5, line 9.

90.0   *For Victor Hugo:*   See note on poem 89, the dedication.

90.20   *like the one that Judas wore:*   Judas, the betrayer of Christ, was often represented with a pointed beard.

90.43   *a foul / phoenix:*   Originally a figure in Egyptian mythology, the phoenix, according to legend, was reborn from its own ashes.

91.0   *For Victor Hugo:*   See note on poem 89, the dedication.

91.6   *Laïs:*   Laïs was an ancient Greek courtesan, famously the lover of Alcibiades.

91.6   *Eponine:*   Eponine was a woman of Gaul who rebelled against the Romans and was executed.

91.37   *Vestal virgin:*   Baudelaire ironically refers to a woman who frequented a gambling house as a vestal virgin—that is, a celibate priestess of the Roman Vesta, goddess of the hearth.

91.40   *everyone's pleasure in Tivoli's shade:*   Tivoli was an expansive pleasure-garden in Paris.

91.44   *they call him Hippogriff:*   Half horse, half griffon, this winged creature could carry a human on its back.

97.0   *Danse Macabre:*   "The Dance of Death."

97.0   *To Ernest Christophe:*   Ernest Christophe's statuette of a female skeleton preparing for a ball was the inspiration for this poem. Christophe also sculpted the statue described in poem 20.

97.50   *Antinoüses:*   A beautiful boy from Bithynia in Asia Minor, Antinoüs was a favorite of the Emperor Hadrian.

99.0   *I still recall the little whitewashed lodging where...:*   The addressee in this and the following is Baudelaire's mother.

99.3   *A plaster Pomona and an aging Queen of Love*:   The Queen of Love is the goddess Venus; Pomona is an ancient Roman fertility goddess.

100.1   *Think of my kind old nurse*:   The nurse referred to here was named Mariette. She was hired by Baudelaire's mother, the addressee of the poem.

102.0   *For Constantin Guys*:   Constantin Guys (1802–1892) was a friend of Baudelaire's and a painter.

102.23   *In them colossal naiads*:   In classical mythology, a naiad is a water nymph who inhabits a spring, a waterfall, or a river.

103.25   *Aurora*:   Aurora is the Roman goddess of the dawn.

105.26   *the dazzling Pactolus*:   After washing off King Midas's golden touch, the river Pactolus acquired a golden tinge; see note on poem 81, line 8.

107.6   *a wanton kiss from skinny Adeline*:   Scholars have identified no allusion or biographical reference here.

110.0   *A Drawing by an Unknown Master*:   Scholars have identified no drawing of which this poem is an ekphrasis.

110x.0   *Lesbos*:   A Greek island in the Aegean off the western coast of what is now Turkey. The female poet Sappho (circa 630–570 BCE) lived there and composed poetry that celebrated female homosexual desire. "Lesbian" sexual orientation takes its name from the fact that Sappho lived on Lesbos.

110x.14   *Paphos*:   A town on the island of Cyprus where Venus (Aphrodite) had a center of worship.

110x.14   *Venus envies Sappho's fame*:   Venus envies Sappho here because Sappho is at least as popular on Lesbos as Venus is at her cult center on Cyprus.

110x.21   *age-old Plato*:   The philosopher Plato (428–347 BCE) is here set up as the antithesis of sensual pleasure.

110x.46   *I look out from Leucadia's top*:   According to legend, Sappho committed suicide by jumping from this peak into the sea. Though she traditionally is said to have done so in an attempt to cure her love for a boatman named Phaon, Baudelaire has her do it because she broke a covenant to have only homosexual affairs.

110xx.0   *Delphine and Hippolyta*:   Scholars have not identified a literary allusion or biographical reference for these names.

110xx.59   *Apollo on the sacred seat*:   Baudelaire compares Delphine to the Pythia, a priestess of the god Apollo, who delivered prophecies while sitting on a tripod in the Temple of Apollo at Delphi.

110xx.79   *the fell Fury*:   The Furies are winged female goddesses of the underworld. They hunt down transgressors and punish them.

111.11   *rose volcanic for Saint Anthony*:   Saint Anthony of Egypt lived around 300 CE and is regarded as the first Christian monastic. After he withdrew to live alone in the desert, demons disguised as women often tempted him.

111.15   *O Bacchus*:   Bacchus is the classical god of wine and ecstasy.

112.14   *sad cypress to her toxic myrtle wreath*:   Myrtle is associated with Venus, the Roman goddess of love; cypress is associated with death.

115.0   *The Beatrice*:   Beatrice Portinari (1265–1290) was the object of adoration for the Italian poet Dante Alighieri (1265–1321).

116.0   *A Voyage to Cythera*:   Cythera is a Greek island south of the Peloponnese, associated with lovers in classical mythology.

117.0   *Love and the Skull*:   This poem is an ekphrasis of two engravings by Hendrick Goltzius (1558–1617).

118.0   *Saint Peter's Denial*:   This poem assumes the reader's knowledge of John 13–19 and Matthew 26.

118.26   *you whipped the wicked merchants in the countinghouse*:   In Mark 11, Jesus casts the money changers out of the temple in Jerusalem.

118.32   *Peter rejected Jesus*:   Peter denied knowing Jesus in order to escape prosecution.

119.0   *Abel and Cain*:   In Genesis, Cain and Abel, the sons of Adam and Eve, are a farmer and a shepherd, respectively. When God rejects Cain's offering, Cain out of envy kills his brother. God condemns Cain to wander the earth as an eternal outcast.

120.0   *The Litanies of Satan*:   A litany is a series of petitions used in a church service and responded to by the congregation.

120.35   *Croesus's brow*:   Croesus was an extravagantly wealthy king of Lydia in the sixth century BCE.

120.50   *the Tree / of Knowledge*:   Traditionally, the Tree of Knowledge with its forbidden fruit is located in the Garden of Eden.

123.12   *the somber Capitol*:   The reference here is to the Capitoline Hill in Rome, representative of classical antiquity.

125.0   *For Félix Nadar*:   Félix Nadar (1820–1910) was a friend of Baudelaire's, a cartoonist and an early photographer.

126.0   *For Maxime du Camp*:   Maxime Du Camp (1822–1894) was a French writer and photographer. He had written a poem entitled "The Voyager" (published in 1855).

126.12   *despotic Circe who has drugs in stock*:   In Homer's *Odyssey*, Circe uses a potion to turn men into animals.

126.38   *El Dorado*:   Spanish for "the Golden Man," El Dorado ends up signifying a city of gold in the New World. Edgar Allan Poe (1809–1849) published his poem "Eldorado" in 1849.

126.47   *his entranced gaze sees a Capua*:   A city in Campania twenty-four miles north of Naples. It was known for luxury in Roman times.

126.117   *the Wandering Jew*:   A figure who, according to legend, was condemned, as a punishment for mocking Christ, to wander the earth until Judgment Day.

126.129   *Lotus flowers*:   In Homer's *Odyssey*, several of Odysseus's men eat the Lotus flower and lose all interest in returning home. Baudelaire was likely familiar with Lord Alfred Tennyson's poem "The Lotos-Eaters" (1832).

126.134   *Pylades*:   In classical mythology, the loyal friend of Orestes.

126.136   *Swim to your Electra*:   The sister of Orestes, Electra, in one version of her story, marries Pylades.

INDEX

All page numbers in roman refer to the English translations.
All page numbers in *italics* refer to the originals.

The Poems in English

The Poems in French